W9-BSU-824

# Stanley ★★ Elkin's Greatest Hits

## ALSO BY STANLEY ELKIN

Boswell
Criers and Kibitzers, Kibitzers and Criers
A Bad Man
The Dick Gibson Show
Searches and Seizures
The Franchiser
The Living End

# Stanley 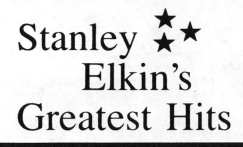 Elkin's Greatest Hits

## STANLEY ELKIN

Foreword by Robert Coover

E. P. Dutton ● New York

Grateful acknowledgment is made to the following for permission to quote from copyrighted material:

Selection from *The Franchiser,* © 1976 by Stanley Elkin. Reprinted by permission of Farrar, Straus and Giroux, Inc.

Copyright © 1964, 1965, 1967, 1970, 1971, 1973, 1976, 1977, 1978, 1979, and 1980 by Stanley Elkin

All rights reserved. Printed in the U.S.A.

No part of this publication may be reproduced or transmitted in any form or by any means, electronic or mechanical, including photocopy, recording or any information storage and retrieval system now known or to be invented, without permission in writing from the publisher, except by a reviewer who wishes to quote brief passages in connection with a review written for inclusion in a magazine, newspaper or broadcast.

For information contact:
Elsevier-Dutton Publishing Co., Inc.,
2 Park Avenue, New York, N.Y. 10016

Library of Congress Cataloging in Publication Data
Elkin, Stanley
Stanley Elkin's greatest hits.
CONTENTS: The Making of Ashenden.—Feldman & Son.
—Bernie Perk.—The Guest.—The Transient.—Mr.
Softee. [etc.]
I. Title.
PZ4.E44St 1980 [PS3555.L47] 813'.54 80-15891

ISBN: O-525-20940-9

Published simultaneously in Canada by Clarke, Irwin & Company Limited, Toronto and Vancouver

Designed by Nicola Mazzella

10 9 8 7 6 5 4 3 2 1
First Edition

*To my sister,*
*Diane Brandwein*

# Contents

# Foreword

## Robert Coover

Welcome, whether newly come here or a seasoned traveler returning to old haunts, to the fictional world of one of America's great tragicomic geniuses. A fictional world, yet real of course, indeed like all masterful fictions more real than our own, a true presence amid ephemerae, and made so through awe and wonder, exceptional skill, perceptive gifts, a love of highwire rhetoric ("I'd rather have a metaphor than a good cigar!"), and the inspired timing of a great stand-up comedian.

Stanley Elkin also shares with comedians a zest for bizarrely elaborated routines, the extended metaphor, prodigious sales pitches, and show-off shaggy-dogging—see Isidore Feldman's madcap lessons to his son, for example, or Bernie Perk's altogether shaggy confession on Dick Gibson's radio show—but his *Greatest Hits,* as you will discover, is no mere anthology of famous Elkin routines. His is a voice unique among all our writers—"Nothing but genre blindness could prevent us from seeing that there is no warmer, wealthier poetry being written in our time," William Gass has declared—and through that voice emerges a whole story about a whole man, a kind of parodic "seven ages of man" (there might have been more, one supposes, if there had been more books) from the Edenic "Making of Ashenden" and Feldman's boyhood through Perk's passion, the midlife crises of the transients Poor Bertie and Jimmy ("The Masked Playboy") Boswell, to Mr. Softee's power failure and Ellerbee's life in the Hereafter.

The voice that sustains this composite tale is vivid, intense, singular ("I allow every character my diction, and may it serve him better than it serves me!"), celebrative, egocentric (*"I want! I want!"*), often clownish, always rich and musical, committed to craft, to calling, to vocation, and unmistakably American, enamored of shop talk, greeterism, advertising hoo-hah, excess of all kinds ("I stand in awe of the outré . . . I eat excess up!"), brand names and clichés and media icons—all the crude stuff of the rude world, "the true American graffiti, the perfect queer calligraphy of the American signature—what gives us meaning and makes us fun." As his franchiser Ben Flesh says: "What I have is my American overview, the stars-and-stripes vision. I'm this mnemonic patriot of place."

Elkin relates rhetorical intensity—what he calls "heroic extravagance"—to a vision, a reach for significance, a spiritual connection to mystery. In his doctoral thesis on the religious themes in William Faulkner, he observed that Faulkner's "stylistic excesses represent a lush spirituality," and what he most admired in the man was "the lost dulled sense of awe suddenly revived." Elkin, too, is committed to that revival, to "looking hard and close at things" in order to "introduce significance into what otherwise may be untouched by significance," to recover "the beauty that sleeps in the vulgar." And though he is more of a skeptic, more

of a clown, he is, like Faulkner, an insistent yea-
sayer. Because: why not? "The only way finally to
make any sense out of the world," he has said, " is simply by saying 'yes' to it, and jumping up and down in
it." And let the pratfalls come where they may.

In that same thesis, he defined tragedy as "the failure
of hope," eternal in its consequences, inexplicable, in-
eluctable, and unfair. This is essentially the world of his
own fictions, though upended by his clown-heroes' refusal to take no for an answer, his felled men's egocentric refusal to stay fallen. In this tragicomic world,
"the hero is not he who rises above it so much as he
who can stand in it," and consequently it's not the
pratfalls that are funny so much as the standings-up.
When Flight Lieutenant Tanner tells Ben Flesh, "Be
hard, Mister Softee," it is not Ben's multiple sclerosis
we are laughing at, but the goofy, spirited, indomitable,
but ultimately hapless confrontation of the sadface
clown with an intransigently hostile universe. "It seems
to me there is only one modern joke," Elkin once
remarked in an interview, "the joke of powerlessness . . ."

I am thinking of a specific line. When Feldman is
closeted with the girl, Mona, in the warden's party
section of *A Bad Man,* he thinks Mona may be the
warden's wife. Oh, God, he thinks, suppose they catch
me with the warden's wife. Yet the woman is very
attractive to him. She says to Feldman, "One of the
things that always bothered me about you stick-up
guys and murderers and thugs is the fact that when
you're driven to the police station in a police car, you
always hold your hats over your faces. Why do you do
that?" And Feldman says, "Yeah, well, we like the way
they smell." Feldman is not really answering her question: that is the answer of powerlessness.

It is a joke Elkin shares with Samuel Beckett—you must go on, I can't go on, I'll go on—just as he shares with him a love for rhetorical flourish and comedy, the pursuit of whimsical strategies, a belief in the alliance of vision and the vulgar; and though Beckett is more cerebral, more demanding, Elkin is more transparently in love with the world. And such is Elkin's art that the reader, too, incurable skeptic though he may be, finds himself often as not jumping up and down in the dreck of the world like a kid in a sandbox, yea-saying everything from hot asphalt to cold pee.

Perhaps you doubt that? Well, come see for yourself. All you guests, you felled men, clowns, all you hapless transients . . .

# Stanley ★★ Elkin's Greatest Hits

# The Making ★★★ of Ashenden

I've been spared a lot, one of the blessed of the earth, at least one of its lucky, that privileged handful of the dramatically prospering, the sort whose secrets are asked, like the hundred-year-old man. There is no secret, of course; most of what happens to us is simple accident. Highish birth and a smooth network of appropriate connection like a tea service written into the will. But surely something in the blood too, locked into good fortune's dominant genes like a blast ripening in a time bomb. Set to go off, my good looks and intelligence, yet exceptional still, take *away* my mouthful of silver spoon and lapful of luxury. Something my own, not passed on or handed down, something seized, wrested—my good character, hopefully, my taste perhaps. What's mine, what's mine? Say taste—the soul's harmless appetite.

I've money, I'm rich. The heir to four fortunes. Grandfather on Mother's side was a Newpert. The family held some good real estate in Rhode Island until they sold it for many times what they gave for it.

(From *Searches and Seizures,* 1973.)

1

Grandmother on Father's side was a Salts, whose bottled mineral water, once available only through prescription and believed indispensable in the cure of all fevers, was the first product ever to be reviewed by the Food and Drug Administration, a famous and controversial case. The government found it to contain nothing that was actually *detrimental* to human beings, and it went public, so to speak. Available now over the counter, the Salts made more money from it than ever.

Mother was an Oh. *Her* mother was the chemical engineer who first discovered a feasible way to store oxygen in tanks. And Father was Noel Ashenden, who though he did not actually invent the matchbook, went into the field when it was still a not very flourishing novelty, and whose slogan, almost a poem, "Close Cover Before Striking" (a simple stroke, as Father liked to say), obvious only after someone else has already thought of it (the Patent Office refused to issue a patent on what it claimed was merely an instruction, but Father's company had the message on its matchbooks before his competitors even knew what was happening), removed the hazard from book matches and turned the industry and Father's firm particularly into a flaming success overnight—Father's joke, not mine. Later, when the inroads of Ronson and Zippo threatened the business, Father went into seclusion for six months and when he returned to us he had produced another slogan: "For Our Matchless Friends." It saved the industry a second time and was the second and last piece of work in Father's life.

There are people who gather in the spas and watering places of this world who pooh-pooh our fortune. Après ski, cozy in their wools, handsome before their open hearths, they scandalize amongst themselves in whispers. "Imagine," they say, "saved from ruin because of some cornball sentiment available in every bar and grill and truck stop in the country. It's not, not . . ."

Not what? Snobs! Phooey on the First Families. On railroad, steel mill, automotive, public utility, banking and shipping fortunes, on all hermetic legacy, morganatic and blockbuster bloodlines that change the maps and landscapes and alter the mobility patterns, your jungle wheeling and downtown dealing a stone's throw from warfare. I come of good stock—real estate, mineral water, oxygen, matchbooks: earth, water, air and fire, the old elementals of the material universe, a bellybutton economics, a linchpin one.

It is as I see it a perfect genealogy, and if I can be bought and sold a hundred times over by a thousand men in this country—people in your own town could do it, providents and trailers of hunch, I bless them, who got into this or went into that when it was eight cents a share—I am satisfied with my thirteen or fourteen million. Wealth is not after all the point. The genealogy is. That bridge-trick nexus that brought Newpert to Oh, Salts to Ashenden and Ashenden to Oh, love's lucky longshots which, paying off, permitted me as they permit every human life! (I have this simple, harmless paranoia of the good-natured man, this cheerful awe.) Forgive my enthusiasm, that I go on like some secular patriot wrapped in the simple flag of self, a professional descendant, every day the closed-for-the-holiday banks and post offices of the heart. And why not? Aren't my circumstances superb? Whose are better? No boast, no boast. I've had it easy, served up on all life's silver platters like a satrap. And if my money is managed for me and I do no work— less work even than Father, who at least came up with those two slogans, the latter in a six-month solitude that must have been hell for that gregarious man

("For Our Matchless Friends": no slogan finally but a
broken code, an extension of his own hospitable being,
simply the Promethean gift of fire to a guest)—at least
I am not "spoiled" and have in me still alive the nerve
endings of gratitude. If it's miserly to count one's
blessings, Brewster Ashenden's a miser.

This will give you some idea of what I'm like:

On Having an Account in a Swiss Bank: I never had
one, and suggest you stay away from them too. Oh, the
mystery and romance is all very well, but never forget
that your Swiss bank offers no premiums, whereas for
opening a savings account for $5,000 or more at First
National City Bank of New York or other fine institu-
tions you get wonderful premiums—picnic hampers,
Scotch coolers, Polaroid cameras, Hudson's Bay blankets from L. L. Bean, electric shavers, even lawn
furniture. My managers always leave me a million or
so to play with, and this is how I do it. I suppose I've
received hundreds of such bonuses. Usually I give
them to friends or as gifts at Christmas to doormen
and other loosely connected personnel of the household, but often I keep them and use them myself. I'm
not stingy. Of course I can afford to buy any of these
things—and I do, I enjoy making purchases—but
somehow nothing brings the joy of existence home to
me more than these premiums. Something from nothing—the two-suiter from Chase Manhattan and my
own existence, luggage a bonus and life a bonus too.
Like having a film star next to you on your flight from
the Coast. There are treats of high order, adventure
like cash in the street.

Let's enjoy ourselves, I say; let's have fun. Lord, let
us live in the sand by the surf of the sea and play till the
cows come home. We'll have a house on the Vineyard
and a brownstone in the Seventies and a *pied-à-terre* in
a world capital when something big is about to break.

(Put the Cardinal in the back bedroom where the sun
gilds the bay at afternoon tea and give us the courage
to stand up to secret police at the door, to top all
threats with threats of our own, the nicknames of
mayors and ministers, the fast comeback at the front
stairs, authority on us like the funny squiggle the
counterfeiters miss.) Re-Columbus us. Engage us with
the overlooked, a knowledge of optics, say, or a gift for
the tides. (My pal, the heir to most of the vegetables in
inland Nebraska, has become a superb amateur ocean-
ographer. The marine studies people invite him to
Wood's Hole each year. He has a wave named for him.)
Make us good at things, the countertenor and the
German language, and teach us to be as easy in our
amateur standing as the best man at a roommate's
wedding. Give us hard tummies behind the cummer-
bund and long swimmer's muscles under the hound's
tooth so that we may enjoy our long life. And may all
our stocks rise to the occasion of our best possibilities,
and our humanness be bullish too.

Speaking personally I am glad to be a heroic man.

I am pleased that I am attractive to women but
grateful I'm no bounder. Though I'm touched when
married women fall in love with me, as frequently they
do, I am rarely to blame. I never encourage these fits
and do my best to get them over their derangements so
as not to lose the friendships of their husbands when
they are known to me, or the neutral friendship of the
ladies themselves. This happens less than you might
think, however, for whenever I am a houseguest of a
married friend I usually make it a point to bring along
a girl. These girls are from all walks of life—models,
show girls, starlets, actresses, tennis professionals, sing-
ers, heiresses and the daughters of the diplomats of
most of the nations of the free world. *All* walks. They
tend, however, to conform to a single physical type,

and are almost always tall, tan, slender and blond, the girl from Ipanema as a wag friend of mine has it. They are always sensitive and intelligent and good at sailing and the Australian crawl. They are never blemished in any way, for even something like a tiny beauty mark on the inside of a thigh or above the shoulder blade is enough to put me off, and their breaths must be as sweet at three in the morning as they are at noon. (I never see a woman who is dieting for diet sours the breath.) Arm hair, of course, is repellent to me though a soft blond down is now and then acceptable. I know I sound a prig. I'm not. I am—well, classical, drawn by perfection as to some magnetic, Platonic pole, idealism and beauty's true North.

But if I'm demanding about the type I fall in love with—I *do* fall in love, I'm not Don Juan—I try to be charming to all women, the flawed as well as the unflawed. I know that times have changed and that less is expected of gentlemen these days, that there's more "openness" between the sexes and that in the main, this is a healthy development. Still, in certain respects I am old-fashioned—I'm the first to admit it—and not only find myself incapable of strong language in the presence of a lady (I rarely use it myself at any time, even a "damn" even a "hell") but become enraged when someone else uses it and immediately want to call him out. I'm the same if there's a child about or a man over the age of fifty-seven if he is not vigorous. The leopard cannot change his spots. I'm a gentleman, an opener of doors and doffer of hats and after you firster, meek in the elevator and kind to the help. I maintain a fund which I use for the abortions of girls other men have gotten into trouble; if the young lady prefers, I have a heart-to-heart with the young man. And although I've no sisters, I have a brother's temperament, all good counsel and real concern. Even without a sister of my own—or a brother either for that matter; I'm an only child—I lend an ear and do for other fellows' sisses the moral forks.

Still, there's fun in me, and danger too. I'm this orphan now but that's recent (Father and Mother died early this year, Mother first and Father a few days later—Father, too, was courteous to women), and I'm afraid that when they were alive I gave my parents some grisly moments with my exploits, put their hearts in their mouths and gray in their hair. I have been a fighter pilot for the RAF (I saw some action at Suez) and a mercenary on the *Biafran* side, as well as a sort of free-lance spy against some of your South American and Greek juntas. (I'm not political, but the average generalissimo cheats at cards. It's curious, I've noticed that though they steal the picture cards they rarely play them; I suppose it's a class thing—your military man would rather beat you with a nine than a king.) I am Johnny-on-the-spot at disasters—I was in Managua for the earthquake—lending a hand, pulling my oar, the sort of man who knocks your teeth out if he catches you abusing the water ration in the lifeboat and then turns around and offers his own meager mouthful to a woman or a man over fifty-seven. Chavez is my friend and the Chicago Seven, though I had to stop seeing them because of the foul language. (I love Jerry Rubin too much to tear his head off, and I could see that's what it would come to.) And here and there I've had Mafiosi for friends—wonderful family men, the Cosa Nostra, I respect that. And the astronauts, of course; I spent a weightless weekend with them in an anti-gravity chamber in Houston one time, coming down only to take a long-distance phone call from a girl in trouble. And, let's see, sixty hours in the

bathysphere with Cousteau, fathoms below where the
ordinary fish run. So I have been weightless and I have
been gravid, falling in free-fall like a spider down its
filament and payed out in rappel. And in the Prix de
this and Prix de t'other, all the classic combats of moving parts (my own moving parts loose as a toy yet to be
assembled), uninsurable at last, taking a stunt man's
risks, a darer gone first, blinded in the world's uncharted caves and deafened beneath its waterfalls, the earth
itself a sort of Jungle Gym finally, my playground,
swimming at your own risk.

Last winter I fought a duel. I saw a man whipping
his dog and called him out. Pistols at fourteen paces.
The fellow—a prince, a wastrel—could get no one to
act as his second so I did it myself, giving him point-
ers, calling the adjustments for windage, and at last
standing still for him as one of those FBI paper silhou-
ettes, my vitals (we were on a beach, I wore no shirt,
just my bathing suit, the sun, rising over his shoulder,
spotlighting me) clear as marked meat on a butcher's
diagram, my Valentine heart vaulting toward the barrel
of his pistol. He fired and missed and I threw my pistol
into the sea. He wept, and I took him back to the
house and gave him a good price for his dog. And
running with the bulls at Pamplona—not in front of
them, *with* them—and strolling at two A.M. through
the Casbah like a fellow down Main Street, and standing on top of a patrol car in Harlem talking through
the bull horn to the sniper. And dumb things too.

Father called me home from Tel Aviv a few weeks
before he died.

He was sitting on a new bed in his room wearing
only his pajama tops. He hadn't shaved, the gray
stubble latticing his lower face in an old man's way,

like some snood of mortality. There was a glass in his hand, his hundred-dollar bill rolled tight around the condensation. (He always fingered one, a tic.)

"Say hello to your mother."

I hadn't seen her. Like many people who have learned the secret of living together, Father and Mother slept in separate suites, but now twin beds, Father in one, Mother in the other, had replaced Father's four-poster. A nightstand stood between them—I remembered it from Grandmother Newpert's summer house in Edgarton—on which, arranged like two entrenched armies, were two sets of medicines, Father's bright ceremonial pills and May Day capsules, and Mother's liquids in their antique apothecary bottles (she supplied the druggist with these bottles herself, insisting out of her willful aesthetic sense that all her prescriptions be placed in them), with their water glasses and a shiny artillery of teaspoons. Mother herself seemed to be sleeping. Perhaps that's why I hadn't noticed her, or perhaps it was the angle, Father's bed being the closer as I walked into the room. Or perhaps it was her condition itself, sickness an effacement. I hesitated.

"It's all right," Father said. "She's awake. You're not disturbing her."

"Her eyes are closed," I said softly to Father.

"I have been seeing double in the morning, Brewster darling," Mother said. "It gives me megrim to open them."

"Mother, you naughty slugabed," I teased. Sometimes being a gentleman can be a pain in the you-know-where, to oneself as well as to others. Well, it's often fatuous, and in emergency it always is, as anything is in emergency short of an uncivilized scream, but what can you do, a code is a code. One dresses for dinner in the jungle and surrenders one's sword to the enemy

and says thank you very much and refuses the blind-
fold. "Shame on you, sweetheart, the sun up these
several hours and you still tucked in."

"It's cancer, Son," Father said in a low tone not
meant for Mother.

"Lazybones," I scolded, swallowing hard.

"Oh, I *do* want to see you, Brewster," Mother said.
"Perhaps if I opened just *one* little eye—"

"Not at all, you sweet dear. If you must lie in bed
all day I think it best that you do some honest sleeping. I'll still be here when you finally decide to get
up."

"There, that's better," Mother said, opening her
right eye and scowling at me.

"Please, honeybunch, you'll see double and get megrim."

"Brewster, it's lovely. It makes you twice as handsome, twice as tall."

"Please, Mother—"

"Let her, Brew. This is a deathbed."

"Father!"

"Why are you so shocked, Brewster? It had to
happen someday."

"I think I'll close it now."

"Really, Father, a *death*bed . . ."

"Since it upsets him so."

"Well, death*beds* then."

"But I reserve the right to open it again whenever I
choose. If a cat can look at a king . . ."

"Father, aren't you being—that's right, darling, shut
it, shut it tight—the slightest bit melodramatic?"

"Oh, for Lord's sake, Brew, don't be prissy. Mother
and I are going, she of cancer, I of everything. Rather
than waste the little time we have left together, we
might try to get certain things straight."

"When Father called you back from overseas he

arranged with Mrs. Lucas to have these twin deathbeds set up in here."

Mrs. Lucas is the housekeeper. She used to give me my baths when I was a child. I always try to remember to bring her a picnic hamper or some other especially nice premium from the bank when I come home for a visit. Over the years Mrs. Lucas has had *chaises longues,* card tables, hammocks and many powerful flashlights from me—a small fortune in merchandise.

"What were you doing in the Middle East in the first place? Those people aren't your sort, Brew."

"He did it for you, darling. He thought that by putting both deathbeds in the same room you wouldn't have to shuffle back and forth between one chamber and the next. It's a time-space thing, Noel said. Isn't that right, Noel?"

"Something like that. Yes, Nora."

"Father, the Jewish are darned impressive. They run their military like a small family business. The Arabs can't touch them."

"Arabs, Jews. In my time a country club was a country club. I don't understand anything anymore."

"Don't quarrel, Noel, Brew. Brew, you're the reason we decided to have deathbeds in the first place. Well, my family has always had them, of course. None of this hole-and-corner hospital stuff for them. I don't speak against hospitals, mind you, they're all very well if you're going to get better, but, goodness, if you're really dying it's so much more pleasant for the immediate family if they can be saved from those drafty, smelly hospital corridors. Grandmother Oh herself, though she invented the oxygen tank, refused the tent when her time came if it meant going to a hospital."

"Brr."

"Are you addressing me, Father?"

"What? No, no, I have a chill."

"Let me help you." I lifted his legs into the bed gently, took the glass out of his hand and set it down, unpeeling the hundred-dollar bill as if it were a beer label. I placed his head back on the pillow and, smoothing the sheets, started to cover him when he grinned.

"Close cover before striking," he said hoarsely. That broke the ice and we all laughed.

"Nothing important ever gets said in a hospital," Father said after a while. "There's too much distraction. The room, the gadgets, the flowers and who sent what, the nurses coming in for one thing or another. Nothing important gets said."

I nodded.

"Mother's right, Brewster. The deathbed has been a tradition in our family. This twin bed business is a little vulgar, perhaps, but it can't be helped. We'll have a deathbed vigil. It's a leisure thing. It's elegant."

"Please, Father, let's not have any more of this morbid stuff about dying," I said, getting the upper hand on myself. "It's my notion you're both gold-bricking, that you'll be out on the links again in no time, your handicap lower than ever."

"It's heart, Brew," Father said gloomily. "It's Ménière's disease. It's TB and a touch of MS that hangs on like a summer cold. It's a spot of Black Lung."

"Black Lung?"

"Do you know how many matches I've struck in my time?"

"I wouldn't be surprised, Father, if there were another slogan in you yet. 'I Would Rather Light an Ashenden Match Than Curse the Darkness.' How's that?"

"Too literary. What the smoker wants is something

short and sweet. No, there'll be no more slogans. Let
others carry on my work. I'm tired."

"There's this Israeli ace," I said as a stopgap, "Izzy
Heskovitz, who's . . ."

"What's this about a duel, Brewster?" Father asked.

"Oh, did you hear about that? I should have
thought the Prince would have wanted it hushed up,
after what happened."

"After what happened? He thinks you're mad. And
so do I. Exposing yourself like that, offering a target
like a statesman in an open car, then tossing your
pistol into the sea. It was irresponsible. Were you
trying to kill yourself?"

"It was a question of honor."

"With you, Brewster, everything is a question of
honor."

"Everything is."

"Stuff and nonsense."

"I'm looking for myself."

"Brewster, you are probably the last young man in
America still looking for himself," Father said. "As a
man who has a certain experience with slogans, I have
some sense of when they have lost their currency."

"Father, you are probably the last *old* man in
America to take to a deathbed."

"Touché, Brew. He's got you there, Noel," Mother
said.

"Thank you, Mother, but all I intended was to point
out that obsolescence runs in our family. I am the
earth, water, fire and air heir. Let the neon, tin and
tungsten scions prepare themselves for the newfangled.
I have pride and I have honor. My word is my bond
and I'll marry a virgin. And I agree with you, Father,
about the sanctity of the deathbed, though I shall
continue, out of chivalry and delicacy, to maintain the

imposture that this . . . these"—I took in the twin
beds—"is . . . are . . . not that . . . those."

"You're marvelous, Brewster. I . . ."

"Is something wrong, Father?"

" . . . we . . . your mother and I . . ."

"Father?"

"I love you, Son."

"I love *you,* sir," I told him. I turned to Mother. She
had opened one eye again. It was wet and darting from
one side to the other like an eye in REM sleep. I
understood that she was trying to choose my real
image from the two that stood before her. In a moment
her eye had decided. It stared off, focused about four
yards to my right. I smiled to reassure her that she had
chosen correctly and edged slowly to my right, an
Indian in reverse, unhiding, trying to appear in her line
of sight like a magician's volunteer in an illusion. "And
all I have to say to *you,* you great silly, is that if you're
not out of bed soon I'll not answer for your zinnias and
foxgloves. I noticed when the taxi brought me up the
drive that Franklin, as usual, has managed to make a
botch of the front beds."

"Franklin is old, Son," Mother said. "He isn't well."

"Franklin's a rogue, Mother. I don't know why you
encourage him. I'm certain he's going to try to trade
Mrs. Lucas the three hundred feet of lovely rubber
garden hose I brought him for her Scotch cooler so
that he can have a place to hide his liquor."

Mother closed her eye; Father grinned. I wrung out
Father's hundred-dollar bill and handed it back to him.
Excusing myself, I promised to return when they had
rested. "Brr," Father said.

"Were you speaking to me, Father?"

"It's the chill again," he said.

I went to my room, called up their doctors and had
long, discouraging talks with them. Then I phoned

some specialist friends of mine at Mass General and a
good man at Barnes in St. Louis and got some additional opinions. I asked about Franklin, too.

I kept the vigil. It was awful, but satisfying, too, in a
way. It lasted five weeks and in that time we had truth
and we had banter, and right up to the end each of us
was able to tell the difference. Only once, a few days
after Mother's death (her vision returned at the end:
"I can see, Brewster," she said, "I can see far and I
can see straight." These were not her last words; I'll
not tell you her last words, for they were meant only
for Father and myself, though I have written them
down elsewhere to preserve for my children should I
ever have them) did Father's spirits flag. He had
gotten up from his bed to attend the funeral—through
a signal courtesy to an out-of-stater, the Governor of
Massachusetts permitted Mother to be buried on
Copp's Hill Burying Ground near the Old North
Church in Boston—and we had just returned to the
house. Mrs. Lucas and Franklin were weeping, and I
helped Father upstairs and back into his deathbed. He
was too weak to put his pajamas on. "You know,
Brew," he said, "I sure wish you hadn't thrown that
d——d pistol into the ocean."

"Oh Father," I said, "never mind. Tomorrow when
you're stronger we'll go to town and buy a fresh brace
and stroll the woods and shoot the birds from their
trees just as we used to."

He was dead in his own tree a few days later. I
sensed it coming and had moved into the room with
him, where I lay next to him all night in the twin bed,
only Grandmother Newpert's nightstand between us,
Mother's effects—the lovely old apothecary bottles and
her drinking glass and medicine spoons—having been
cleared away. I was awake the entire night, hanging on
his broken breath and old man's groans like a detective

in films on the croaks of a victim. I listened for a
message from the coma and tried to parse delirium as
if it were only a sort of French. Shall a man of honor
and pride still searching for himself in his late thirties
deny the sibyl in a goner's gasps? (I even asked one or
two questions, pressing him in his terminal pain, pursuing him through the mazes of his dissolution, his
deathbed my Ouija board.)

Then, once, just before dawn, a bird twittered in the
garden and Father came out of it. For fifteen minutes
he talked sense, speaking rapidly and with an astonishing cogency that was more mysterious somehow than
all his moans and nightmares. He spoke of ways to
expedite the probating of the two wills, of flaws in the
nature of his estate, instructing me where to consoli-
date and where to trim. He told me the names of what
lawyers to trust, which brokers to fire. In five minutes
he laid down principles which would guarantee our
fortune for a hundred years. Then, at the end, there
was something personal, but after what had gone before, I thought it a touch lame, like a **P.S.** inquiring
about your family's health at the end of a business
letter. He wished me well and hoped I would find some
nice girl, settle down, and raise fine children. I was to
give them his love.

I thought this was the end, but in a few moments he
came round again.

"Franklin *is* a rogue," he said. "For many years now
he and Mrs. Lucas have been carrying on an affair
below stairs. That time during the war when Mrs.
Lucas was supposed to have gone to stay with her
sister in Delaware she really went away to have Franklin's child. The scoundrel refused to marry her and
would have had money from us to abort the poor
thing. It was Mrs. Lucas who wouldn't hear of it, but

the baby died anyway. Mrs. Lucas loves him. It's for her sake we never let him go when he screws up in the garden."

Those were Father's last words. Then he beckoned me to rise from my bed and approach him. He put out his right hand. I shook it and he died. The hundred-dollar bill he always held came off in my palm when the final paroxysm splayed his fingers.

The grief of the rich is clubby, expensive. (I don't mean *my* grief. My grief was a long gloom, persistent as grudge.) We are born weekenders anyway, but in death we are particularly good to each other, traveling thousands of miles to funerals, flying up from Rio or jamming the oceanic cables with our expensive consolation. (Those wires from the President to the important bereaved—that's our style, too.) We say it with flowers, wreaths, memorial libraries, offering the wing of a hospital as casually as someone else a chicken leg at a picnic. And why not? There aren't that many of us—never mind that there are a thousand who can buy and sell me. Scarcer we are than the Eskimaux, vanishing Americans who got rich slow.

So I did not wonder at the crowds who turned up at Mother's funeral and then went away the long distances only to return a few days later for Father's. Or at the clothes. Couturiers of Paris and London and New York—those three splendid cities, listed always together and making a sound on the page like a label on scent—taxed to the breaking point to come up with dresses in death's delicious high fashion, the rich taking big casualties that season, two new mourning originals in less than two weeks and the fitter in fits. The men splendid in their decent dark. Suits cunningly not black, *off* black, proper, the longitudes of their decency in their wiry pinstripes, a gent's torso bound up in vest

and crisscrossed by watch chains and Phi Beta Kappa
keys in the innocent para-militarism of the civilian
respectable, men somehow more vital at the graveside
in the burdensome clothes than in Bermudas on
beaches or dinner jackets in hotel suites with cocktails
in their hands, the band playing on the beach below
and the telephone ringing.

And all the women were beautiful, gorgeous, griev-
ing's colors good for them, aloof mantles which made
them seem (though I knew better) unattainable vir-
gins again, yet sexy still as secret drinkers. God, how I
lusted when I was with them! I could barely put two
words together for them or accept their condolences
without feeling my importunate, inopportune blood
thicken, my senses as ticklish as if Persian whores had
gotten to them. Which added to my gloom, of course,
because I was dishonoring my parents in their death as
I never had while they lived.

Only the necessity to cope saved me from some
sacrilege. (Oh, the confidence of lust! Surely that's the
basis of its evil. The assumptions it permits one,
glossing reality like a boy in the dark, touching himself
and thinking of his mother's bridge guests.) Somehow
however, I managed to see my tailor, somehow got the
arrangements made, somehow wrote the necessary
checks and visited the near-at-hand safe-deposit boxes
before they were red-flagged, somehow got through the
inventories, spoke to the obituary people at the *Times,*
prepared the eulogies somehow, and fielded all the
questions of the well-meaning that are asked at times
like these.

"Will there be a foundation, do you suppose, Ashenden?" asked an old friend of the family who had
himself been an heir for as long as we had known him.
(And oh, the effect of that "Ashenden"! It was the

first time one had been thus addressed, at least officially, since one's roommates at boarding school and
college, thinking of their own inheritances, had used
it.)

"I don't know, sir. It's too early to tell. I shall have
to wait until the estate is properly probated before I
can be certain what there is."

"Of course, of course," he said, "but it's never too
soon to start *thinking* about a foundation, fixing your
goals."

"Yes, sir."

"Let me give you a little advice on that score. The
arts. There are those who swear by diseases and the
various social ills, but I'm not one of them. And of the
arts I think the *performing* arts give you your best
return. You get invited backstage."

"I'll have to look into it."

"Look into it."

And one of Mother's friends wondered if marriage
was in the offing. "Now you really *are* eligible, Brewster," she said. "Oh, you were before, of course, but
now you must certainly feel a bit of pressure to put
your affairs in order and begin to think about the next
generation."

It was a rude thing to say (though something like
these had been almost Father's last words to me), but
the truth was I did feel it. Perhaps that was what my
shameful lust had been about, nature's way of pointing
me to my duty. My search for myself seemed trivial
child's play now. Honor did subsist in doing right by
the generations. I know what you're thinking: Who's
this impostor, this namby with no will of his own? If
he's so rich, why ain't he smart? Meaning glacial,
indifferent, unconscious of the swath of world he cuts
as the blade of what it leaves bleeding—the cosmos as

rich man's butter pat. Listen, disdain's easy, a mug's game, but look close at anything and you'll break your heart.

I was inconsolable, grave at the graveside, beside myself like a fulfillment of Mother's prophetic double vision.

"People lose parents," a Securities and Exchange Commission cousin told me. (Yes, yes, it's nothing, only nature bottoming out.) "Sons lose mothers," he said, his gray hair trimmed that morning, wet looking. "Fathers die."

"Don't look," I said wildly, "shut an eye. I am beside myself."

I keened like a widow, a refugee from hardest times, a daughter with the Cossacks, a son chopped in the thresher. I would go about in black, I thought, and be superstitious. My features will thicken and no one will know how old I am.

"There, there," he told me, "there, there."

"There, there. There, there," said this one and that.

My pals did not know what to make of me.

"My God, Ashenden," one said, a roommate from boarding school, "have you seen the will? Is it awful?"

"I've been left everything," I told him coolly.

He nudged me in the ribs. I would have called him out had I not been in mourning.

Only the sight of Mrs. Lucas saved me. The thought of that brave woman's travail enabled me to control myself at last. I no longer wept openly and settled into a silent, standoffish grimness, despair like an ingrown toenail on a man of fashion.

The weekends began.

All my adult life I have been a guest in other people's houses, following the sun and seasons like a migratory bird, an instinct in me, the rich man's cun-

ning feel for ripeness, some oyster-in-an-r-month notion working there which knows without reference to
anything outside itself when to pack the tennis racquet,
when to bring along the German field glasses to look at
a friend's birds, the telescope to stare at his stars, the
wet suit to swim in beneath his waters when the exotic
fish are running. It's not in the *Times* when the black
dinner jacket comes off and the white one goes on; it's
something surer, subtler, the delicate guidance system
of the privileged, my playboy astronomy.

The weekends began, and the midweeks and week-
and two-week stretches in the country. I was very
grateful to my friends' sense of what I needed then.
Where I was welcome before, I was now actively
pursued. My friends were marvelous, and not a mean
motive between them. If I can't say as much for
myself.

In the luggage now with the bandboxes of equipment, the riding boots and golf clubs and hiker's gear,
was a lover's wardrobe: shirts like the breasts of birds,
custom ties that camouflaged themselves against their
backgrounds or stood out like dye in the sea, ascots
like bunting for the throat's centennial, the handmade
jackets and perfect trousers and tack-room leathers. I
dressed to kill, slay should I meet her, the mother of
my children. (These were my mourning togs, mind.)
And if I brought the best that could be had, it was not
out of vanity but only respect for that phantom girl
who would be so exquisite herself, so refined and
blessed with taste that it would have been as dangerous
for her to look at the undistinguished as for another to
stare directly into the eclipse. So it was actually humility that made me dress as I did, simple self-effacement,
the old knight's old modesty, shyness so capitulative
that prostration was only a kind of militant attention, a
death-defying leap to the earth. And since I had never

met her, nor knew her name, nor had a clue to where
she might be, I traveled alone, for the first time taking
along no guest of the guest. Which my friends put
down to decency, the thirty- or sixty- or ninety-day
celibacy of the orphaned. But it wasn't that.

It was a strange period of my life. My friends,
innocent of my intentions and honoring what they
supposed to be my bereavement, omitted to invite any
girls for me at all, and I found myself on this odd
bachelor circuit, several times meeting the same male
guest I had met at someone else's house a few weeks
before. We crossed each other's paths like traveling
salesmen with identical territories. And I rode and
hunted and fished and stayed up all hours playing
whist or backgammon or chess with my hosts or the
other male guest, settled before fires with sherry and
cognac, oddly domestic, as if what I owed the generations was a debt already paid, a trip in the time
machine, keeping late hours in libraries until the odor
of leather actually became offensive to me. On the few
occasions I retired early it was at my host's instructions. (I am an obedient guest.) The next morning
there was to be an excursion in the four-wheel drive to
investigate property he had acquired in backwoods
forty miles off—a lodge, an abandoned watchtower,
twice an old lighthouse. And always, nodding my approval if the purchase had been made or giving my
judicious advice if it hadn't, I had this sense that I'd
had the night before in the library: that the property in
question was *my* property, that I was already what I
was dressed to become.

I was not bored; I was distraught.

A strange thing happened. It occurred to me that
perhaps my old fastidiousness regarding the inviolabili-
ty of a friend's wife was wrong, morally wrong. Had
not these women made overtures, dropped hints, left

doors ajar so that returning to my room with a book I could see them in nightgowns beside bedlamps; hadn't they smiled sweetly and raised arms? Perhaps I had been a prig, had placed too high a value on myself by insisting on the virginity of my intended. Perhaps it was my fate to figure in a divorce. I decided that henceforth I must not be so standoffish with my friends' wives.

So I stroked their knees beneath the whist table and put down their alarm to surprise. I begged off going on the excursions and stayed home with them when my friend and the other guest climbed into the jeep. I followed the wife all about the house and cornered her in stairwells and gardens.

"I'm no prig," I told Nan Bridge, and clasped her breast and bit her ear.

"What the hell do you think you're doing, buster?" she shouted.

"Four months ago I would have called you out for that," I told her lamely and left her house that afternoon and went to the next three days early, determined to be more careful.

I was staying with Courtney and Buffy Surface in Connecticut. Claiming a tennis elbow, I excused myself from the doubles early in the first set. Courtney and I were partners against Buffy and Oscar Bobrinage, the other houseguest. My plan was for Buffy to drop out and join me. I sat under a wide umbrella in the garden, and in a few minutes someone came up behind me. "Where does it hurt? I'll rub it for you."

"No thank you, Oscar."

"No trouble, Brewster."

"I've a heating pad from Chase Manhattan in my suitcase, Osc," I told him dejectedly.

That night I was more obvious. I left the library and mentioned as casually as I could that I was going out for a bit of air. It has been my observation that the predisposition for encounter precedes encounter, that one must set oneself as one would a table. I never stroll the strand in moonlight except when I'm about the heart's business, or cross bridges toward dawn unless I mean to save the suicides. There are natural laws, magnetism. A wish pulls fate.

I passed the gazebo and wondered about the colors of the flowers in the dark, the queer consolidation of noon's bright pigment, yellow sunk in on yellow a thousand times as if struck by gravity. I thought of popular songs, their tunes and words. I meant for once to do away with polite conversation should Buffy appear, to stun her with my need and force. (Of all my friends Buffy was the most royally aloof. She had maddening ways of turning aside any question or statement that was the least bit threatening.)

I heard the soft crunch of gravel. "Oscar?"

"No, it's Buffy. Were you looking for Oscar?"

"I thought he might be looking for me."

*"Voilà du joli,"* Buffy said. She knew the idioms of eleven modern languages.

I gazed into her eyes. "How are you and Courtney, Buffy?"

*"Mon dieu! ¿Qué pasa? Il est onze heures et demi,"* she said.

"Buffy, how are you and *Courtney*?"

"Courtney's been off erythromycin five days now and General Parker says there's no sign of redness. God bless wonder drugs. *Darauf kannst du Gift nehmen.*"

"Do you ever think of Madrid, Buffy? "Once in a nightclub in Madrid on New Year's Eve she had kissed me. It was before she and Courtney met, but my memory of such things is long lasting and profound. I never forget the blandest intimacy. *"Do* you?"

"Oh, Brewster, I have every hope that when Juan Carlos is restored the people will accept him."

"Buffy, we kissed each other on New Year's Eve in Madrid in 1966 before you ever heard of Courtney Surface."

*"Autres temps, autres moeurs."*

"I can't accept that, Buff. Forgive me, dear, but when I left the game this morning you stayed behind to finish out the set *against* Courtney. Yes, and before that you were Oscar's partner. Doesn't this indicate to you a certain aberrant competitiveness between you and your husband?"

"Oh, but darling, we play for *money. Pisica blậndiă pgarie raŭ.* Didn't you know that? We earn each other's birthday presents. We've an agreement: we don't buy a gift unless we win the money for it from the other fellow. I'll tell you something, *entre nous.* I get ripped off because I throw games. I do. I take dives. I go into the tank. *Damit kannst du keinen Blumetopf verlieren.* Isn't that *awful?* Aren't I *terrible?* But that's how Courtney got the money together to buy me Nancy's Treehouse. Have you seen her? She's the *most* marvelous beast. I was just going out to the stables to check on her when I ran into you. If you'd like to accompany me come along *lo más pronto posible.*"

"No."

*"De gustibus."*

"That's *not* a modern language, Buffy."

"People *grow,* darling."

"Buffy, as your houseguest I *demand* that you listen to me. I am almost forty years old and I am one of the three or four dozen truly civilized men in the world and I have been left a fortune. A fortune! And though I have always had the use of the money, I have never till now had the control of it. Up to now I have been

an adventurer. The adventures, God save me, were
meant to teach me life. Danger builds strong bodies
twelve ways, I thought. Action and respite have been
the pattern of my existence, Buffy. Through shot and
shell on hands and knees one day, and breakfast in bed
at Claridge's the next. I have lived my life like a fighter
pilot, beefed up as a gladiator, like a stuffed goose,
like a Thanksgiving turkey. I am this civilized . . .
*thing.* Trained and skilled and good. I mean *good,*
Buffy, a strict observer till night before last of every
commandment there is. Plus an eleventh—honor thy
world, I mean. I've done that. I'm versed in it, up to
my ears in it as you are in idioms. I was an environ-
mentalist a decade before it was an issue. When I first
noticed the deer were scrawnier than they'd been when
I was a boy and the water in the rivers where I swam
no longer tasted like peaches.

"I've been a scholar of the world—oh, an amateur, I
grant you, but a scholar just the same. I understand
things. I know literature and math and science and art.
I know *everything.* How paper is made, glass blown,
marble carved, things about furniture, stuff about
cheese. This isn't a boast. With forty years to do it in
and nothing to distract you like earning a living or
raising a family, you can learn almost all there is *to*
learn if you leave out the mystery and the ambiguity. If
you omit the riddles and finesse the existential.

"No, *wait!* I'm perfectly aware that I'm barking up
the wrong tree—do you have that idiom, my dear?—
but looky, looky, I'm speaking my heart. I'm in
mourning, Buff. Here's how I do it. By changing my
life. By taking this precious, solipsistic civilization of
mine—Buffy, listen to me, dear; *it's not enough that
there are only three or four dozen truly civilized men
in the world*—this precious civilization of mine and
passing it on to sons, daughters, all I can get."

*"Was ist los?"* she said miserably.

"Time and tide."

*"Pauvre garçon."*

"Buffy, *pauvre garçon* me no *pauvres garçons.*"

She looked at me for a moment with as much feeling as I had looked at her. "Jane Löes Lipton."

"What?"

"Jane Löes Lipton. A friend of my sister Milly."

"What about her?"

"Ah."

"Ah?"

"She'll be Comte de Survillieur's houseguest this month. Do you know the Comte?"

"We did a hitch together in the Foreign Legion."

"Go. Pack. I'll phone Paris. Perhaps Milly can get you an invitation. *In bocca al lupo.*"

I missed her at the Comte de Survillieur's, and again at Liège, and once more at Cap Thérèse and the Oktoberfest at München. All Europe was talking about her—the fabulous Jane Löes Lipton. One had only to mention her name to elicit one of those round Henry James "Ah's." Nor did it surprise me that until the evening in Buffy Surface's garden I had never heard of her: I had been out of society for three or four months. These things happen quickly, these brush fires of personality, some girl suddenly taken up and turned into a household word (if you can call a seventy-room castle a household or "Ah" a word). Once or twice I had seen an old woman or even a child given this treatment. Normally I avoided such persons. When their fame was justified at all it was usually predicated on some quirkishness, nothing more substantial than some lisp of the character—a commitment to astrology, perhaps, or a knack for mimicry, or skill at bridge. I despise society, but who else will deal with me? I can't run loose in the street with the sailors or drink with the whores. I would put off everyone but a peer.

Still . . . Jane Löes Lipton. Ah. I hadn't met her, but from what I could gather from my peers' collective inarticulateness when it came to Miss (that much was established) Lipton, she was an "authentic," an original," a "beauty," a "prize." And it was intriguing, too, how I happened to keep missing her, for once invited to the Comte's—where I behaved; where, recovering my senses, I no longer coveted my neighbor's wife and rededicated myself to carrying on the good work of my genes and environment in honorable ways—I had joined a regular touring company of the rich and favored. We were like the Ice Capades, like an old-time circus, occasionally taking on personnel, once in a while dropping someone off—a car pool of the heavily leisured. How I happened, as I say, to keep on missing her though we were on the same circuit now, going around—no metaphor but a literal description—in the same circles—and it is *too* a small world, at our heights, way up there where true North consolidates and collects like fog, it is—was uncanny, purest contretemps, a melodrama of bad timing. We were on the same guest lists, often the same floors or wings (dowagers showed me house plans, duchesses did; I saw the seating arrangements and croquet combinations), co-sponsors of the same charity balls and dinners. Twice it was I who fell out of lockstep and had to stay longer than I expected or leave a few days early, but every other time it was Jane who canceled out at the last minute. Was this her claim on them, I wondered? A Monroeish temperament, some pathological inability to keep appointments, honor commitments (though always her check for charity arrived, folded in her letter of regret), the old high school strategy of playing hard to get? No. And try to imagine how *this* struck me, knowing what you do about me, when I heard it. "Miss Löes Lipton called to say she will not be able to join your Lordship this weekend due to an emergency outbreak of cholera among the children at the Sisters of Cecilia Mission in Lobos de Afuera." That was the message the Duke's secretary brought him at Liège.

"She's Catholic?" I asked.

"What? Jane? Good Lord, I shouldn't think so."

Then, at Cap Thérèse, I learned that she had again begged off. I expressed disappointment and inquired of Mrs. Steppington whether Miss Lipton were ill.

"Ah, Jane. Ill? Jane's strong as a horse. No, dear boy, there was a plane crash at Dar es Salaam and Jane went there to help the survivors. She's visiting in hospital with them now. For those of them who have children—mostly wogs, I expect—she's volunteered to act as a sort of governess. I can almost see her, going about with a lot of nig-nog kids in tow, teaching them French, telling them the Greek myths, carrying them to whatever museums they have in such places, giving them lectures in art history, then fetching them water-colors—and oils too, I shouldn't doubt—so they can have a go at it. Oh, it *will* be a bore not having her with us. She's a frightfully good sailor and I had hoped to get her to wear my silks in the regatta."

Though it was two in the morning in Paris, I went to my room and called the Comte de Survillieur.

"Comte. Why couldn't Jane Löes Lipton make it month before last?"

"What's that?" The connection was bad.

"Why did Miss Löes Lipton fail to show up when she was expected at Deux Oiseaux?"

"Who?"

"Jane Löes Lipton."

"Ah."

"Why wasn't she there?"

"Who's this?"

"Brewster Ashenden. I apologize for ringing up so late, but I have to know."

"Indians."

"Indians?"

"Yes. American Indians I think it was. Had to do some special pleading for them in Washington when a bill came up before your Congress."

"HR eleven seventy-four."

*"Qu'est-ce que c'est?"*

"The bill. Law now. So Jane was into HR eleven seventy-four."

"Ah, what isn't Jane into? You know, I think she's become something of a snob? She has no time for her old friends since undertaking these crusades of hers. She told the Comtesse as much—something about finding herself."

"She said *that*?"

"Well, she was more poetic, possibly, but that's how it came down to me. I know what *you're* after," the Comte said roguishly. "You're in love with her."

"I've never even met her."

"You're in love with her. Half Europe is. But unless you're a black or redskin, or have arranged in some other way to cripple yourself, you haven't a chance. Arse over tip in love, *mon cher* old comrade."

We rang off.

In the following weeks I heard that Jane Löes Lipton had turned up in Hanoi to see if there weren't some way of getting negotiations off dead center; that she had published a book that broke the code in Oriental rugs; that she had directed an underground movie in Sweden which despite its frank language and graphic detail was so sensitive it was to be distributed with a G rating; and that she was back in America visiting outdoor fairs and buying up paintings depicting clowns and rowboats turned over on beaches for a show she was putting together for the Metropolitan entitled "Shopping Center Primitive: Collectors' Items for the Twenty-Third Century." One man said she could be seen in Dacca on Bangladesh Television in a series called "Cooking Nutritious Meals on the Pavement for Large Families from Garbage and Without Fire," and another that she had become a sort of spiritual adviser to the statesmen of overdeveloped nations. Newspapers reported her on the scene wherever the earth quaked or the ships foundered or the forests burned.

Certainly she could not have had so many avatars. Certainly most was rumor, speculation knit from Jane's motives and sympathies. Yet I heard people never known to lie, Rock-of-Gibraltarish types who didn't get the point of jokes, swear to their testimony. Where there's smoke there's fire. If most was exaggerated, much was true.

Ah, Jane, Candy Striper to the Cosmos, Gray Lady of the Ineffable, when would I meet you, swap traveler's tales of what was to be found in those hot jungles of self-seeking, those voyages to the center of the soul and other uncharted places, the steeps and deeps and lost coves and far shelves of being? Ah, Jane, oh Löes Lipton, half Europe loves you.

I went to London and stayed at the Bottom, the tall new hotel there. Lonely as Frank Sinatra on an album cover I went up to their revolving cocktail lounge on the fiftieth floor, the Top of the Bottom, and ran into Freddy Plympton.

"She's here."

"Jane Löes Lipton? I've heard *that* one before." (We hadn't been talking of her. How did I know that's who he meant? I don't know, I knew.)

"No, no, not here, she's at my country place. She's there now. She's exhausted, poor dear, and tells me her doctor has commanded her to resign temporarily from all volunteer fire departments. So she's here. I've got her. She's with Lady Plympton right this moment. I had to come to town on business or I'd be with her. I'm going back in the morning. Ever meet her? Want to come down?"

"She's there? She's really there?"

"Want to come down?"

There's been too much pedigree in this account, I think. (Be kind. Put it down to metaphysics, not vanity. In asking Who? I'm wondering What? Even the trees have names, the rocks and clouds and grasses do. The world's a picture post card sent from a far hotel. "Here's my room, this is what the stamps in this country look like, that's the strange color of the sand here, the people all wear these curious hats.") Bear with me.

Freddy Plympton is noble. The family is old—whose isn't, eh? we were none of us born yesterday; look it up in *Burke's Peerage* where it gets three pages, in *Debrett* where it gets four—and his great estate, Duluth, is one of the finest in England. Though he could build a grander if he chose. Freddy's real wealth comes from the gambling casinos he owns. He is an entrepreneur of chance, a fortune teller. The biggest gaming palaces and highest stakes in Europe, to say nothing of hotels in Aruba and boats beyond the twelve-mile limit and a piece of the action in church bingo basements and punchboards all over the world, the newsprint for which is supplied from his own forests in Norway and is printed on his own presses. Starting from scratch, from choosing odds-or-evens for cash with his roommate at Harrow, a sheikh's son with a finger missing from his left hand—he was left-handed—which made him constitutionally unable to play the game ("He thought 'even,' you see," Freddy explains), taking the boy, neither of them more than fourteen, to the cleaners in the third form. It, the young sheikh's deformity, was Freddy's initial lesson in what it means to have the house odds in your favor and taught him never to enter any contest in which he did not have the edge.

Freddy has one passion, and it is not gambling. "Gambling's my work, old bean," he says. (He uses these corny aristocratic epithets. They make him seem fatuous but are as functional to his profession as a drawl to a hired gun.) "I'm no gambler at all, actually. I'm this sort of mathematician. Please don't gamble with me, please don't accept my bets. We're friends and I'm ruthless. Not vicious—ruthless. I will never surrender an advantage. Since I know the odds and respect them, to ignore them would be a sort of cheating, and since I'm honorable I couldn't think of that. Don't play with me. We're friends. I was never the sheikh's friend, never the friend of any of those feet-off-the-ground *Fleugenmensch* sons of rich men I lived with at Harrow and Cambridge and who gave me my stake. Where I was meditative they were speculative. I like you, as I like anyone who doesn't confuse his need with his evidence. Let's never gamble. Promise. *Promise?*"

So he has a passion, but it isn't gambling. It's animals—beasts, rather. Duluth contains perhaps the most superb private zoo in the world, a huge game park, larger than Whipsnade and much more dangerous. Where Whipsnade hedges with moats and illusions, at Duluth the animals are given absolute freedom. An enormous, camouflaged electrified fence, the largest in the world, runs about the entire estate. ("We control the current. The jolt merely braces the larger animals and only stuns the smaller, puts them unconscious. I've installed an auxiliary electrical plant for when there are power failures.") Although from time to time a few of the animals have fought and occasionally killed each other, an attempt has been made to introduce as near perfect an ecological balance as possible, vegetarians and carnivores who find the flesh of the beasts with whom they must live inimical, some almost religious constraint in the jaws and digestion, some once-burned, twice-sorry instinct passed on from generation to generation that protects and preserves his herds.

It was an ancestor of Plympton's who began the park, and as a result of the care he and his successors put into selecting and arranging the animals, some of the most incredible and lovely juxtapositions in the world are to be found there. (Freddy told me that Henri Rousseau painted his *Sleeping Gypsy* while he was a guest on the estate.) From the beginning a single rule has determined the constituency of the zoo: all the beasts collected there must have appeared on the Plympton heraldry. Lions, bears, elephants, unicorns ("a pure white rhinoceros actually"), leopards, jackals ("one old boy helped to do in Becket, old boy"), pandas, camels, sheep and apes. The family is an old one, the list long.

Though Plympton and I had known each other for years—we're the same age—this was the first time I had been invited to Duluth. I drove down with him the next morning, and of course it was not of the fabulous game park that I was thinking—I was not sure I even approved of it—but of Jane. I gave myself away with my questions.

"She's ill, you say?"

"Did I? I thought I said tired. What she told me,

anyway. Looks ruddy healthy, in fact. Tanner than
I've ever seen her."

"Is she alone?"

"What, is there a *man* with her, you mean? No, no,
Ashenden. She's quite singular."

"How did she happen to drop in on you?"

"I'm not in it at all, dear chap. I'm a businessman
and gamekeeper. My life's quite full. I suppose that
may actually have had something to do with it, in fact.
She called from Heathrow day before yesterday. Said
she was in England and wanted someplace to rest.
Lord, I hope she's not put off by my bringing you
down. Never thought of that aspect of it before."

"I won't bother her."

"No, of course you won't," he said smiling. "Sorry I
suggested that. Just thinking out loud. A man con-
cerned with animals must always be conscious of who
goes into the cage with whom. It's a social science,
zoology is, very helpful in making up parties. I suppose
mine, when I trouble to give them, are among the most
*gemütlich* in Europe. Indeed, now I think of it, I must
have realized as soon as I saw you last night that you'd
be acceptable to Jane, or I'd never have asked you.
Have you known her long?"

"We've never met."

"What, never met and so keen?" I smiled lamely
and Freddy patted my knee. "I understand. I do. I feel
you hoping. And I quite approve. Just don't confuse
your hope with your evidence." He studied me for a
moment. "But then you wouldn't, would you, or I'd
not be so fond of you."

"You do understand quite a lot, Freddy."

"Who, me? I'm objective, is all. Yearning, I can
smell yearning a mile off."

"I shall have to shower."

"Not at all, not at all. It stinks only when untempered by reason. In your case I smell reason a mile off, too. Eminently suitable, eminently," he pronounced. "I wouldn't bet against it," he added seriously, and I felt so good about this last that I had to change the subject. I questioned him about Duluth, which till then I hadn't even thought of. Now, almost superstitiously, I refused to think about Jane. Every time he gave me an opening I closed it, choosing, as one does who has so much at stake and success seems within his grasp, to steer clear of the single thing that is of any interest to him. We spoke trivially the whole time, and my excitement and happiness were incandescent.

"How many miles do you get to the gallon in this Bentley of yours, Plympton?" I asked, and even before he could answer I turned to look out the window and exclaim, "Look, look at the grass, so green it is. That's your English climate for you. If rain's the price a nation must pay to achieve a grass that green, then one must just as well pay up and be still about it. Who's your tailor? I'm thinking of having some things made."

When we left the M-4 and came to the turnoff that would bring us at last to Duluth I put my hand on Plympton's sleeve. "Freddy, listen, I know I must sound like a fool, but could you just introduce us and give me some time alone with her? We've so many friends in common—and perhaps other things as well—that I know there won't be any awkwardness. My God, I've been pursuing her for months. Who knows when I'll have such an opportunity again? I know my hope's showing, and I hope—look, there I go again—you won't despise me for it, but I have to talk to her. I have to."

"Then you shall," he said, and we turned onto the road that took us across the perimeter of the estate and drove for five miles and came to a gate where a gatekeeper greeted Lord Plympton and a chauffeur

who seemed to materialize out of the woods got in and
took the wheel while Freddy and I moved to the back
seat, and we drove together through the lovely grounds
for another fifteen or twenty minutes and passed
through another gate, though I did not see it until we
were almost on it—the queer, camouflaged electric
fence—and through the windows I could hear the
coughing of apes and the roar of lions and the bleating
of lambs and the wheezes and grunts and trebles and
basses of a hundred beasts—though I saw none—and
at last, passing through a final gate, came to the long,
curving, beautiful driveway of the beautiful house and
servants came to take our bags and others to open
doors and an older woman in a long gown—Plympton
kissed her and introduced her as his wife, the Lady
Plympton I'd never met ("She came with guanacos on
her crest, dear fellow, with the funny panda and the
gravid slug. I married her—ha ha—to fill out the set"),
and he bolted upstairs beckoning me to follow.
"Come on, come on," he said, "can't wait to get here,
then hangs back like a boy at his first ball," and I
bounded up the stairs behind him, and overtook him.
"Wherever are you going? You don't know the way.
Go on, go on, left, left," he called. "When you come to
the end of the hall turn right into the Richard Five
wing. It's the first apartment past the Ballroom of
Time. You'll see the clocks," and I left him behind,
only to come to the door, *her* door, and stop outside
it.

Plympton came up behind me. "I knew you
wouldn't," he said, and knocked on the door gently,
"Jane," he called softly. "Jane? Are you decent, darling?"

"Yes," she said. Her voice was beautiful.

"Shall I push open the door?"

"Yes," she said, "would you just?"

He shoved me gently inside, but did not cross the threshold himself. "Here's Brewster Ashenden for you," he said, and turned and left.

I could not see her clearly. No lights were on and the curtains were still drawn. I stood in the center of the room and waited for a command. I was physically excited, a fact which I trusted the darkness to shield from Jane. Neither of us said anything.

Then I spoke boldly. "He's right. I trust he's right. I pray he is."

"He?"

"Plympton. 'Here's Brewster Ashenden for you,' he said."

"Did he? That was presumptuous of him, then."

"I am Brewster Ashenden of the earth, air, fire and water Ashendens and this moment is very important to me. I'm first among eligible men, Miss Löes Lipton. Though that sounds a boast, it is not. I have heard of your beauty and your character. Perhaps you have heard something of mine."

"I never listen to gossip. And anyway hearsay is inadmissible in court . . . ship."

I knew she was going to say that. *It was exactly what I would have replied had she made the speech I had just made!* Do you know what it means to have so profound a confirmation—to have, that is, all one's notions, beliefs, hunches and hypotheses suddenly and entirely endorsed? My God, I was like Columbus standing in the New round World, like the Wrights right and aloft over Kitty Hawk! For someone like myself it was like having my name cleared! I'm talking about redemption. *To be right!* That's everything in life, you know. To be right, absolutely right, one hundred percent correct in all the essentials, that's all we want. And whoever is? Brewster Ashenden—once. I had so much to tell her.

I began to talk, a mile a minute, filling her in, breathlessly bringing her up to date, a Greek stranger's after-dinner talk in a king's gold palace on an inaccessible island in a red and distant sea. A necessary entertainment. Until then I had not known my life had been a story.

Then, though I could not see it in the dark room, she held up her hand for me to stop. It was exactly where I would have held up *my* hand had Jane been speaking.

"Yes," she said of my life, "it was the same with me."

Neither of us could speak for a time. Then, gaily, "Oh, Brewster, think of all the—"

"—coastlines?" I said.

"Yes," she said, "yes. All the coastlines, bays, sounds, capes and peninsulas, the world's beaches scribbled round all the countries and continents and islands. All the Cannes and Hamptons yet to be. Shores in Norway like a golden lovely dust. Spain's wild hairline, Portugal's long face like an impression on coins. The nubbed antlers of Scandinavia and the great South American porterhouse. The French teapot and Italian boot and Australia like a Scottie in profile."

"Asia running like a watercolor, dripping Japan and all the rest," we said together.

"Yes, yes," she said. "God, I love the world."

"There's no place like it."

"Let me wash up on seashores and eat the local specialties, one fish giving way to another every two or three hundred miles along the great continuous coasts like an exquisite, delicious evolution. Thank God for money and jet airplanes. Let me out at the outpost. Do you feel that way?"

"What, are you kidding? An earth, fire, air and water guy like me? I do, I do."

"Family's important," she said.

"You bet it is."

She giggled. "My grandfather, a New Yorker, was told to go west for his health. Grandfather hated newspapers, he didn't trust them and said all news— even of wars, heavy weather and the closing markets— was just cheap gossip. He thought all they were good for, since he held that calendars were vulgar, was the date printed at the top of the page. In Arizona he had the *New York Times* sent to him daily, though of course it always arrived a day or two late. So for him the eleventh was the ninth or the tenth, and he went through the last four years of his life a day or two behind actual time. Grandfather's Christmas and New Year's were celebrated after everyone else's. He went to church on Easter Tuesday."

"Easter Tuesday, that's very funny."

"I love the idiosyncratic; it is all that constitutes integrity. Difference, nuance, hues and shade. Spectra, Brewster. That's why we travel, perhaps, why we're found on all this planet's exotic strands, cherishing peculiarities, finding lost causes, chipping in to save the primitive wherever it occurs—"

"Listen to her talk. Is that a sweetheart?"

"—refusing to let it die, though the old ways are the worst ways and unhealthy, bad for the teeth and the balanced diet and the comfort and the longevity. Is that selfish?"

"I think so."

"Yes," she said pensively. "Of course it is. All taste's a cruelty at last. We impede history with our Sierra Clubs and our closed societies. We'll have to answer for that, I suppose. Oh, well . . . Brewster, do you have uncles? Tell me about your uncles."

"I had an Uncle Clifford who believed that disease could be communicated only by a draft when one was traveling at high speeds. He wore a paper bag over his head even in a closed car. He cut out holes for the eyes, for despite his odd notion he dearly loved to travel and watch the scenery go by. Even going up in elevators he wore his paper bag, though he strolled at ease through the contagion wards of hospitals dispensing charity to the poor."

"Marvelous."

"Yes."

"Brewster, this is important. Do you know things? People should know facts."

"I know them."

"I knew you knew them."

"I love you, Miss Löes Lipton."

"Jane," she said.

"Jane."

She was weeping. I didn't try to comfort her, but stood silently in place until she was through. I knew she was going to tell me to open the curtains, for this part of the interview was finished.

"Open the curtains, Brewster."

I went to the bay and pulled the drawstring and light came into the room and flooded it and I turned to the chair in which Jane was sitting and saw her face for the first time. She looked exactly as I knew she would look, though I had never seen a photograph of her or yet been to any of the houses in which her portraits were hung. All that was different was that there was a darkish region under her eyes and her skin had an odd tan.

"Oh," I said, "you've a spot of *lupus erythematosus* there, don't you?"

"You *do* know things, Brewster."

"I recognized the wolflike shadow across the eyes."

"It's always fatal."

"I know."

"The body develops antibodies against itself."

"I know."

"It's as if I were allergic to my own chemistry."

"I know, I know." I went toward her blinded by my tears. I kissed her, her lips and the intelligent, wolfish mask across her beautiful face. "How much time is there?" I asked.

Jane shrugged.

"It isn't fair. It isn't."

"Yes. Well," she said.

"Marry me, Jane."

She shook her head.

"You've got to."

"No," she said.

"Because of this fatal disease? That doesn't matter to me. I beg your pardon, Jane, if that sounds callous. I don't mean that your mortality doesn't matter to me. I mean that now that I've found you I can't let you go, no matter how little time you might have left."

"Do you think that's why I refused you? Because I'm going to die? Everyone dies. I refuse you because of what you are and because of what I am."

"But we're the same. We know each other inside out."

"No. There's a vast gulf between us."

"No, Jane. I know what you're going to say before you say it, what you're going to do before you do it."

"No."

"Yes. I swear. Yes." She smiled, and the wolf mask signal of her disease made her uncanny. "You mean because I don't know why you refuse me? Is that what you mean?" She nodded. "Then you see I *do* know. I knew that it was because I didn't know why you refused me. Oh, I'm so confused. I'm—wait. Oh. Is it what I think it is?" She nodded. "Oh, my God. Jane,

*please*. I wasn't thinking. You let me go on. I was too
hasty in telling you my life. It's because you're pure
and I'm not. That's it, isn't it? Isn't that it?" She
nodded. "Jane, I'm a *man,*" I pleaded. "It's different
with a man. Listen," I said, "I *can* be pure. I can be
again. I *will* be."

"There isn't time."

"There *is,* there *is.*"

"If I thought there were . . . Oh, Brewster, if I really
thought there *were*—" she said, and broke off.

"There *is*. I make a vow. I make a holy vow." I
crossed my heart.

She studied me. "I believe you," she said finally.
"That is, I believe you seriously *wish* to undo what you
have done to yourself. I believe in your penitent spirit,
I mean. No. Don't kiss me. You must be continent
henceforth. Then . . ."

"We'll see?"

"We'll see."

"The next time, Jane, the next time you see me, I
swear I will have met your conditions."

I bowed and left and was told where I was to sleep
by a grinning Plympton. He asked if, now that I had
seen Jane, I would like to go with him on a tour of the
estate.

"Not just yet, Freddy, I think."

"Jane gave you something to think about, did she?"

"Something like that."

Was ever any man set such a task by a woman? To
undo defilement and regain innocence, to take an historical corruption and will it annulled, whisking it out
of time as if it were a damaged egg going by on a
conveyor belt. And not given years—Jane's disease
was progressive, the mask a manifestation of one of its
last stages—nor deserts to do it in. Not telling beads or
contemplating from some Himalayan hillside God's

extensive Oneness. No, nor chanting a long, cunning train of boxcar mantras as it moves across the mind's trestle and over the soul's deep, dangerous drop. No, no, and no question either of simply distributing the wealth or embracing the leper or going about in rags (I still wore my mourning togs, that lover's wardrobe, those Savile Row whippery flags of self) or doing those bows and scrapes that were only courtesy's moral minuet, and no time, no time at all for the long Yoga life, the self's spring cleaning that could drag on years. What had to be done had to be done now, in these comfortable Victorian quarters on a velvet love seat or in the high fourposter, naked cherubs climbing the bedposts, the burnished dimples of their wooden behinds glistening in the light from the fresh-laid fire. By a gilded chamber pot, beneath a silken awning, next to a window with one of the loveliest views in England.

That, at least, I could change. I drew the thick drapes across the bayed glass and, influenced perhaps by the firelight and the Baker Street ambience, got out my carpet slippers and red smoking jacket. I really had to laugh. This won't do, I thought. How do you expect to bring about these important structural changes and get that dear dying girl to marry you if the first thing you do is to impersonate Sherlock Holmes? Next you'll be smoking opium and scratching on a fiddle. Get down to it, Ashenden, get down to it.

But it was pointless to scold when no alternative presented itself to me. How *did* one get down to it? How does one undefile the defiled? What acts of *kosher* and exorcism? Religion (though I am not *ir*religious) struck me as beside the point. It was Jane I had offended, not God. What good would it have done to pray for His forgiveness? And what sacrilege to have prayed for hers! Anyway, I understood that I already

had her forgiveness. Jane wanted a virgin. In the few
hours that remained I had to become one.

I thought pure thoughts for three hours. Images of
my mother: one summer day when I was a child and
we collected berries together for beach-plum jelly; a
time in winter when I held a simple cat's cradle of
wool which my mother was carding. I thought of my
tall father in a Paris park when I was ten, and of the
pictures we posed each other for, waiting for the sun to
come out before we tripped the shutter. And recollect-
ed mornings in chapel in school in New England—I
was seven, I was eight—the chaplain describing the
lovely landscapes of Heaven and I, believing, wanting
to die. I recalled the voices of guides in museums I
toured with my classmates, and thought about World's
Fairs I had attended. The '36 Olympics, sitting on the
bench beside the New Zealand pole vaulter. I remembered perfect picnics, Saturday matinees in Broadway
theaters, looking out the window lying awake in comfortable compartment berths on trains, horseback riding
on a fall morning in mountains, sailing with Father. All
the idylls. I remembered, that is, my virginity, sorting
out for the first time in years the decent pleasures of
comfort and wonder and respect. But—and I was
enjoying myself, I could feel the smile on my face—
what did it amount to? I was no better than a gangster
pleading his innocence because he had once *been* innocent.

I thought *impure* thoughts, reading off my long-time
bachelor's hundred conquests, parsing past, puberty
and old fantasy, reliving all the engrams of lust in
gazebo, band shell, yacht and penthouse, night beaches
at low tide, rooms, suites, shower stalls, bedrooms on
crack trains, at the carpeted turnings of stairs, and
once in a taxi and once on a butcher's block at dawn in

Les Halles—all the bachelor's emergency landing fields, all his makeshift landscapes, propinquitous to grandeur and history, in Flanders Fields, rooms with views, by this ocean or by that, this tall building or that public monument, my backstage lovemaking tangential as a town at the edge of a map. Oh love's landmarks, oh its milestones, sex altering place like sunset. Oh the beds and oh the walls, the floors and bridges—and me a gentleman!—the surfaces softened by Eros, contour stones and foam-rubber floors of forests, everywhere but the sky itself a zone for dalliance, my waterfalls of sperm, our La Guardias of hum and droned groan. Recalling the settings first, the circumstances, peopling them only afterwards and even then only piecemeal, a jigsaw, Jack-the-Ripper memory of hatcheck girl thigh and nightclub singer throat and heiress breast, the salty hairs of channel swimmers and buttocks of horseback riders and knuckles of pianists and strapless tans of models—sex like flesh's crossword, this limb and that private like the fragments in a multiple choice. And only after that gradually joining arm to shoulder, shoulder to neck, neck to face, Ezekielizing my partners, dem bones, dem bones gon' walk aroun'.

Yes? No. The smile was *still* on my face. And there in that Victorian counting house, I, lust's miser, its Midas, touching gold and having it gold still, an ancient Pelagian, could not overcome my old unholy gratitude for flesh, and so lost innocence again, even as I resisted, the blood rushing where it would, filling the locks of my body. "Make me clean," I prayed, "help me to make one perfect act of contrition, break my nasty history's hold on me, pull a fast one at this eleventh hour."

A strange thing happened. The impure thoughts left me and my blood retreated and I began to remember

those original idylls, my calendar youth, the picnic and
berry hunts, and all those placid times before fires,
dozing on a couch, my head in Mother's lap and her
hands in my hair like rain on the roof and, My God,
my little weewee was stiff, and it was stiff now too!

It was what I'd prayed for: shame like a thermal
inversion, the self-loathing that *is* purity. The sailing
lessons and horseback rides and lectures and daytrips
came back tainted. I saw how pleased I'd been, how
smug. Why, I'm free, I thought, and was. "I've licked it,
Jane," I said. "I'm pure, holy as a wafer, my heart
pink as rare meat. I was crap. Look at me now."

If she won't have me, I thought, it's not my fault. I
rushed out to show myself to her and tell her what I'd
discovered. I ran over it again to see if I had it
straight. "Jane," I'd say, "I'm bad, unsavory from the
word go, hold your nose. To be good subsists in such
understanding. So innocence is knowledge, not its lack.
See, morality's easy, clear, what's the mystery?" But
when I stepped outside my suite the house was dark.
Time had left me behind. The long night of the soul
goes by in a minute. It must have been three or four in
the morning. I couldn't wake Jane; she was dying of
*lupus erythematosus* and needed her rest. I didn't
know where Plympton slept or I would have roused
him. Too exhilarated by my virtue to sleep, I went
outside.

But it was not "outside" as you and I know it. Say
rather it was a condition, like the out-of-doors in a
photograph, the colors fixed and temperature unfelt,
simply not factors, the wind stilled and the air light,
and so wide somehow that he could walk without
touching it. It was as if he moved in an enormous
diorama of nature, a crèche of the elements. Brewster
Ashenden was rich. He had lain on his back on On-

tario turf farms and played the greens of St. Andrews
and Burning Tree, but he had never felt anything like
Duluth's perfect grass, soft and springy as theater
seats, and even in moonlight green as billiard cloth.
The moon, perfectly round and bright as a tennis
shoe—he could make out its craters, like the eternally
curving seams of a Spalding—enabled him to see perfectly, the night no more than the vaguest atmosphere,
distant objects gyroscopically stilled like things
glimpsed through the whirling blades of a fan.

What he saw was like the landscapes behind madon-
nas in classical paintings—one missed only the carefu-
ly drawn pillars and far, tiny palaces—blue-hilled hori-
zons, knolls at the end of space, complex shores that
trailed eccentrically about flat, blackish planes of water
with boulders rising from them. He thought he perceived distant fields, a mild husbandry, the hay in, the
crops a sloping green and blue debris in the open
fields, here and there ledges keyholed with caves, trees
in the middle distance as straight as the land they grew
from. It was a geography of eclectic styles and landscapes, even the sky a hybrid—here clear and black
and starred, there roiling with a brusque signature of
cloud or piled in strata like folded linen or the interior
of rock.

He walked away from the castle, pulled toward the
odd, distant galleries. His mood was a fusion of virtue
and wonder. He felt solitary but not lonely, and if he
remembered that he walked unprotected through the
largest game preserve this side of the Kenyan savan-
nah, there was nothing in his bold step to indicate this.
He strode powerfully toward those vistas he had seen
stretching away in every direction from the manor.
Never had he seemed to himself so fulfilled, and never,
unless in dreams, had such seeming distances been so
easily negotiated, the scenery changing every hundred

yards or so, the hills that had appeared so remote easily climbed and giving way at their crests to tiny valleys and plains or thick, sudden clots of jungle. This trick of perspective was astonishing, reminding him of cunning golf courses, sudden doglegs, sand traps, unexpected waterholes. Everything was as distinctively charactered as foreign countries, natural borders. He remembered miniature golf courses to which he had been taken as a child, each hole dominated by some monolithic feature, a windmill, perhaps, a gingerbread house, a bridge, complicated networks of banked plains that turned on themselves, culs-de-sac. He thought that Duluth might be deceptively large or deceptively small, and he several miles or only a few thousand feet from the main house—which had already disappeared behind him.

As he came, effortlessly as in any paradise, to each seamed, successive landscape, the ease of his arrivals added to his sense of strength, and each increment of strength to his sense of purity, so that his exercise fed his feelings about his health and happiness. Though he had that day made the long drive from London, had his interview with Jane (as exhausting as it was stimulating) and done the hardest thinking of his life, though he had not slept (even in London he had tossed and turned all night, kept awake by the prospect of finally meeting Jane) in perhaps forty hours, he wasn't tired. He wondered if he would ever be tired again. Or less gay than now. For what he felt, he was certain, was not mood but something deeper, a stability, as the out-of-doors was, as space was. He could make plans. If Jane would have him (she would; they had spoken code this afternoon, signaled each other a high language of commitment, no small talk but the cryptic, sacred speech of government flashing its secret observations over mountains and under seas, the serious ventriloquism of outpost), they could plan not to plan, simply to live, to be. In his joy he had forgotten her death, her rare, personal disease in which self fled self in ultimate allergy. *Lupus erythematosus.* It was not catching, but he would catch it. He would catch *her.* There was no need to survive her. Together they would grow the wolf mask across their eyes, death's big spreading butterfly. It didn't matter. They'd have their morality together, the blessed link-up between appropriate humans, anything permissible between consenting man and consenting woman—anything, any bold or timid configuration, whatever the one craved and the other yielded, whatever whatsoever, love's sanctified arrangements, not excluding the deathbed itself. What need had he to survive her—though he'd probably not die until she did—now that he had at last a vehicle for his taste, his marriage?

He was in a sort of clearing. Though he knew he had not retraced his steps nor circulated around it, seemed familiar. He stood on uneven ground and could see a line of low frigid mountains in the distance. High above him and to his right the great tear of the moon, like the drain of day, sucked light. At his feet there appeared the remains of—what? A feast? A picnic? He bent down to investigate and found a few clay shards of an old jug, a bit of yellow wood like the facing on some stringed instrument and a swatch of faded, faintly Biblical cloth, broadly striped as the robe of a prophet. As he fingered this debris he smelled what was unmistakably bowel.

"Have I stepped in something?" He stood and raised his shoe, but his glance slid off it to the ground where he saw two undisturbed lumps, round as hamburger, of congealing lion waste. It came to him at once. "I *knew* it was familiar! *The Sleeping Gypsy.* This is where it was painted!" He looked suspiciously at the mangled mandolin facing, the smashed jug and the tough cloth, which he now perceived had been forcibly torn. My God, he thought, the lion must have eaten the poor fellow. The picture had been painted almost seventy-five years earlier, but he understood from his reading that lions often returned to the scenes of their most splendid kills, somehow passing on to succeeding generations this odd, historical instinct of theirs. Nervously he edged away, and though the odor of lion dung still stung his nostrils, it was gradually replaced by more neutral smells. Clearly, however, he was near the beasts.

He turned but still could not see the castle. He was not yet frightened. From what he had already seen of Duluth he understood that it was a series of cunningly stitched enclaves, of formal transistorized prospects that swallowed each other transitionlessly. It seemed to be the antithesis of a maze, a surface of turned corners that opened up on fresh surprises. He thought of himself as walking along an enormous Möbius strip, and sooner or later he would automatically be brought back to his starting point. If he was a little uneasy it was only because of the proximity of the animals, whose presence he felt and smelled rather than saw or heard.

Meanwhile, quickening his pace, he came with increasing frequency to experience a series of déjà vus, puzzling at first but then suddenly and disappointingly explicable. He had hoped, as scenes became familiar to him, that he was already retracing his steps, but a few seconds' perusal of each place indicated otherwise. These were not places he had ever been, only places he had seen. Certainly, he thought, the paintings! Here's Cranach the Elder's *Stag Hunt*. Unmistakably. And a few moments later—I'll be darned, Jean Honoré Fragonard's *A Game of Hot Cockles*. And then Watteau's

*Embarking for Cythera,* will you look at that? There
was E. Melvin Bolstad's *Sunday in the Country* and
then El Greco's *View of Toledo* without Toledo. Astonishing, Ashenden thought, really worthwhile. Uh
oh, I don't think I care for that Constable, he thought;
why'd they use that? Perhaps because it was here.
Gosh, isn't that a Thomas Hart Benton? However did
they manage that odd rolling effect? That's really lovely. I'll have to ask Plympton the name of his land-
scaper. Jane and I will certainly be able to use him
once we're settled. Now he was more determined than
ever to get rid of Franklin.

And so it went. He strolled through wide-windowed
Wyeths and gay, open-doored Dufys and through Hop-
pers—I'll have to come back and see that one with the
sun on it—scratchy Segonzacs and dappled Renoirs
and faintly heaving Cézannes, and across twilled Van
Gogh grasses and faint Utrillo fields and precise Audu-
bon fens, and one perfect, wild Bosch dell. It was
thrilling. I am in art, thought Brewster Ashenden,
pleased to have been prepared for it by his education
and taste.

He continued on until he came to a small jewel of a
pond mounted in a setting of scalloped shoreline with
low thin trees that came up almost to the water. It was
the Botticelli *Birth of Venus,* which, like El Greco's
*View of Toledo* without Toledo, was without either
Venus, Zephyr, Chloris, or the Hour of Spring. Nevertheless it was delightful, and he took a seat on a
mound of earth and rested, thinking of Jane and listening to the sea in a large shell he had found on the
beach.

"I'm glad," he said, speaking from the impulse of
his mood now that his wanderings were done and the
prospect of his—their—death had become a part of
his taste and filled his eyes with tears, "I'm glad to

have lived in the age of jet travel, and to have had the money for tickets." He grew contemplative. "There has never been a time in my life," he said, "when I have not had my own passport, and never a period of more than four months when I was not immune to all the indigenous diseases of place for which there are shots. I am grateful—not that I'd ever lord it over my fore-bears—that I did not live in the time of sailing ships. Noble as those barks were, they were slow, slow. And Dramamine not invented. This, for all its problems, is the best age to be rich in. I've seen a lot in my time."

Then, though he couldn't have told you the connec-tion, Ashenden said a strange thing for someone at that moment and in that setting. *"I am not a jerk,"* he said, "I am not so easily written off. Profound guys like me often seem naïve. Perhaps I'm a fool of the gods. That remains to be seen. But answers are mostly simple, wisdom is." He was melancholy now and rose, as if by changing position he hoped to shake off this new turn in his mood. He looked once more at the odd pool and spoke a sort of valedictory. "This is a nice place. Jane would enjoy it. I wish I still had those two folding chairs the Bank of America gave me for opening an account of five thousand dollars. We could come here tomorrow on a picnic."

He did not know whether to go around the pond or cut through the thin trees, but finally determined not to go deeper into the forest. Though he suspected the animals must be all around him, it was very quiet and he wondered again about them. They would be asleep, of course, but didn't his presence mean anything to them? Had their queer captivity and the unusual cir-cumstances in which they lived so accustomed them to man that one could walk among them without disturb-ing them at all? But I am in art, he thought, and thus in nature too, and perhaps I've already caught Jane's illness and the wolf mask is working someplace under my skin, making me no more significant here than the presence of the trees or the angles of the hills.

Walking around the other side of the pond, he noticed that the trees had changed. They were sparser, more ordinary. Ahead he spied a bluff and moved toward it. Soon he was again in a sort of clearing and here he smelled the smells.

The odor of beasts is itself a kind of meat—a dream avatar of alien sirloin, strange chops and necks, oblique joints and hidden livers and secret roasts. There are nude juices in it, and licy furs, and all the flesh's vegetation. It is friction which rubs the fleshly chemistry, releasing it, sending sky-high the queer subversive gasses of oblique life forms. It is noxious. Separated as we are from animals in zoos by glass cages and fenced-off moats, and by the counter odors of human crowds, melting ice cream, peanut shells crushed underfoot, snow cones, mustard, butts of bun—all the detritus of a Sunday outing—we rarely smell it. What gets through is dissipated, for a beast in civilization does not even smell like a beast in the wild. Already evolution has begun its gentling work, as though the animals might actually feel compunction, some subtle, aggravating modesty. But in Plympton's jungle the smells were uninhibited, biological, profane. Their acidity brought tears to Ashenden's eyes and he had to rub them.

When he took his hands away he saw where he was. He had entered, he knew, the last of the pictures. Although he could not at first identify it, much was familiar. The vegetation, for example, was unmistakably Rousseau, with here and there a Gauguin calabash or stringy palm. There were other palms, hybrid

as the setting itself, queer gigantic leaves flying from
conventional European trunks. The odor was fierce but
he couldn't leave. At his feet were thick Rousseauvian
candelabra of grass, and before him vertical pagoda
clusters of enormous flowers, branches dangerously
bent under the weight of heavy leaves like the notched
ears of elephants. Everywhere were fernlike trees, ar-
ticulated as spine or rib cage, a wide net of the greenly
skeletal and the crossed swords of tall grasses. There
were rusts and tawns and huge wigwam shapes and
shadows like the entrances to caves, black as yawns.
The odor was even more overpowering than before, and
had he not seen the vegetation he would have thought
himself at the fermented source of the winish world.
Yet the leaves and grasses and bushes and flowers were
ripe. He reached out and touched a leaf in a low
branch and licked his hand: it was sweet. Still, the
place stank. The smell was acrid, actually hot. Here
the forest was made impenetrable by its very odor and
he started to back off. Unable either to turn away from
it completely or to look at it directly, he was forced to
squint, and immediately he had a striking perception.

Seen through his almost closed eyes, the trees and
vegetation lost their weird precision and articulation
and became conventional, transformed into an ordinary arbor. Only then, half blinded, he saw at last where
he was. It was Edward Hicks's *The Peaceable Kingdom*, and unquestionably the painter had himself been
squinting when he painted it. It was one of Ashenden's
favorite paintings, and he was thrilled to be where lion
and fox and leopard and lamb and musk ox and goat
and tiger and steer had all lain together. The animals
were gone now but must have been here shortly before.
He guessed that the odor was the collective conflagra-
tion of their bowels, their guts' bonfire. I'll have to be

careful where I step, he thought, and an enormous
bear came out of the woods toward him.

It was a Kamchatkan Brown from the northeastern
peninsula of the U.S.S.R. between the Bering and Ok-
hotsk seas, and though it was not yet full grown it
weighed perhaps seven hundred pounds and was already taller than Ashenden. It was female, and what he
had been smelling was its estrus, not shit but lust, not
bowel but love's gassy chemistry, the atoms and hor-
mones and molecules of passion, vapors of impulse
and the endocrinous spray of desire. What he had been
smelling was secret, underground rivers flowing from
hidden sources of intimate gland, and what the bear
smelled on Brewster was the same.

Ashenden did not know this; indeed, he did not even
know that it was female, or what sort of bear it was.
Nor did he know that where he stood was not the
setting for Hicks's painting (that was actually in a part
of the estate where he had not yet been), but had
he discovered his mistake he would still have told you
that he was in art, that his error had been one of grace,
ego's flashy optimism, its heroic awe. He would have
been proud of having given the benefit of the doubt to
the world, his precious blank check to possibility.

All this changed with the sudden appearance of the
bear. Not *all*. He still believed—this in split seconds,
more a reaction than a belief, a first-impression chemical as the she-bear's musk—that the confrontation was
noble, a challenge (there's going to be a hell of a
contest, he thought), a coming to grips of disparate
principles. In these first split seconds operating on that
edge of instinct which is still the will, he believed not
that the bear was emblematic, or even that he was, but
that the two of them there in the clearing—remember,
he thought he stood in *The Peaceable Kingdom*—

somehow made for symbolism, or at least for meaning.
As the bear came closer, however, he was disabused of
even this thin hope, and in that sense the contest was
already over and the bear had won.

He was terrified, but it must be said that there was
in his terror (an emotion entirely new to him, nothing
like his grief for his parents nor his early anxieties
about the value of his usefulness or life's, nor even his
fears that he would never find Jane Löes Lipton, and
so inexpert at terror, so boyish with it that he was
actually like someone experiencing a new drive) a
determination to survive that was rooted in principle,
as though he dedicated his survival to Jane, reserving
his life as a holdup victim withholds the photographs of
loved ones. Even as the bear came closer this did not
leave him. So there was something noble and generous
even in his decision to bolt. He turned and fled. The
bear would have closed the gap between them and
been on him in seconds had he not stopped. For-
tunately, however, he realized almost as soon as he
began his sprint that he could never outrun it. (This
was the first time, incidentally, that he thought of the
bear as *bear,* the first time he used his man's knowledge of his adversary.) He remembered that bears
could cruise at thirty miles an hour, that they could
climb trees. (And even if they couldn't would any of
those frail branches already bowed under their enormous leaves have supported his weight?) The brief
data he recalled drove him to have more. (This also
reflex, subliminal, as he jockeyed for room and position in the clearing, a rough bowl shape perhaps fifty
feet across, as his eye sought possible exits, narrow
places in the trees that the bear might have difficulty
negotiating, as he considered the water—but of course
they swam, too—a hundred yards off through a slender
neck of path like a firebreak in the jungle.) He turned

and faced the bear and it stopped short. They were no
more than fifteen feet from each other.

It suddenly occurred to him that perhaps the bear
was tame.

"Easy, Ivan," he crooned, "easy boy, easy Ivan,"
and the bear hearing his voice, a gentle, low, masculine
voice, whined. Misconstruing the response, recalling
another fact, that bears have weak eyesight, at the
same time that he failed to recall its corollary, that
they have keen hearing and a sharp sense of smell like
perfect pitch, Ashenden took it to be the bear's normal
conversational tone with Plympton. "No, no, Ivan," he
said, "it isn't Freddy, it's not your master. Freddy's
sleeping. I'm Brewster, I'm your master's friend, old
Bruin. I'm Brewster Ashenden. I won't hurt you, fellow." The bear, excited by Ashenden's playful tone,
whined once more, and Brewster, who had admitted he
wasn't Plympton out of that same stockpile of gentle-
manly forthrightness that forbade deception of any
creature, even this bear, moved cautiously closer so
that the animal might see him better and correct any
false impression it might still have of him.

It was Ashenden's false impression that was corrected. He halted before he reached the bear (he was
ten feet away and had just remembered its keen hearing and honed smell) and knew, not from anything it
did, not from any bearish lurch or bearish bearing, that
it was not tame. This is what he saw:

A black patent-leather snout like an electric socket.

A long and even elegant run of purplish tongue,
mottled, seasoned as rare delicatessen meat, that lolled
idiotic inches out of the side of its mouth.

A commitment of claw (they were non-retractile, he
remembered) the color of the heads of hammers.

A low black piping of lip.

A shallow mouth, a logjam of teeth.

Its solemn oval of face, direct and expressionless as a goblin's.

Ears, high on its head and discrete as antlers.

Its stolid, plantigrade stance, a flash as it took a step toward him of the underside of its smooth, hairless paws, vaguely like the bottoms of carpet slippers.

A battering ram of head and neck, pendent from a hump of muscle on its back, high as a bull's or buffalo's.

The coarse shag upholstery of its blunt body, greasy as furniture.

He knew it was not tame even when it settled dog fashion on the ground and its short, thick limbs seemed to disappear, its body hiding in its body. And he whirled suddenly and ran again and the bear was after him. Over his shoulder he could see, despite its speed, the slow, ponderous meshing of muscle and fat behind its fur like children rustling a curtain, and while he was still looking at this the bear felled him. He was not sure whether it had raised its paw or butted him or collided with him, but he was sent sprawling—a grand, amusing, almost painless fall.

He found himself on the ground, his limbs spraddled, like someone old and sitting on a beach, and it was terrible to Ashenden that for all his sudden speed and the advantage of surprise and the fact that the bear had been settled dog fashion and even the distance he had been sent flying, he was no more than a few feet from the place where he had begun his run.

Actually, it took him several seconds before he realized that he no longer saw the bear.

"Thank God," he said, "I'm saved," and with a lightning stroke the bear reached down from behind Ashenden's back and tore away his fly, including the underwear. Then, just as quickly, it was in front of

him. "Hey," Ashenden cried, bringing his legs together
and covering himself with his hands. The tear in his
trousers was exactly like the inside seam along the
thigh and crotch of riding pants.

"əəŋ̂g," said the bear in the International Phonetic
Alphabet.

Brewster scrambled to his knees while the bear
watched him.

"o͡ohwm."

"All right," Ashenden said, "back off!" His voice
was as sharp and commanding as he could make it.
"Back *off,* I said!"

"ᴋʜᴀēr ᴋʜo͝onn."

"Go," he commanded. "Go on. Shoo, Shoo, you."
And still barking orders at it—he had adopted the
masterful, no-nonsense style of the animal trainer—he
rose to his feet and actually shoved the bear as hard as
he could. Surprisingly it yielded and Brewster, encour-
aged, punched it with all his considerable strength on the
side of its head. It shook itself briefly and, as if it meant
to do no more than simply alter its position, dropped
to the ground, rolled over—the movement like the
practiced effort of a cripple, clumsy yet incredibly
powerful—and sat up. It was sitting in much the same
position as Ashenden's a moment before, and it was
only then that he saw its sex billowing the heavy
curtain of hair that hung above its groin: a swollen,
grotesque ring of vulva the color and texture of an ear
and crosshatched with long loose hairs; a distended
pucker of vagina, a black tunnel of oviduct, an inner
tube of cunt. Suddenly the she-bear strummed itself
with a brusque downbeat of claw and moaned. Ashenden moved back and the bear made another gesture,
oddly whorish and insistent. It was as if it beckoned
Ashenden across a barrier not of animal and man but
of language—Chinese, say, or Rumanian. Again it

made its strange movement, and this time barked its moan, a command, a grammar of high complication, of difficult, irregular case and gender and tense, a classic of aberrant syntax. Which was exactly as Ashenden took it, like a student of language who for the first time finds himself hearing in real and ordinary life a unique textbook usage. O God, he thought, I understand Bear!

He did not know what to do, and felt in his pockets for weapons and scanned the ground for rocks. The bear, watching him, emitted a queer growl and Ashenden understood *that,* too. She had mistaken his rapid, reflexive frisking for courtship, and perhaps his hurried glances at the ground for some stagy, bumpkin shyness.

"Look here," Ashenden said, 'I'm a man and you're a bear," and it was precisely as he had addressed those wives of his hosts and fellow guests who had made overtures to him, exactly as he might put off all those girls whose station in life, inferior to his own, made them ineligible. There was reproof in his declaration, yet also an acknowledgment that he was flattered, and even, to soften his rejection, a touch of gallant regret. He turned as he might have turned in a drawing room or at the landing of a staircase, but the bear roared and Ashenden, terrorized, turned back to face it. If before he had made blunders of grace, now, inspired by his opportunities—close calls arbitrarily exalted or debased men—he corrected them and made a remarkable speech.

"You're in rut. There are evidently no male bears here. Listen, you look familiar. I've seen your kind in circuses. You must be Kamchatkan. You stand on your hind legs in the center ring and wear an apron and a dowdy hat with flowers on it that stand up stiff as pipes. You wheel a cub in a carriage and do jointed,

clumsy curtseys, and the muzzle's just for show, reas-
surance, state law and municipal ordinance and an
increment of the awful to suggest your beastliness as
the apron and hat your matronliness. Your decals are
on the walls of playrooms and nurseries and in the
anterooms of pediatricians' offices. So there must be
something domestic in you to begin with, and it is to
that which I now appeal, madam."

The bear, seated and whimpering throughout
Ashenden's speech, was in a frenzy now, still of noise,
not yet of motion, though it strummed its genitalia like
a guitar, and Brewster, the concomitant insights of
danger on him like prophecy, shuddered, understanding that though he now appreciated his situation he
had still made one mistake. No, he thought, *not* madam. If there were no male bears—and wouldn't there
be if she were in estrus?—it was because the bear was
not yet full-grown and had not till now needed mates.
It was this which alarmed him more than anything he
had yet realized. It meant that these feelings were new
to her, horrid sensations of mad need, ecstasy *in extremis*. She would kill him.

The bear shook itself and came toward him, and
Brewster realized that he would have to wrestle it. Oh,
Jesus, he thought, is this how I'm to be purified? Is *this*
the test? Oh, Lord, first I was in art and now I am in
allegory. Jane, I swear, I shall this day be with you in
Paradise! When the bear was inches away it threw itself
up on its hind legs and the two embraced each other,
the tall man and the slightly taller bear, and Brewster,
surprised at how light the bear's paws seemed on his
shoulders, forgot his fear and began to ruminate. See
how strong I am, how easily I support this beast. But
then I am beast too, he thought. There's wolf in me
now, and that gives me strength. What this means, he

thought, is that my life has been too crammed with civilization.

Meanwhile they went round and round like partners in a slow dance. I have been too proud of my humanism, perhaps, and all along not paid enough attention to the base. This is probably a good lesson for me. I'm very privileged. I think I won't be too gentle with poor dying Jane. That would be wrong. On her deathbed we'll roll in the hay. Yes, he thought, there must be positions not too uncomfortable for dying persons. I'll find out what these are and send her out in style. We must not be too fastidious about ourselves, or stuck-up because we aren't dogs.

All the time he was thinking this he and the bear continued to circle, though Ashenden had almost forgotten where he was, and with whom. But then the bear leaned on him with all her weight and he began to buckle, his dreamy confidence and the thought of his strength deserting him. The bear whipped its paw behind Ashenden's back to keep him from falling, and it was like being dipped, supported in a dance, the she-bear leading and Brewster balanced against the huge beamy strength of her paw. With her free paw she snagged one sleeve of Ashenden's Harris tweed jacket and started to drag his hand toward her cunt.

He kneed her stomach and kicked at her crotch.

"ärng."

"Let go," he cried, "let go of me," but the bear, provoked by the pleasure of Ashenden's harmless, off-balance blows and homing in on itself, continued to pull at his arm caught in the sling of his sleeve, and in seconds had plunged Brewster's hand into her wet nest.

There was a quality of steamy mound, a transitional texture between skin and meat, as if the bear's twat

were something butchered perhaps, a mysterious cut
tumid with blood and the color of a strawberry ice-
cream soda, a sexual steak. Those were its lips. He had
grazed them with his knuckles going in, and the bear
jerked forward, a shudder of flesh, a spasm, a bump, a
grind. Frenzied, it drew his hand on. He made a fist
but the bear groaned and tugged more fiercely at
Ashenden's sleeve. He was inside. It was like being up
to his wrist in dung, in a hot jello of baking brick
fretted with awful straw. The bear's vaginal muscles
contracted; the pressure was terrific, and the bones in
his hand massively cramped. He tried to pull his fist
out but it was welded to the bear's cunt. Then the
bear's muscles relaxed and he forced his fist open
inside her, his hand opening in a thick medium of
mucoid strings, wet gutty filaments, moist pipes like the
fingers for terrible gloves. Appalled, he pulled back
with all his might and his wrist and hand, greased by
bear, slid out, trailing a horrible suction, a concupis-
cent comet. He waved the hand in front of his face and
the stink came off his fingertips like flames from a
shaken candelabrum, an odor of metal fruit, of something boiled years, of the center of the earth, filthy
laundry, powerful as the stench of jewels and rare
metals, of atoms and the waves of light.

"Oh Jesus," he said, gagging, "oh Jesus, oh God."

"û(r)m," the bear said, "wrənff."

Brewster sank to his knees in a position of prayer
and the bear abruptly sat, its stubby legs spread, her
swollen cunt in her lap like a bouquet of flowers.

It was as if he had looked up the dress of someone
old. He couldn't look away and the bear, making
powerful internal adjustments, obscenely posed, flexing
her muscular rut, shivering, her genitalia suddenly and
invisibly engined, a performance coy and proud. Finally he managed to turn his head, and with an almost

lazy power and swiftness the bear reached out with one paw and plucked his cock out of his torn trousers. Ashenden winced—not in pain, the paw's blow had been gentle and as accurate as a surgical thrust, his penis hooked, almost comfortable, a heel in a shoe, snug in the bear's curved claws smooth and cool as piano keys—and looked down.

"OERƏKH."

His penis was erect. "That's Jane's, not yours!" he shouted. "My left hand doesn't know what my right hand is doing!"

The bear snorted and swiped with the broad edge of her forepaw against each side of Ashenden's peter. Her fur, lanolized by estrus, was incredibly soft, the two swift strokes gestures of forbidden brunette possibility.

*And of all the things he'd said and thought and felt that night, this was the most reasonable, the most elegantly strategic: that he would have to satisfy the bear, make love to the bear, fuck the bear. And this was the challenge which had at last defined itself, the test he'd longed for and was now to have.* Here was the problem: *Not whether it was possible for a mere man of something less than one hundred and eighty pounds to make love to an enormous monster of almost half a ton; not whether a normal man like himself could negotiate the barbarous terrains of the beast or bring the bear off before it killed him; but merely how he, Brewster Ashenden of the air, water, fire and earth Ashendens, one of the most fastidious men alive, could bring himself to do it—how, in short, he could get it up for a bear!*

But he had forgotten, and now remembered: it was *already* up. And if he had told the bear it was for Jane and not for it, he had spoken in frenzy, in terror and error and shock. It occurred to him that he had not been thinking of Jane at all, that she was as distant from his mind at this moment as the warranties he possessed for all the electric blankets, clock radios and space heaters he'd picked up for opening accounts in banks, as distant as the owner's manuals stuffed into drawers for all that stuff, as forgotten as all the tennis matches he'd played on the grass courts of his friends, as the faults in those matches, as all the strolls to fences and nets to retrieve opponents' balls, the miles he'd walked doing such things. Then why was he hard? And he thought of hanged men, of bowels slipped *in extremis*, of the erectile pressures of the doomed, of men in electric chairs or sinking in ships or singed in burning buildings, of men struck by lightning in open fields, and of all the random, irrelevant erections he'd had as an adolescent (once as he leaned forward to pick up a bowling ball in the basement alley of a friend from boarding school), hardness there when you woke up in the morning, pressures on the kidney that triggered the organ next to it, that signaled the one next to *it,* that gave the blood its go-ahead, the invisible nexus of conditions. "That's Jane's," he'd said, "not yours. My left hand doesn't know what my right hand is doing." Oh, God. It *didn't.* He'd lied to a bear! He'd brought Jane's name into it like a lout in a parlor car. There was sin around like weather, like knots in shoes.

*"What the hell am I talking about?"* he yelled, and charged the bear.

And it leaned back from its sitting position and went down on its back slowly, slowly, its body sighing backward, ajar as a door stirred by wind, and Ashenden belly-flopped on top of it—with its paws in the air he was a foot taller than the bear at either end, and this contributed to his sin, as if it were some child he tumbled—pressed on its swollen pussy as over a barrel. He felt nothing.

His erection had withered. The bear growled contemptuously. *"Foreplay, foreplay,"* Brewster hissed, and plunged his hand inside the bear. I'm doing this to save my life, he thought. I'm doing this to pass tests. This is what I call a challenge and a half.

The bear permitted the introduction of his hand and hugged him firmly, yet with a kind of reserve as though conscious of Ashenden's eggshell mortality. His free hand was around her neck while the other moved around inside the bear insinuatingly. He felt a clit like a baseball. One hand high and one low, his head, mouth closed, buried in the mound of fur just to the side of the bear's neck, he was like a man doing the Australian crawl.

The bear shifted. Still locked together, the two of them rolled over and over through the peaceable kingdom. For Ashenden it was like being run over, but she permitted him to come out on top. His hand had taken a terrific wrenching however, and he knew he had to get it out before it swelled and he was unable to move it. Jesus, I've stubbed my hand, he thought, and began to withdraw it gently, gingerly, through a booby-trapped channel of obstacle grown agonizing by his injury, a minefield of pain. The bear lay stock still as he reeled in his hand, climbing out of her cunt as up a rope. (Perhaps this feels good to her, he thought tenderly.) At last, love's Little Jack Horner, it was out and Ashenden, his hand bent at almost a right angle to his wrist, felt disarmed. What he had counted on—without realizing he counted on it—was no longer available to him. He would not be able to manipulate the bear, would not be able to get away with merely jerking it off. It was another illusion stripped away. He would have to screw the animal conventionally.

Come on, he urged his cock, wax, grow, *grow.* He pleaded with his penis, taking it in his good hand and rubbing it desperately, polishing it like an heirloom,

Aladdinizing it uselessly. Meanwhile, tears in his own, he looked deep into the bear's eyes and stalled by blowing crazy kisses to it off his broken hand, saying foolish things, making it incredible promises, keeping up a lame chatter like the pepper talk around an infield.

"Just a minute. Hold on a sec. I'm almost ready. It's going to be something. It's really . . . I've just got to . . . Look, there's really nothing to worry about. Everything's going to work out fine. I'm going to be a man for you, darling. Just give me a chance, will you? Listen," he said, "I love you. I don't think I can live without you. I want you to marry me." He didn't know what he was saying, unconsciously selecting, with a sort of sexual guile he hadn't known he possessed, phrases from love, the compromising sales talk of romantic stall. He had been maidenized, a game, scared bride at the bedside. Then he began to hear himself, to listen to what he was saying. He'd never spoken this way to a woman in his life. Where did he get this stuff? Where did it come from? It was the shallow language of two-timers, of drummers with farm girls, of whores holding out the gigolos holding in, the conversation of cuckoldry, of all amorous greed. It was base and cheap and tremendously exciting and suddenly Ashenden felt a stirring, the beginning of a faint lust. He moved to the spark like an arsonist and gazed steadily at the enormous hulk of impatient bear, at its black eyes cute as checkers on a snowman. Yes, he thought, afraid he'd lose it, *yes. I am the wuver of the teddy bear, big bwown bear's wittle white man.*

He unbuckled his pants and let them drop and stepped out of his underwear feeling moonlight on his ass. He moved out of his jacket and tore off his shirt, his undershirt. He ran up against the bear. He slapped at it with his dick. He turned his back to it and moved the spread cheeks of his behind up and down the pelt. He climbed it, impaling himself on the strange softness of the enormous toy. He kissed it.

Pet, pet, he thought. *"Pet,"* he moaned, his eyes closed now. "My pet, my pet." Yes, he thought, yes. And remembered, suddenly, *saw,* all the animals he had ever petted, all the furry underbellies, writhing, inviting his nails, all the babies whose rubbery behinds he'd squeezed, the little girls he'd drawn toward him and held between his knees to comfort or tell a secret to, their hair tickling his face, all small boys whose heads he'd rubbed and cheeks pinched between his fingers. We are all sodomites, he thought. There is disparity at the source of love. We are all sodomites, all pederasts, all dikes and queens and mother fuckers.

"Hey bear," he whispered, "d'ja ever notice how all the short, bald, fat men get all the tall, good-looking blondes?" He was stiffening fast. "Hey bear, ma'am," he said, leaning naked against her fur, bare-assed and upright on a bear rug, "there's something darling in a difference. Why me—take *me.* There's somethin' dar-lin' in a difference, how else would water come to fire or earth to air?" He cupped his hand over one of its cute little ears and rubbed his palm gently over the bristling fur as over the breast buds of a twelve-year-old girl. "My life, if you want to know, has been a sodomy. What fingers in what pies, what toes in what seas! I have the tourist's imagination, the day-tripper's vision. Fleeing the ordinary, crossing state lines, greedy at Customs and impatient for the red stamps on my passports like lipstick kisses on an envelope from a kid in the summer camp. Yes, and there's wolf in me too now. God, how I honor a difference and crave the unusual, life like a link of mixed boxcars." He put a finger in the lining of the bear's silken ear. He kissed its mouth and vaulted his tongue over her teeth, prob-

ing with it for the roof of her mouth. Then the bear's
tongue was in his throat, not horrible, only strange,
the cunning length and marvelous flexibility an avatar
of flesh, as if life were in it like an essence sealed in a
tube, and even the breath, the taste of living, rutting
bear, delicious to him as the taste of poisons vouch-
safed not to kill him, as the taste of a pal's bowel or a
parent's fats and privates.

He mooned with the giant bear, insinuating it backwards, guiding it as he would a horse with subtle
pressures, squeezes, words and hugs. The bear re-
sponded, but you do not screw a bear as you would a
woman and, seeing what he was about to do, she
suddenly resisted. Now he was the horse—this too—
and the bear the guide, and she crouched, a sort of
semi-squat, and somehow shifted her cunt, sending it
down her body and up behind her as a tap dancer
sends a top hat down the length of her arm. With her
head stretching out, pushing up and outward like the
thrust of a shriek, cantilevering impossibly and looking
over her shoulder, she signaled Ashenden behind her.

He entered her from the rear, and oddly he had
never felt so male, so much the man, as when he was
inside her. Their position reinforced this, the bear
before him, stooped, gymnastically leaning forward as
in the beginning of a handstand, and he behind as if he
drove sled dogs. He might have been upright in a
chariot, some Greek combination of man and bear
exiled in stars for a broken rule. So good was it all that
he did not even pause to wonder how he fit. He fit,
that's all. Whether swollen beyond ordinary length
himself or adjusted tô by some stretch-sock principle
of bear cunt (like a ring in a dime store that snugs any
finger), he fit. "He fit, he fit and that was it," he
crooned happily, and moved this way and that in the
warm syrups of the beast, united with her, ecstatic,

transcendent, not knowing where his cock left off and the bear began. Not deadened, however, not like a novocained presence of tongue in the mouth or the alien feel of a scar, in fact never so filled with sensation, every nerve in his body alive with delight, even his broken hand, even that, the nerves rearing, it seemed, hind-legged almost, revolting under their impossible burden of pleasure, vertiginous at the prospect of such orgasm, counseling Ashenden to back off, go slow, back off or the nerves would burst, a new lovely energy like love's atoms split. And even before he came, he felt addicted, hooked; where would his next high come from, he wondered almost in despair, and how you gonna keep 'em down on the farm, and what awfulness must follow such rising expectations?

And they went at it for ten minutes more and he and the bear came together.

"uəōōŏŏŭ(r)reñg hwhu ä ä c̱ẖ ouhw ouhw nnng," said the bear.

"uəōōŏŏŭ(r)reñg hwhu ä ä c̱ẖc̱ẖ *ouhw* ouhw *nnñg*!" groaned Ashenden, and fell out of the bear and lay on his back and looked at the stars.

And he lay like that for half an hour, catching his breath, feeling his nerves coalesce, consolidating once more as a man, his hard-on declining, his flesh turning back into flesh, the pleasure lifting slow as fever. And thinking. So. I'm a sodomite. But not just any ordinary sodomite with a taste for sheep or a thing for cows, some carnivore's harmless extension of appetite that drives him to sleep with what he eats. No. I'm kinky for bears.

And then, when he was ready, when at last he could once more feel his injured hand, he pushed himself up on his elbows and looked around. The bear was gone, though he thought he saw its shape reclined beside a tree. He stood up and looked down and examined himself. When he put his clothes back on, they hung on him like flayed skin and he was conscious of vague withdrawal symptoms in his nuts. He moved into the moonlight. His penis looked as if it had been dipped in blood. Had it still been erect the blood might perhaps have gone unnoticed, a faint flush; no longer distended, it seemed horrid, wet, thick as paint. He cupped his hand beneath himself and caught one drop in his palm. He shook his head. "My God," he said, "I haven't just screwed a bear, I've fucked a virgin!"

Now his old honor came back to chide him. He thought of Jane dying in the castle, of the wolf mask binding her eyes like a dark handkerchief on the vision of a condemned prisoner, of it binding his own and of the tan beard across his face like a robber's bandanna. Ashenden shuddered. But perhaps it was not contagious unless from love and honor's self-inflicted homeopathy. Surely he would not *have* to die with her. All he had to do was tell her that he had failed the test, that he had not met her conditions. Then he knew that he would never tell her this, that he would tell her nothing, that he would not even see her, that tomorrow—today, in an hour or so when the sun was up—he would have Plympton's man take him to the station, that he would board a train, go to London, rest there for a day or two, take in a show, perhaps go to the zoo, book passage to someplace far, someplace wild, further and wilder than he had ever been, look it over, get its feel, with an idea of maybe settling down one day. He'd better get started. He had to change.

He remembered that he was still exposed and thought to cover himself lest someone see him, but first he'd better wipe the blood off his penis. There was a fresh handkerchief in his pocket, and he took it out, unfolded it and strolled over to the pond. He dipped the handkerchief in the water and rubbed himself briskly, his organ suddenly tingling with a new surge of pleasure, but a pleasure mitigated by twinges of pain. There was soreness, a bruise. He placed the handkerchief back in his pocket and handled himself lightly, as one goes over a tire to find a puncture. There was a small cut on the underside of his penis that he must have acquired from the bear. Then the blood could have been mine, he thought. Maybe *I* was the virgin. Maybe *I* was. It was good news. Though he was a little sad. *Post-coitum tristesse,* he thought. It'll pass.

He started back through art to the house, but first he looked over his shoulder for a last glimpse of the sleeping bear. And he thought again of how grand it had been, and wondered if it was possible that something might come of it. And seeing ahead, speculating about the generations that would follow his own, he thought, Air. Water, he thought. Fire, Earth, he thought . . . And *honey.*

# Feldman ★ ★★
# & Son

For the first twelve years they fled the *minyan*. They hid from it in Maine, in Vermont, in Pennsylvania, in Ohio, in Indiana. Once his father had seen a film of ranchers in Montana, but they never got that far. At last they came to southern Illinois' Little Egypt.

His father rebuilt his peddler's wagon for a fifth time, nailing the old lumber with the old nails. "Test it, test it," his father said, and Feldman climbed inside, stretching out on his back in the gentile sun, the goyish heat. His father stepped inside the long handles. "Old clothes," he called, "rags, first-born Jews." A woman stood on her porch and stared at them. "Go inside, lady," Feldman's father said, "it's only a rehearsal. Out, kid."

Feldman sprang from the wagon. "What a leap, what a jump," his father said. "Soon *I* ride in the wagon, you get a good offer and you sell me." He stooped and picked up the paintbrush and threw it to his son. "Paint for the hicks a sign. In English make a legend: ISIDORE FELDMAN AND SON." His father

(From *A Bad Man,* 1967.)

74

watched him make the letters. "It's very strange," he
said, "I have forgotten how to write English. But I can
still read it, so no tricks." When Feldman had finished,
his father took the brush, saying, "And now I will do
the same in Hebrew on the other side. For the Tal-
mudic scholars of southern Illinois." His son climbed
into the wagon and lay back against the planks with
their faded, flaking legends, the thick Hebrew letters
like the tips of ancient, heavy keys. "This afternoon it
dries, and tomorrow it is opening day in America."

His father was insane. For five years Feldman had
been old enough to recognize this; for three years he
had been old enough to toy with the idea of escaping;
for two weeks he had been brave enough to try. But he
had hesitated, and for a week he had realized with
despair that he loved his father.

They had rented a house. It was like all the houses
they had ever lived in. "Look at it," his father said,
climbing up on the porch. "White frame." He touched
the wood. "Steps. A railing. A swing. Here, when
you're old enough, you'll court Americans in that
swing. And *screen* doors. Look, look, Leo, at the
*screen* doors. A far cry from the East Side. No screen
doors on the East Side. Smell the flowers. I wish I
knew their names. Get the American girl in the swing
to tell you their names. That way, if they die, we will
know what seeds to ask for. Good. Then it's settled."

While the paint was drying they walked in the town.
His father showed him the feed store, the courthouse,
the tavern. They went inside and Feldman's father
drank a beer and spoke with the bartender. "Neighbor," his father said, "a Jew is a luxury that God
affords Himself. He is not serious when He makes a
Jew. He is only playing. Look, you got a wife?"

"Sure," the man said uneasily.

"Tell her today you met Feldman and Son." He

leaned across the bar and winked. "If a Jew wants to get ahead," he whispered, "he must get ahead of the other Jews. He must go where there are no Jews. A Jew is a novelty." He turned to his son. "Tell the neighbor our word," he said.

"Please, Papa," Feldman said, embarrassed.

"In the first place, papa me no papas, pop me no pops. This is America. Dad me a dad. Father me a father. Now—the word."

"Diaspora," Feldman said.

"Louder, please."

"Diaspora," he said again.

"Diaspora, delicious."

The bartender stared at them.

"Explain. Tell the fellow."

"It means dispersion," Feldman said.

"It *says* dispersion, and it *means* dispersion," his father said. "I tell you, ours is a destiny of emergency. How do you like that? You see me sitting here fulfilling God's will. I bring God's will to the Midwest. I don't lift a finger. I have dispersed. Soon the kid is older, *he* disperses. Scatter, He said." He looked around the tavern significantly, and going to the front window, made an oval in the Venetian blinds for his face and peered out. "To the ends of the earth. Yes, Lord." He rushed back to the bar. "Who owns the big store here?" he asked suddenly.

"That would be Peterson," the bartender said.

"Peterson, perfect."

The bartender started to move away, but Feldman's father reached across the bar and held his elbow. "The jewelry store? Quickly."

"Mr. Stitt."

"Stitt, stupendous."

"Come, Father," Feldman said.

"There's no *shul,* no Jew?" his father said.

"I don't know none, mister."

"Know none, nice." He stood up. At the door he turned to all of them in the tavern. Huge men in faded overalls looked down at him from enormous stools. "Farmers, townsmen—*friends:* I am your new neighbor, Isidore Feldman, the peddler. In the last phase of the Diaspora. I have come to the end of the trail in your cornfields. I can go no further. Here I hope to do business when the pushcart dries. I have scouted the community and can see that there is a crying need for a ragman. The old-clothes industry is not so hot here either. Never mind, we will grow together. Tell the wife. Meanwhile, look for me in the street!"

Going home, his father, elated, taught him the calls as they walked along. "Not 'ra*gs*,' not 'o*ld* clo*thes*.' What are you, an announcer on the radio? You're in a street! Say 'regs, all cloze.' Shout it. Sing it. I want to hear steerage, Ellis Island in that throat. I'll give you the pitch. Ready, begin: *Rugs, oil cloths!* Wait, stop the music. *Greenhorn,* you're supposed to be a greenhorn! What, you never saw the Statue of Liberty through the fringes of a prayer shawl?"

He hadn't and neither had his father.

"All right, from the top. *Rocks, ill clots.* Better, beautiful, very nice, you have a flair."

*"Rex, wild clits,"* Feldman sang out. A hick stared at him from behind a lawn mower. He could smell preserves in the air.

"Terrific," Feldman's father shouted, " 'wild clits' is very good. We'll make our way. I *feel* it. *I* know it's a depression, once I built a railroad, made it run. *I* know this is Illinois, America. *I* know the rubble is not the destruction of the second temple, but just today's ashes. Never *mind!* We are traveling Jews in the latest phase of the new Diaspora. We will be terr*if*ic."

He stopped and pulled his son close to him. "Listen,

if anything happens you'll need wisdom. I can't help
you. Father's a fathead. Dad's a dope. But in lieu of
wisdom—*cunning.* These are bad times—bad, *dreck-
ish,* phooey! But bad times make a bullish market for
cunning. I'm no Red. From me you don't hear 'from
each according to his ability, to each according to his
need.' From me you hear 'from them to me.' I know
the world. I *know* it. I fight it one day at a time. This
is your father speaking. This is advice.
  *"Rogues, wooled clouds,"* he roared down the
American street.


  So they sold and sold. "It's the big sellout," his
father said. "What did you sell today?" he would ask
people he met in the street. "Trade, traffic, barter,
exchange, deal, peddle, purvey," he called ecstatically
to the house fronts.
  They'd go into Woolworth's—Woolworth's was one
of his father's chief suppliers; "My wholesaler," he'd
say—and his father would gasp at the abundances
there, the tiers of goods, the full shelves, the boxes on
high platforms lining the walls. "Commodities," he'd
sigh. "Things. Thing City." Staring like a stricken poet
at an ideal beauty. "Some operation you've got here,"
he said to the girl who sold the clusters of chocolate
peanuts. He stared passionately at the penny weighing
machine, the Foot-Eze machine. "Nothing for something," he groaned jealously.
  He turned to his son. "The beggars. Ah, the beggars
and cripples. The men who sit armless and stumpless
on a spread-out sheet of newspaper with the pencils in
their caps. They have it made. *They* do. Take the
nickel and keep the pencil! Delicious, delightful! The
freaks stashed in cages, getting *gelt* for a gape. My son,
my son, forgive me your health, your arms and your
legs, your size and strong breathing, your unblemished

skin. I chain you forever to invoice and lading, to rate
of exchange, to wholesale, to cost." He'd wink. "Sell
seconds," he'd say, "irregulars. Sell damaged and
smoke-stained and fire-torn things. Sell the marred and
impared, the defective and soiled. Sell remnants, re-
mainders, the used and the odd lot. Sell broken sets.
That's where the money is."

He would pick up a pair of ladies' panties from the
lingerie counter. "Look, look at the craftsmanship,"
he'd say distastefully, plunging his big hand inside and
splaying his fingers in the silky seat, "the crotchman-
ship." He'd snap the elastic. "No sag, no give," he'd
say to the startled salesgirl. 'Give me give, the sec-
ond-rate. Schlock, give me. They're doing some wonderful things in Japan.

*"Because,"* he'd say, explaining, "where's the contest in sound merchandise? You sell a sound piece of
merchandise, what's the big deal? Demand has nothing
to do with good business, not *good* business. Need,
who needs it? In England—come closer, miss, you'll
enjoy this—they have a slang term for selling. 'Flogging,' they call it. Flogging, fantastic. But that's it,
that's it exactly. Beating, whipping. Every sale a
scourge. Sell me envelopes."

"That's the stationery counter. Aisle four."

"You hear, Leo? A *stationary* counter. Wonderful,
wonderful. Not like with us with the wheels on the
wagon, the rolling Diaspora. What a thing it is to be a
gentile! A goy, gorgeous!"

He leaned across the counter and took the girl's
hands in his own. He moved with her like this to the
break in the counter and pulled her toward him gently.
They were like sedate figures in an old dance.

"It's not my department," the girl objected.

"You drive a hard bargain," his father said. "It's a
pleasure to do business with you."

"No, really—listen—"

"Envelopes, forty. One pack, wide white. Here's the quarter. It's a flog. Now, please, beat me a box pencils."

Then, incredibly, he would sell the envelopes. One at a time. He would go into the office of the farm agent. "Have you written Mother this week?" he might ask, and sell him an envelope for two cents.

"What have you got for us today, Isidore?" an old man would call from the bench at the courthouse. His father sold him an envelope.

He lived by sufferance, his son saw. His father saw too. "They owe me," he explained. "Fuck them."

Little children suffered him. He would stride up to them in their games in the schoolyard. Perhaps he would intercept the ball, running after it clumsily, knees high, awry, hugging it ineptly. Holding it high. "Want to buy a ball?" he shouted. The children laughed. "What did *you* sell today?" Leering awfully, asking Helen, a girl in his son's class, eleven and breasted, eleven and haired. The children roared and touched each other.

"What have you got for us today, Isidore?" a child yelled. It was what the old men called.

He tossed the ball aside, pushing it as a girl would, and reached into his pocket. *"White,"* he whispered, pulling a crayon from the pocket, holding it out to them, a waxy wand. "White!"

"I'll tell you about white. White," he'd say, his loose, enormous lids heavy, slack wrappings for his eyes, "is the first thing. White is light, great God's let was, void's null. You can't go wrong with white. You wouldn't be sorry you took white. Ask your teacher, you don't believe me. It reflects to the eye all the colors in the solar spectrum. How do you like that? This is the *solar* spectrum I'm talking about, not your small-time local stuff. You take the white—the blue, yellow, red and green go with it. Some white! A nickel for the rainbow, I'm closing it out."

"What could you do with it?" a boy asked.

"Color an elephant and sell it," his father said. "Put up a flag. Tell a lie. Ah, kid, you know too much. You've seen the truth. It's the color of excuse and burden. I've got a nerve. You're too young. Why should I saddle you with white? But have you got a big brother maybe? Nah, nah, it's a grownup's color. Buy better brown. Go green, green's grand. You want green? Here—" He stuck his hand into his pocket and without looking pulled out a green crayon. The boy gasped and moved back. "No? Still thinking about the white? Naughty kid, you grow up too fast today. White-hot for white, are you? All right, you win, I *said* white for sale and I *meant* white for sale. White sale here. *All right, who wants it?"*

A boy offered three cents, another four. A child said a nickel. He sold it to a girl for six.

"Done," he said, and took the money and reached back into his pocket. His eyes were closed. *"Purple,"* he said.

They lived on what his father earned from the sales. Maybe fifteen dollars came into the house in a week, and although it was the Depression his son felt poor. Perhaps he would have felt poor no matter what his father earned, for all he needed to remind him of their strange penury was one sight of his father at his card table in what would normally be the parlor. (A card table and chairs in the American Home; they had brought the Diaspora into the front room.) It was the countinghouse of a madman. On the table, on the chairs, on the floor—there were only the card table and two chairs for furniture—were the queer, changed products and by-products, the neo-junk his father dealt in.

There were stamped lead soldiers, reheated on the kitchen stove and bent into positions of agony, decapitated, arms torn from the lead sides, the torsos and heads and limbs in mass cigar-box graves. His father would sell these as "a limited edition, a special series from the losing side" ("An educational toy," he explained to the children. "What, you think it's all victories and parades and boys home on furlough? This is why they *give* medals. A head is two cents, an arm a penny. It's supply and demand"). There were four identical decks of Bicycle cards into which his father had inserted extra aces, kings, queens. These he carried in an inside pocket of his coat and took with him into the pool hall for soft interviews with the high school boys ("Everybody needs a head start in life. You, fool, how would you keep up otherwise?"). There were single sheets torn from calendars ("April," he called in February, "just out. Get your April here"). There were collections of pressed flowers, leaves ("The kids need this stuff for school"). There was a shapeless heap of dull rags, a great disreputable mound of the permanently soiled and scarred, of slips that might have been pulled from corpses in auto wrecks, of shorts that could have come from dying men, sheets ripped from fatal childbeds, straps pulled from brassieres—the mutilated and abused and dishonored. Shards from things of the self, the rags of rage they seemed. Or as if they grew there, in the room, use's crop. "Stuff, stuff," his father said, climbing the rags, wading into them as one might wade into a mound of autumn's felled debris. "Someday you'll wear a suit from this." There were old magazines, chapters from books, broken pencils, bladders from ruined pens, eraser ends in small piles, cork scraped from the inside of bottle caps, ballistical shapes of tinfoil, the worn straps from watches, wires, strings, ropes, broken glass—things' nubbins.

*"Splinters,"* his father said, "there's a fortune in splinters."

*"Where's the fortune in splinters already?"* his father said. Looking at the collection, the card table, the two chairs, the room which for all its clutter seemed barren. "Look alive there. Your father, the merchant prince, is talking. What, you think I'll live forever? We're in a crisis situation, I tell you. I have brought the Diaspora this far and no further. Though I'll tell you the truth, even now things fly outward, my arms and my heart, pulling to scatter. I don't want to go, I don't want to go. There are horses inside me and they are stampeding. Run, run for the doctor. Get cowboys with ropes. Talk to me. *Talk!"*

"What do you want me to say?" his son asked.

"Yielder, head bower, say what you mean."

The boy didn't know what he meant.

"It's not moving, it's not moving," his father moaned. "Business is terrible. Are you hungry?"

"No."

"Are you cold?"

"No."

"Nevertheless, business is terrible. It stinks, business." He brushed a pile of canceled stamps from the table. "Everything is vendible. It *must* be. That's religion. Your father is a deeply religious man. He believes in vendibility. To date, however, he has failed to move the unsalable thing. The bottom has dropped out of his market look out below."

They lived like this for three years.

For three years he was on the verge of fleeing his father. What prevented him now was not love (love goes, he thought) so much as an illusion that the

Diaspora *had* brought him to an end of the earth, an
edge of the world. For all that there were telephone
poles about him, newspapers, machines, cars, neon in
the windows of the taverns, he seemed to live in a
world that might have been charted on an old map, the
spiky spines of serpents rising like waves from wine-
dark seas, personified zephyrs mump-cheeked and
fierce—a distant Praetorianed land, unamiable and
harsh. There might have been monkeys in its trees,
burning bushes in its summers. He lived in a constant
fear of miracles that could go against him. The wide
waters of the Ohio and the Mississippi that he had seen
meld from a bluff just below Cairo, Illinois, would
have turned red in an instant had he entered them,
split once and drowned him had he taken flight. There
was the turtle death beyond, he vaguely felt, and so,
like one who has come safely through danger to a
given clearing, he feared to go on or to retrace his
steps. He was content to stay still.

Content but embarrassed.

His father was famous now, and they seemed to live
under the special dispensation of their neighbors. "I
would make them eat the Jew," he would confide
defiantly.

Like anyone famous, however, they lived like cap-
tives. (He didn't really mean "they"; surprisingly, he
was untouched—a captive's captive.) It must have
been a task even for his father to have always to come
up to the mark of his madness. Once he bored them he
was through. It was what had happened in Vermont, in
Maine, elsewhere. Once he repeated himself—not the
pattern; the pattern was immune, classic—it would be
over. "There's a fortune in eccentricity, a fortune. I'm
*alive,*" his father said in honest wonder, weird pride.
"It's no joke, it costs to live. Consumers, we're consumers. Hence our mortality. I consume, therefore I

am." He would smile. *"I hate them,"* he'd say. "They
don't buy enough. Read Shylock. What a wisdom!
That was some Diaspora they had there in Venice."

It was not hate, but something darker. Contempt.
But not for him. For him there were, even at thirteen
and fourteen and fifteen, pinches, hugs, squeezes. They
slept together in the same bed ("It cuts coal costs. It
develops the heart"). Awakened in the declining night
with a rough kiss ("Come, chicken, cluck cluck cluck.
If you cannot tell me, hold me"). Whispers, declara-
tions, manifestoes in the just unhearing ear. Bedtime
stories: "Your mother was a gentile and one of my
best customers. I laid her in my first wagon by pots
and by pans and you were born and she died. You think
I hate you, you think so? You think I hate you, you
took away my *shiksa* and a good customer? Nah, nah,
treasure, I love you. She would have slowed down the
Diaspora. We had a truck, and she couldn't read the
road maps. Wake up, I'll tell you the meaning of life.
Can you hear me? Are you listening? This is rich." (At
first he was terrified, but gradually he accommodated
to madness, so that madness made no difference and
words were like melodies, all speech as meaningless as
tunes. He lied, even today. He said what he wanted,
whatever occurred to him. Talk is cheap, talk is
cheap.) "Get what there is and turn it over quick.
Dump and dump, mark down and close out. Have
specials, my dear. The thing in life is to sell, but if no
one will buy, listen, listen, *give* it away! Flee the
*minyan*. Be naked. Travel light. Because there will
come catastrophe. Every night expect the flood, the
earthquake, the fire, and think of the stock. Be in a
position to lose nothing by it when the bombs fall. But
what oh what shall be done with the unsalable thing?"

Madness made no difference. It was like living by
the railroad tracks. After a while you didn't hear the

trains. His father's status there, a harmless, astonishing madman, provided him with a curious immunity. As the boy became indifferent to his father, so the town became indifferent to the boy, each making an accommodation to what did not matter. It was not, however, that madness made sense to him. It was just that since he'd grown up with madness, nothing made sense. (His father might even be right about things; he was probably right.) He had been raised by wolves, he saw; a growl was a high enough rhetoric. But he could not be mad himself. Perhaps he did not have the energy for obsession. He had lived so close to another's passion, his own would have been redundant. "You have a locked heart," his father told him. Perhaps, perhaps he did. But now if he failed to abandon him ("When do you go?" his father sometimes asked. "When do you embark, entrain, enbus? When do you have the shoes resoled for the long voyage out? And what's to be done with the unsalable thing?"), it was not a sudden reloving, and it was no longer fear. The seas had long since been scraped of their dragons; no turtle death lay waiting for him. The Diaspora had been disposed of, and the tricky double sense that he lived a somehow old-timey life in a strange world. It was *his* world; he was, by having served his time in it, its naturalized citizen. He had never seen a tenement, a subway, a tall building. As far as he knew he had never seen a Jew except for his father. What was strange about there being a cannon on the courthouse lawn, or a sheriff who wore a star on his shirt? What was strange about anything? Life was these things too. Life was anything, anything at all. Things were of a piece.

He went to a county fair and ate a hot dog. (Nothing strange *there,* he thought.) He chewed cotton candy. He looked at pigs, stared at cows. He came into a

hall of 4-H exhibits. Joan Stizek had hooked a rug;
Helen Prish had sewn a dress; Mary Stellamancy had
put up tomatoes. He knew these girls. They said,
"How are you, Leo?" when they saw him. (Nothing
strange *there*.)

He went outside and walked up the Midway. A man
in a booth called him over. "Drop the ring over the
block and take home a prize," he said. He showed him
how easy it was. "Three tosses for a dime."

"The blocks are magnets," he said. "There are tiny
magnets in the rings. You control the fields by pressing
a button under the counter. I couldn't win. There's
nothing strange."

"Beat it, kid," the man said. "Get out of here."

"I am my papa's son," he said.

A woman extended three darts. "Bust two balloons
and win a prize."

"Insufficient volume of air. The darts glance off
harmlessly. My father told me," he said.

"I'll guess your birthday," a man said.

"It's fifteen cents. You miss and give a prize worth
five. Dad warned me."

"Odds or evens," a man said, snapping two fingers
from a fist.

He hesitated. "It's a trick," he said, and walked
away.

A sign said: LIVE! NAKED ARTIST'S MODEL! He
handed fifty cents to a man in a wide felt hat and went
inside a tent. A woman sat naked in a chair.

"Three times around the chair at an eight-foot distance at a reasonable pace. No stalling," a man standing inside the entrance said. "You get to give her one
direction for a pose. Where's your pencil? Nobody
goes around the chair without a pencil."

"I haven't got one," he said.

"Here," the man said. "I rent pencils. Give a dime."

"Nobody said anything about a pencil," he said. "It's a gyp."

"The sign says '*Artist's* Model,' don't it? How you going to draw her without a pencil?" He narrowed his eyes and made himself taller. "If you ain't an artist what are you doing in here? Or are you some jerk pervert?"

Feldman's son put his hand in his pocket. "Green," he said, showing a crayon from the inventory. "I work in green crayon."

"Where's your paper?" the man said. "Paper's a nickel."

"I don't have paper," he admitted.

"Here, Rembrandt," the man said. He held out a sheet of ringed, lined notebook paper.

"Are we related," Feldman's son asked, handing him a nickel.

He joined a sparse circle of men walking around the woman in a loose shuffle.

The man at the entrance flap called directions. "Speed it up there, New Overalls."

"Hold your left tit and point your finger at the nipple," a man in a brown jacket said.

"That's your third trip, Yellow Shoes. Get out of the line," called the man at the entrance. "*Eight-foot distance,* Green Crayon. I told you once."

"Spread your legs."

"Boy, oh boy, I got to keep watching you artists, don't I, Bow Tie?" the man said. "You already said she should grab her behind with both hands. One pose, *one* pose. Put the pencil in the hat, Yellow Shoes. You just rented that."

"Spread your legs," Feldman's son said. Nothing strange there, he thought.

"Keep it moving, keep it moving. You're falling behind, Brown Jacket."

He left the tent, still holding the unused sheet of notebook paper that had cost him a nickel.

There was an ox-pulling contest. He found a seat in the stands near the judge's platform and stared at the beasts. Beneath him several disqualified teams of oxen had been unyoked and sprawled like Sphinxes, their legs and haunches disappearing into their bodies, lush and fat and opulent. He gazed at the behinds of standing animals, seeing their round ball-less patches. They leaned together in the great wooden yokes, patient, almost professional.

"The load is eight thousand five hundred pounds," the announcer said, drawling easily, familiarly, a vague first-name hint in his voice. "Joe Huncher's matched yellows at the sled for a try, Joe leading, Willy Stoop making the hitch. Move those boys back there, William. Just a little more. A *lit*tle more. You did it, William. Clean hitch."

The man jumped aside as the oxen stamped jerkily backwards, moving at a sharp left angle to their hitch.

"Gee, gee there, you." The leader slapped an ox across the poll with his hat. He beat against the beast's muzzle. "Gee, you. Gee, gee."

"Turn them, Joseph. Walk them around. Those lads are excited," the announcer said.

The leader looked up toward the announcer and said something Feldman's son couldn't hear. The announcer's easy laugh came over the loudspeaker. He laughed along with him. I'm a hick, he thought. I'm a hick too. I'm a Jewish hick. What's so strange? He leaned back and brushed against a woman's knee behind him. " 'Scuse me, Miz Johnson," he said, not recognizing her.

"Hmph," she said.

Spread your legs, he thought. Touch your right tit with your left instep.

The oxen were in line now and the farmer stepped back. "Gee-*up,*" he yelled, waving his hat at them. "Gee-UP!" The animals stepped forward powerfully, taking up the slack on their chain harness. They strained at the heavy sled, stumbling, their muscles jumping suddenly under their thick flesh. "Gee-*UP!* Whoosh whoosh whoosh whoosh whoosh, whoosh whoosh whoosh whoosh whoosh!" The burdened sled slid nine feet forward in the dirt.

The crowd applauded, Feldman's son clapping with them.

"Thataway, William, good work there, Joe," he called. Hey, Willy, yo, Joe, he wanted to call aloud. Hey hey. Hi yo. Hee hee. Yo yo. Hey hi yo hee ho! Whoosh, boys. Whoosh whoosh whoosh whoosh whoosh.

"I thought I saw William spit there, Joe. No fair greasing the runners," the announcer said.

Feldman's son laughed.

"All right, folks," the announcer said, "next up's a pair of brown Swiss from the Stubb-Logan farm over county in Leeds. That's George Stubb up front, Mr. Gumm at the hitch. You been feeding them roosters, George? They look to me like they did some growing since the last pull."

At 9,500 pounds only Huncher and Stoop and the Leggings brothers were still in the contest. The matched yellows, his favorites because they were the crowd's, were unable to move the sled even after three tries.

He applauded as Joe Huncher led the team away. He leaned forward and cupping his hands shouted

down at them. "That was near five tons on that sled
there, Joseph. Hose those boys down now, William.
Hose those boys down." Stoop waved vaguely toward
the unfamiliar voice, and Feldman's son smiled. "A
man works up a sweat doing that kind of pulling," he
said to his neighbor.

The Leggings brothers led their oxen, sleek and
black as massive seals, toward the sled to make the
hitch. They maneuvered them back carefully and one
brother slapped the ring solidly onto the peg.

"Come," the other brother commanded. "Come.
Come. Come." The two beasts struggled viciously forward. It seemed they would strangle themselves against
the yoke. They stretched their necks; their bodies
queerly lengthened. There was a moment of furious
stasis when Feldman's son thought that either the
chain must break or the beasts themselves snap back
against the sled, breaking their legs. Then he saw the
thick wooden runners scrape briefly sideways, and the
animals dragged the load five feet.

The announcer called the brothers up to collect their
prize.

"Just a minute. Hold your oxes," a voice called. It
was his father, standing in front of the judge's stand
looking up. "Your Honor," he called, "Your Hon-
or."

The crowd recognized him, laughing. The boy heard
his father's name repeated like a rumor up and down
the grandstands.

"What is it?" the announcer asked over the loudspeaker.

"Your Honor," Feldman said, "the contest ain't
over."

"Of course it's over. What do you mean it's not
over?"

It sounded like a routine. The son wondered if it

was. "It's part of the show," he turned around and told the woman behind him. "It's part of the show, Miz Johnson."

"Now what's the meaning of this interruption, Isidore?" the announcer asked.

Yeah, Isidore, what? the son thought. Vat iz diz?

"These Leggings brothers are waiting for their check," said the announcer.

"It's not fair," Feldman shouted. "Anyway, the little one pushed from behind." The crowd roared. "Let it stand, but give a man a chance, Your Honor."

"What are you saying, Isidore? You mean you want to be in the contest too?"

His father flexed his arm, and the crowd laughed harder than before.

"Do you folks think Isidore Feldman here should take his turn?" They cheered. "All right, Isidore, let's see what you can do then," the announcer said.

Feldman walked past the sled and looked at it for a moment but did not stop. "Cement," he called roughly, pointing to the massive blocks chain-belted to the sled. "Cement for sale. Cash and carry."

"Make your hitch there, Isidore," the announcer called. He seemed annoyed. The son had an idea now it might not be an act.

Alarmingly, Feldman suddenly began to run. As he ran he shouted up to them, blowing out his phrases in gasps. "Wait, wait—while you're here—I've got— something to show you." He ran across the small stadium and pushed open a gate in the low wall. Feldman's son recognized the wagon, piled incredibly high. His father placed himself inside the long wood handles and bent far forward, like one in a storm. A tarpaulin had been spread over the load, so that it looked like a mountain. He seemed heroic. The people gasped as the wheels began slowly to turn and the wagon, the mountain inside it, began to move. He came steadily forward. "Talk about strength," he intoned as he came, "heavy as earth, terrible tons, see how I pull it, drag it along, I break all the records, an ant of a man, prudent as squirrel, thrifty as greed, they'll be a winter, who'll make me warm?"

He brought the wagon to rest a few feet from the grandstand and straightened up. He turned around, and grabbing one corner of the tarpaulin, pulled at it fiercely. "Ladies and gentleman," he announced, shouting, *"THE INVENTORY!"*

"Things," he called, "things here. Things as they are. Thingamabobs and thingamajigs, dinguses and whatsits. Whatdayacallits, whatchamacallits. Gadgets and gewgaws. Kits and caboodle. Stuff. Stuff here!" He stood beside the pile, studying it. "What's to be done with the unsalable thing?" He pulled at his sleeve like one reaching into dishwater for a sunken spoon and slipped his hand with gingerly gentleness into the center of the pile. "Teakettle," he said. He pulled out a teakettle.

"We will trade together," he said seriously. He advanced to the railing at the foot of the stands, the small kettle swinging like a censer before him. "Diaspora," he called. "America, Midwest, Bible Belt, corn country, county fairgrounds, grandstand. Last stop for the Diaspora, everyone off." He recognized his son in the stands and winked hugely. "All right," he said, "I just blew in on the trade winds, and I'm hot see, and dusty see, and I'm smelling of profit and smelling of loss, and it's heady stuff, heady. I could probably use a shower and a good night's sleep, but business is business and a deal is a deal." He held out the kettle. "All right," he said, "This from the East. All from the East, where commerce begins. Consumers, consumers, purchasers, folks. I bring the bazaar. I've spared no expense. Down from the mountains, over the deserts, up from the seas. On the hump of a camel, the back of an ass. All right. Here is the kettle, who drinks the tea?" He leaped over the low rail and rushed into the stands. "Buy," he demanded, "buy, damnit, *buy, I say!*" He chose a farmer and thrust the kettle into the man's hand. He waited. The man tried to give the kettle back, but Feldman's father wouldn't take it; he folded his arms and dodged, bobbing and weaving like a boxer. "Pay up," he shouted, "a deal is a deal." The man made one more attempt to give it back. "All sales final," his father said. "Read your contract." At last the man, embarrassed, dug into his overalls and gave him a coin. His father held it up for the crowd to see. "Object's no money," he said scornfully. Passing his son, he took the sheet of notebook paper the boy still held. He sold it, then returned to the wagon. "Come," he said over his shoulder. "Come. Come. Come." Several followed him.

Again and again Feldman dipped into his pile. He pulled things out, handling, caressing, rubbing value into everything he touched. He signaled them closer. "Come," he called to those still in the stands. "Come. Come. Come." One by one they left the stands to crowd round his wagon. In ten minutes only his son was still in the stands. His father climbed into the wagon and yelled to the announcer. "I win, Your Honor." He indicated the large crowd beneath him that he had brought from the stands. He pointed suddenly to his son. "I can't move *that* item," he confessed.

He disappeared behind his inventory. "I've got the goods," he shouted, "and that ain't bad." In half an hour the pile had diminished, and his father, still in the wagon, seemed to have grown taller. He waved to his

son. "Are you learning anything?" he called to him
over the heads of the crowd.

Gradually the people began to drift away. There
were still two or three things unsold, and Feldman
reached down and held a man's arm. "Wait," he
roared, "where are you going? You think I'm through
with you? This is winter I'm talking about. This is the
cold, sad solstice. Just because the sun is shining over
us now, you think it's stuck up there? You take too
much for granted. You buy something, you hear me?"
He bent down and picked up a carved, heavy leg from
an old dining-room table. "Here," he said. "A wonderful club. For your enemies. You got enemies? No?
Then build a table over it and invite your friends to
supper."

Finally there was nothing left to sell and the people
had all gone. His father still stood in the wagon, tall,
forlorn as a giant. The oxen passed beside him, led by
their owners. "What's to be done with the unsalable
thing?" Feldman crooned.

His son, in the stands, stared at him without moving.
"What *is* the unsalable thing?" he called.

"The unsalable thing? My God, don't you know?"

"No."

"No?"

"You never told me."

They were shouting to each other.

"I didn't?"

"Not once."

"Never?"

"No."

"I had to tell you? You couldn't guess?"

"I never bothered."

"Some son."

"Well?"

"Well what? What well?"
"What is it?"
"What is what?"
"What's that?"
"The unsalable thing."
"It's me," he said.

A year later his father began to cough. The boy was always with him now on the wagon. During the choking, heavy seizures, brought on, it seemed, by the swelling, passionate spiels themselves, his son would take over the cries, shouting madder and madder things into the streets. The cough grew worse; it would begin as soon as he started to speak.

Feldman went to the doctor. "It's cancer," he told his son. "I'm dying."

"Can he operate?"

His father shook his head. "It's terminal." He coughed.

"Terminal," his son repeated the word.

"Sure," his father said, coughing so that he could hardly be understood. "Last stop for the Diaspora. Everyone off."

The boy went to the doctor and conferred with him.

Three months later, when the old man died, his son got in touch with the doctor. They argued some more, but it was no use. The doctor, on behalf of the tiny hospital, could offer him only ten dollars for the body.

# Bernie ★★★ Perk

★ ★ ★

Among the guests in the studio all hell broke loose during the station break. They talked excitedly to one another, and called back and forth along the row of theater seats like picnickers across their tables. Though they had nothing to say themselves, Behr-Bleibtreau's people turned back and forth trying to follow the conversation of the others. Indeed, there was a sort of lunatic joy in the room, a sense of free-for-all that was not so much an exercise of liberty as of respite—as if someone had temporarily released them from vows. School was out in Studio A, and Dick had an impression of its also being out throughout the two or three New England states that could pick up the show. He saw people raiding refrigerators, gulping beers, grabbing tangerines, slashing margarine on slices of bread, ravenously tearing chicken wings, jellied handfuls of leftover stews.

Pepper Steep had joined Jack Patterson in exhausted detachment; though he said nothing, Mel Son

(From *The Dick Gibson Show,* 1971.)

looked animatedly from one to the other. Behr-Bleibtreau also seemed exhausted.

Of the members of his panel, only Bernie Perk
seemed keyed up. He jabbered away a mile a minute,
so that Dick couldn't really follow all that he was
saying. The druggist wanted to know what had happened to everyone. "What's got into Pepper?" he
asked. "What's got into Jack?"

Dick couldn't tell him. He had no notion of what
had gotten into his comrades. All he knew was that he
was impatient for the commercial to be finished and
for the show to go back on the air. He couldn't wait to
hear what would happen next, though having some
dim sense of the masquelike qualities of the evening,
and realizing that thus far his guests had "performed"
in the order that they had been introduced, he had a
hunch that it would involve Bernie.

It did.

BERNIE PERK:    May I say something?
DICK GIBSON:    Sure thing.
BERNIE PERK:    Okay, then. What's going on here?
    What's got into everyone? What's got into Pepper?
    What's got into Jack? I came here tonight to talk
    about psychology with an expert in the field. But all
    anyone's done so far is grab the limelight for himself.
    Everyone is too excited. Once a person gets started
    talking about himself all sorts of things come out that
    aren't anybody's business. I understand enough about
    human nature to know that much. Everybody has his
    secret. Who hasn't? We're all human beings. Who
    isn't a human being? Listen, I'm a mild person. I'm
    not very interesting, maybe, and I don't blow my own
    horn, but even someone like myself, good old Bernie
    Perk, corner druggist, "Doc" to one and "Pop" to
    another, could put on a regular horror show if he
    wanted to. *But it isn't people's business.*

Look, my son and his charming wife are guests in
the studio tonight. Pepper Steep's sister is here. How
do you think it must be for them when an intimate
relative sticks his foot in his mouth? If you love people you've got to have consideration.

DICK GIBSON:    Bernie, don't be so upset. Take it easy.

BERNIE PERK:    Dick, I *am* upset about this. No, I mean
it. What's it supposed to be, "Can You Top This?"

DICK GIBSON:    Come on, Bernie—

BERNIE PERK:    Because the temptation is always the one
they yielded to. To give up one's secrets. La. La la.
The soul's espionage, its secret papers. *Know* me.
No, thank you. I'm pretty worked up. Call on
Mel.

DICK GIBSON:    Take it easy.

BERNIE PERK:    Call on Mel.

DICK GIBSON:    Mel? *(no answer)*

BERNIE PERK:    Mel passes. *(He giggles.)* Well, that's too
bad, for thereby hangs a tale, I bet. The truth is
Well, okay, I'll tell the audience something maybe
everybody likes to see his friends with their hair down.
they don't know. We don't see each other off the air.
The illusion is we're mates. You want us to be, but
we're not.

JACK PATTERSON:    Here goes Bernie.

BERNIE PERK:    *(fiercely)* You *had* your turn. You were
*first*. Don't hog everything. You had your turn. Just
because you couldn't do any better than that canned
ardor, don't try to ruin it for everyone else.

The truth of the matter is, I had to laugh. The
man's a schoolteacher. Big deal. He sees up coeds'
skirts. Big deal. He has them in for conferences, he
goes over their papers with them, he bends over the
composition and her hair touches his cheek. Enormous! Call the police, passion's circuits are blown.
I know all that, I *know* all that. But if you want to
see life in the raw, be a pharmacist, buy a drugstore.
You wouldn't *believe* what goes on. It's a meat market. No wonder they register us. Hickory Dickory

"Doc." Let me fill you in on the prescription. Yow. Wow.

You know what a drugstore is? A temple to the senses. Come down those crowded aisles. Cosmetics first stop. Powders, puffs, a verb-wheel of polished nails on a cardboard, lipstick ballistics, creams and tighteners, suntan lotions, eyeshadow, dyes for hair —love potions, paints, the ladies' paintbox!

Come, come with Pop. The Valentine candy, the greeting cards, the paperbook racks and magazine stands. The confessions and movie magazines dated two months beyond the real month because time, like love, is yet to be. Sit at the fountain. See the confections—banana splits and ice-cream sundaes like statues of the sweet, as if sweetness itself, the sugary molecules of love resided in them. The names—like words for lyrics. Delicious the syrups, the salty storm of nuts and tidal waves of spermy cream. Sing yum! Sing yum yum!

All the shampoos, all the lotions and hair conditioners proteined as egg and meat. Files and emery boards, the heartsick gypsy's tools. Sun lamps, sleep masks, rollers, bath oils and depilatories, massaging lotions. Things for acne, panty hose—the model on the package like a yogi whore. Brushes, rinses, bath oils and shower caps like the fruits that grow on beaches.

To say nothing of the Venus Folding Feminine Syringe, of Kotex in boxes you could set a table for four on. Liquid douches—you can hear the sea. Rubber goods, the queer mysterious elastics, supporters, rupture's ribbons and organ's bows. Now we're into it, hard by diarrhea's plugs and constipation's triggers. There's the druggist, behind the high counter, his bust visible like someone on a postage stamp, immaculate in his priest's white collar. See the symbols—the mortar and pestle and flasks of colored liquid. Once I sipped from the red, the woman's potion. I had expected tasteless vegetable dye, but it was sweet, viscous, thick as oil. There are aphrodisiacs in those flasks to float your heart.

And there *I* am, by the refrigerated drugs, the druggist's small safe, the pharmacopoeia, the ledger with names and dates and numbers. A man of the corner and crossroads, scientist manqué, reader of Greek and Latin, trained to count, to pull a jot from a tittle, lift a tittle from a whit, a man of equilibriums, of grains and half-grains, secret energies locked in the apothecary's ounce.

Fresh from college I took a job—this was the Depression—in another man's store. MacDonald's. Old MacDonald had a pharmacy, eeyi eeyi o! An old joke but the first I ever made. "I'll fill the prescriptions," MacDonald told me. "You're a whippersnapper. You'll wait on trade and make the ice-cream sodas. If that isn't satisfactory, go elsewhere. If I'm to be sued for malpractice I'll be the malpracticer, thank you very much." It was not satisfactory, but what could I do? It was the Depression. How many young men trained for a profession had to settle in those days for something else? And do you know what I found out? (What's got into Bernie?) I found out *everything!*

The first week I stood behind the counter, smiling in my white lab jacket, and a lady came in. A plain woman, middle-aged, her hair gone gray and her figure failing. "Doctor, I need something for my hemorrhoids," she said. "They are like to kill me when I sit. It burns so when I make number two that I've been eating clay to constipate myself."

I gave her Preparation H. Two days later she came back to the store and bought a birthday card for her son. Somehow the knowledge that I alone of all the people in the store knew something about that woman's behind was stirring to me. I was married, the woman was plain; she didn't attract me. I was drawn by her hemorrhoids, in on the secret of her sore behind. Each day in that novice year there were similar experiences. I had never been so happy in my life. Old MacDonald puttering away in the back of the store, I up front—what a team we made.

A young woman came in. Sacrificing her turn she gestured to me to wait on the other customers first. When the store was empty she came up to me.

"I have enuresis," she said.

I gave her some pills.

"Listen," she said, "may I use your toilet?"

I let her come behind the counter. She minced along slowly, her legs in a desperate clamp. I opened the door of the small toilet.

"There's no toilet paper," I said. "I'll have to bring you some."

"Thank you," she said.

I stood outside the door for a moment. I heard the splash. A powerful, incredible discharge. You'd think she'd had an enema. But it was all urine; the woman's bladder was converting every spare bit of moisture into uremic acid. She could have pissed mud puddles, oceans, the drops in clouds, the condensation on the outside of beer bottles. It was beyond chemistry, it was alchemy. Golden. Lovely.

I got the paper for her.

"I have the toilet tissue, Miss." Though she opened the door just enough for me to hand the roll in to her, I saw bare knees, a tangle of panties.

Her name was Miss Wallace, and when she came into the store for her pills—need is beyond embarrassment: only *I* was embarrassed—I grew hard with lust. I made no overtures, you understand; I was always clinical, always professional, always offhand.

"Listen," I told her one day, "I suppose you have rubber sheets."

"No good," she said.

"You'll ruin your mattress."

"It's already ruined. When I tried a rubber sheet,

the water collected in the depression under my behind. I lay in it all night and caught cold."

The thought of that pee-induced cold maddened me. Ah God, the bizarre body awry, messes caught in underwear—love tokens, unhealth a function of love.

There were so many I can't remember them all.

I knew I had to leave Old MacDonald. I was held down, you see. Who knew what secrets might not be unlocked if I could get my hands on the *prescriptions* those ladies brought in! When my father died and left me four thousand dollars, I used it to open the store I have now. I signed notes right and left to get my stock and fixtures together. My wife thought it was madness to gamble this way in the depth of the Depression, but I was pining with love. There were so many . . .

Let's see. *These have been a few of the women in my life:*

Rose Barbara Hacklander, Miss Hartford of 1947, 38–24–36, a matter of public record. What is *not* a matter of public record is that she had gingivitis, a terrible case, almost debilitating, and came near to losing the title because of her reluctance to smile. She wanted to shield her puffy gums, you understand. Only I, Bernie Perk, her druggist, knew. On the night before the finals she came to me in tears. She showed me—in the back of the store—lifting a lip, reluctant as a country girl in the Broadway producer's office raising the hem of her skirt, shy, and yet bold too, wanting to please even with the shame of her beauty. I looked inside her mouth. The gums were filled, tumid with blood and pus, enormous, preternatural, the gums of the fat lady in the circus, obscuring her teeth, in their sheathing effect seeming actually to sharpen them, two rings of blade in her mouth. And there, in the back of her mouth at the back of the store, pulling a cheek, squeezing it as one gathers in a trigger—cankers, cysts like snowflakes.

"Oh, Doc," she cried, "what will I do? It's worse tonight. The salve don't help. It's nerves—I know it's nerves."

"Wait, I can't see in this light. Put your head here. Say 'Ah.' "

"Ah," she said.

"Ah," I said. "Ah!"

"What's to be done? Is there anything you can give me?"

"Advice."

"Advice?"

"Give them the Giaconda smile. Mona Lisa let them have."

And she did. I saw the photograph in the newspaper the morning after the finals. Rose Barbara crowned (I the Queenmaker), holding her flowers, the girls in her court a nimbus behind her, openly smiling, their trim gums flashing. Only Miss Hartford of 1947's lips were locked, her secret in the dimpled parentheticals of her sealed smile. I still have the photograph in my wallet.

Do you know what it means to be always in love? Never to be out of it? Each day loving's gnaw renewed, like hunger or the need for sleep? Worse, the love unfocused, never quite reduced to this one girl or that one woman, but always I, the King of Love, taking to imagination's beds whole harems? I was grateful, I tell you, to the occasional Rose Barbara Hacklander for the refractive edge she lent to lust. There were so many. Too many to think about. My mind was like the waiting room of a brothel. Let them leave my imagination, I prayed, the ones with acne, bad breath, body odor, dandruff, all those whose flyed ointment and niggered woodpile were the commonplace of my ardor.

Grateful also to Miss Sheila Jean Locusmundi who had corns like Chiclets, grateful to the corns themselves, those hard outcroppings of Sheila Jean's synovial bursa. I see her now, blonde, high-heeled, her long, handsome legs bronzed in a second skin of nylon.

I give her foot plasters. She hands them back. "Won't do," she says.

"Won't do? Won't do? But these are our largest. These are the largest there are."

"Pop," she whispers, "I've got a cop's corns."

A cop's corns. A cornucopia. I shake my head in wonder. I want to see them, Sheila Jean. I invite her behind the counter, to the back of the store. If I see them I might be able to help her, a doc like me. Once out of view of the other customers Shelia Jean succumbs: she limps. *I* feel the pinch. That's right, I think, don't let *them* see. In my office she sits down in front of my rolltop desk and takes off her shoes. I watch her face. Ease comes in like the high tide. Tears of painless gratitude appear in her eyes. All day she waits for this moment. She wriggles her toes. I see bunions bulge in her stockings. It's hard for me to maintain my professional distance. "Take off your stockings, Miss Locusmundi," I manage. She turns away in my swivel chair and I hear the soft, electric hiss of the nylon. She swings around, and redundantly points.

"I see," I murmur. "Yes, those are really something." They are. They are knuckles, ankles. They are boulders, mountain ranges.

"May I?" I ask.

She gives me her foot reluctantly. "Oh, God, don't touch them, Pop."

"There, there, Miss Locusmundi, I won't hurt you." I hold her narrow instep, my palm a stirrup. I toss it casually from one hand to the other, getting the heft.

"Ticklish," Sheila Jean says. She giggles.

I peer down closely at the humpy callosities, their dark cores. There is a sour odor. This, I think, is what Miss Hartford's gingivitis tastes like. I nod judiciously; I take their measure. I'm stalling because

I can't stand up yet. When finally I can, I sculpt plasters for her. I daub them with Derma-Soft and apply them. When she walks out she is, to all eyes but mine, just another pretty face.

Grateful too—I thank her here—to Mary Odata, a little Japanese girl whose ears filled with wax. I bless her glands, those sweet secretions, her lovely auditory canal. Filled with wax, did I say? She was a *candle* mine. I saved the detritus from the weekly flushings I administered.

Her father took her to live in Michigan, but before she left she wrote me a note to thank me for all I had done. "Respected R. Ph. Perk," she wrote, "my father have selectioned to take me to his brother whom has a truck farm in the state of Michigan, but before I am going this is to grateful acknowledgment your thousand kindnesses to my humble ears. In my heart I know will I never to find in Michigan an R. Ph. as tender for my ears as you, sir. Mine is a shameful affliction, but you never amusemented them, and for this as for your other benefits to me I thank. Your friend, M. Odata."

When I closed the store that night I went into my office and molded a small candle from the cerumen I had collected from her over the months, ran a wick through it, turned off the lights, and reread Mary's letter by the glow of her wax until it sputtered and went out. Call me a sentimental old fool, but that's what I did.

Not to mention Mrs. Louise Lumen, perpetual wet nurse, whose lacteal glands were an embarrassment to her three or even four years beyond her delivery, or flatulent Cora Moss, a sweet young thing with a sour stomach in the draft of whose farts one could catch cold. There were so many. There was Mrs. Wynona Jost whose unwanted hair no depilatory would ever control. Her back, she gave me to understand, was like an ape's. Super-follicled Mrs.

Jost! And psoriatic Edna Hand. And all the ladies with prescriptions. I knew everybody's secret, the secret of every body. And yet it was never the worm in the apple I loved but only a further and final nakedness, almost the bacteria itself, the cocci and bacilli and spirilla, the shameful source of *their* ailment and my privilege. I was deferential to this principle only: that there exists a nudity beyond *mere* nudity, a covertness which I shielded as any lover husbands his sweet love's mysteries. I did not kiss and tell; I did not kiss at all. Charged with these women's cabala I kept my jealous counsel. I saved them, you see. Honored and honed a sort of virginity in them by my silence. Doc *and* Pop. And knight too in my druggist's gorget. I could have gone on like this forever, content with my privileged condition, satisfied to administer my drugs and patent medicines and honor all confidences, grateful, as I've said, for the impersonal personality of the way I loved, calling them Miss, calling them Missus, protecting them from myself as well as from others, not even masturbating, only looking on from a distance, my desire speculative as an issue of stock.

But something human happens.

One day . . . Where's my *son* going? Why's he leaving? Edward? Connie, *don't* go. Youth should have a perspective on its parents . . . Well, they've gone. I must have shamed them. Isn't that the way with the young? They think the older generation is stodgy and then they've no patience with confession. Oh well, let them go. Where was I?

BEHR-BLEIBTREAU:  "One day—"

BERNIE PERK:  Yes, that's right. One day a woman came into my drugstore I'd never seen before. She was pretty, in her early or middle twenties perhaps, but very small. Not just short—though she was, extremely short; she couldn't have been much more than five feet—but *small*. Dainty, you know? Maybe she wore a size six dress. I don't know sizes. She could probably buy her clothes in the same department school girls do. What do they call that? Junior Miss? Anyway, she was very delicate. Tinier than Mary Odata. A nice face, sweet, a little old-fashioned perhaps, the sort of face you see in an old sepia photograph of your grandmother's sister that died. A *very* pretty little woman.

I saw her looking around, going up and down the aisles. Every once in a while she would stoop down to peer in a low shelf. I have these big round mirrors in the corners to spy on shoplifters. I watched her in the mirrors. If I lost her in one mirror I picked her up again in another. A little doll going up and down the aisles in the convex glass.

I knew what was up. A woman knows where things are. It's an instinct. Have you ever seen them in a supermarket? They understand how it's organized. It has nothing to do with the fact that they shop more than men. A man goes into a grocery, he has to ask where the bread is. Not a woman: she knows where it's *supposed* to be. Well, this woman is obviously confused. She's looking for something which she knows is always in one place, whatever store she goes into. So I *knew* what was up: she was looking for the sanitary napkins.

Most places they keep them on the open shelves to spare the ladies embarrassment. I don't spare anyone anything. I keep them behind the counter with me. I want to know what's going on with their periods. They have to ask.

Finally she came over to me. "I don't see the Kotex," she says.

"This is the Kotex department," I say, and reach under the counter for a box. "Will there be anything else? We have a terrific buy on Midol this week. Or some girls prefer the formula in this. I've been getting good reports; they tell me it's very effective against cramps." I hand her a tin of Monthleaze. "How are you fixed for breath sweetener?" I push a tube of Sour-Off across the counter to her.

She ignores my suggestions but picks up the box of Kotex and looks at it. "This is Junior," she says.

"I'm sorry," I say. I give her Regular.

"Don't you have Super?"

"I thought this was for you," I tell her, and give her the size she asks for.

A month later she came in again. "Super Kotex," she said. I give her the box and don't see her again for another month. This time when she comes in I hand her the Super and start to ring up the sale.

"I'd better take the tampon kind too," she says. She examines the box I give her. "Is there anything larger than this?"

"This is the biggest," I say, swallowing hard.

"All right."

"Tell me," I say, "are these for you?"

She blushes and doesn't answer.

I hadn't dared to think about it, though it had crossed my mind. Now I could think of nothing else. I forgot about the others. This girl inflamed me. Bernie burns. It was astonishing—a girl so small. My life centered on *her* center, on the prodigious size of her female parts.

BEHR-BLEIBTREAU:   Say "cunt."

DICK GIBSON:   Wait a minute—

BEHR-BLEIBTREAU:   It's all right. Say "cunt."

BERNIE PERK:   ... *Cunt.* The size of her cunt. The disproportion was astonishing to me. Kotex *and* Tampax. For all I knew, she used the Kotex *inside.* I *did* know it. I conceived of her smallness now as the result of her largeness. It was as if her largeness *there* sapped size from the rest of her body, or that by some incredible compensation her petiteness lent dimension elsewhere. I don't know. It was all I could think of. Bernie burns.

I had to know about her, at least find out who she was, whether she was married. I tried to recall if I had seen a wedding band, but who could think of fingers, who could think of hands? Bernie burns. Perk percolates.

That night I counted ahead twenty-eight days to figure when I might expect her again. The date fell on September 9, 1956.

She didn't come—not then, not the next month.

Then, one afternoon, I saw her in the street. It was just after Thanksgiving, four or five days before her next period. I raised my hat. "Did you have a pleasant holiday?" I asked. My face was familiar to her but she couldn't place me. I counted on this.

"So so." The little darling didn't want to embarrass me.

"I thought you might be going away for Thanksgiving," I said.

She looked puzzled but still wanted to be polite. "My roommate went home but I stayed on in Hartford," she said. "Actually she invited me to go with her but my boss wouldn't give me Friday off."

Ah, I thought, she has a roommate, she's a working girl. Good.

"I'm very sorry," I said, "but I find myself in a very embarrassing position. I don't seem to be able to remember your name."

"Oh," she said, and laughed. "I can't remember yours either. I know we've seen each other."

"I'm Bernie Perk."

"Yes. Of course. I'm Bea Dellaspero. I still don't—"

"I don't either. You see what happens? Here we are, two old friends and neither of us can— *Wait* a minute. I think I've got it. I've seen you in my store. I'm the druggist—Perk's Drugs on Mutual?"

"Oh." She must have remembered our last conversation for she became very quiet. We were standing outside a coffee shop, and when I invited her to

have a cup with me she said she had to be going
and hurried off.

Her number was in the phone book, and I called
right from the coffee shop. If only her roommate's
in, I thought, crossing my fingers for luck.

"Where's Bea? Is Bea there?"

"No."

"Christ," I said. "What's her number at work?
I've got to get her."

I called the number the roommate gave me; it
was a big insurance company. I told them I was
doing a credit check on Bea Dellaspero and they
connected me to personnel. Personnel was nice as
pie. Bea was twenty-four years old, a typist in the
claims department and a good credit risk.

It was something, but I couldn't live on it. I had
to get her to return to the store.

I conceived the idea of running a sale especially
for Bea. My printer set up a sample handbill. Across
the bottom I had him put in half a dozen simple
coupons, with blank spaces where she could write
in the names of the products she wanted to exchange
them for. She could choose from a list of twenty
items, on which I gave about a 90 percent discount.
I sent the flier in an envelope to Bea's address.

Normally I'm closed on Sunday, but that was the
day I set aside for Bea's sale. I opened up at ten
o'clock, and I didn't have to wait more than an
hour. When she came in holding the pink flier we
were alone in the store.

"How are you?" I asked.

"Fine, thank you." She was still uneasy about me.
"I got your advertisement."

"I see it in your hand."

"Oh. Yes."

She went around the store picking up the items
she wanted and brought them to the counter. When
she gave me her coupons, I saw that she'd chosen
products relating to a woman's periods or to feminine

hygiene. She'd had to: I'd rigged the list with men's shaving equipment, pipe accessories, athletic supporters—things like that.

"What size would these be, madam?"

"Super."

"Beg pardon, I didn't hear you."

*"Super."*

Super *duper,* I thought. I put the big boxes on the counter and added two bottles of douche from the shelf behind me. It won't be enough, I thought. She had a pussy big as all outdoors. Imperial gallons wouldn't be enough. "Let me know how you like the douche," I said, "I've been getting some excellent reports."

God, I was crazy. You know how it is when you're smitten. Smitten? I was in love. Married twenty-three years and all of a sudden I was in love for the first time in my life. Whole bales of cotton I would have placed between her legs. Ah love, set me tasks! Send me for all the corks in Mediterranea, all styptic stymies would I fetch!

In love, did I say? *In* love? That's wrong. *In* love I had been since Old MacDonald's. *In* love is nothing, simple citizenship. Now I was *of* love, no mere citizen but a very governor of the place, a tenant become landlord. And who *falls* in love? Love's an ascent, a rising—touch my hard-on—a soaring. Consider my body, all bald spots haired by imagination, my fats rendered and features firmed, tooth decay for God's sake turned back to candy in my mouth. Heyday! Heyday! And all my feelings collateral to a teen-age boy's!

So I had been in love and now was of it. Bernie burns, the pharmacist on fire. I did not so much forget the others as repudiate them; they were just more wives. Get this straight: love is adulterous, hard on the character. I cuckold those cuties, the Misses Odata and Locusmundi. Horns for Miss Hartford! Miss Moss is dross. Be my love, Bea my love!

I bagged Bea's purchases, punched the register a few times to make it look good, and charged her fifty-seven cents for the nineteen dollars' worth of stuff she'd bought.

"So cheap?"

"It's my special get-acquainted offer," I said. "Also I knocked off a few dollars because you mentioned the secret word."

"I did? What was it?"

"I can't tell you. It's a secret."

"You know, it's really a terrific sale," she said. "I'm surprised more people aren't here to take advantage of it."

"They're coming by when church gets out."

"I see."

As she took the two bags in her thin arms and turned to go, it occurred to me that she might never come back to the store. I raced around the counter. I had no idea what I would do; all love's stratagems and games whistled in my head.

"I'll help you," I said, taking one of her bags.

"I can manage."

"No, I couldn't think of it. A little thing like you? Let me have the other one as well."

She refused to give it up. "I'm very capable," she said. We were on the sidewalk. "You better go back. Your store's open. Anyone could just walk off with all your stock."

"They're in church. Even the thieves. I'll take you to your car."

"I don't have a car. I'm going to catch the bus at the corner."

"I'll wait with you."

"It's not necessary."

"It isn't safe."

"They're all in church."

"Just the thieves, not the rapers."

"But it's the dead of winter. You don't even have a coat. You'll catch cold."

"Not cold."

"What?"

"Not cold. Bernie burns."

"Excuse me?"

"Not cold. The pharmacist on fire."

"I'm sorry?"

"Don't worry about me," I said. "I'm hale." I jumped up and down with the bag in my arms. "See?" I said. "See how hale? I'm strong. I huff and I puff." I hit myself in the chest with my fist. "Me? Me sick? There are things on my shelves to cure anything."

Bea was becoming alarmed. I checked myself, and we stood quietly in the cold together waiting for the bus.

Finally I had to speak or burst. " 'There's naught so sweet as love's young dream,' " I said.

"What was that?"

"It's a saying. It's one of my favorite sayings."

"Oh."

" 'Who ever loved that loved not at first sight?' "

"I beg your pardon?"

"It's another saying."

"Do you see the bus coming?"

" 'Love makes the world go round.' "

"I've heard that one."

" 'Love is smoke raised with the fume of sighs.' " The fume of *size:* super. " 'Take away love and earth is tomb.' 'Love indeed is anything, yet is nothing.' "

"I think I hear it coming. Are you *sure* you can't see it?"

" 'Love is blind,' " I said gloomily. She *had* heard it; it lumbered toward us irresistibly. Soon it would be there and I would never see her again. She was very nervous and went into the street and began to signal while the bus was still three blocks off. I watched her performance disconsolately. " 'And yet I love her till I die,' " I murmured softly.

When the driver came abreast, Bea darted up the steps and I handed her bag to her. "Will I see you again?" I said.

"What's that?"

"Will I see you again? Promise when you've used up what you've bought you'll come back."

"Well, it's so *far*," she said. The driver closed the door.

*"I deliver!"* I shouted after her and waved and blew kisses off my fingertips.

DICK GIBSON:    Remarkable!

BERNIE PERK:    So's love, so are lovers. Now I saw them.

DICK GIBSON:    Saw whom?

BERNIE PERK:    Why, lovers. For if love is bad for the character it's good for it too. Now that I was of love, I was also of lovers. I looked around and saw that the whole world was in love. When a man came in to pick up penicillin for his wife—that was a love errand. I tried to cheer him. "She'll be okay," I told him. "The pills will work. She'll come round. Her fever will break. Her sore throat will get better." "Why are you telling me this?" he'd ask. "I like you," I'd say. " 'All the world loves a lover.' "

For the first time I saw what my drugstore was all about. It was love's way station. In free moments I would read the verses on my greeting cards, and my eyes would brim with tears. Or I would pore over the true confessions in my magazine racks. "Aye aye," I'd mutter, "too true this true confession." I blessed the lipstick: "Kiss, kiss," I droned over the little torpedoes. "Free the man in frogs and bogs. Telltales be gone, stay off shirt collars and pocket handkerchiefs." All love was sacred. I pored over my customers' photographs after they were developed. I held a magnifying glass over them— the ones of sweethearts holding hands in the national parks or on the steps of historic buildings, the posed wives on the beach, fathers waving goodbye, small in the distance, as they go up the steps into airplanes. People take the same pictures, did you know that? We are all brothers.

Love was everywhere, commoner than loneliness. I had never realized before what a terrific business I did in rubbers. And it isn't even spring; no one's on a blanket in the woods, or in a rowboat's bottom, or on a hayride. I'm talking about the dead of winter, a high of twenty, a low of three. And you can count on the fingers of one hand the high-school kids' pipe-dream purchase. My customers meant business. There were irons in these lovers' fires. And connoisseurs they were, I tell you, prophylactic more tactic than safeguard, their condoms counters and confections. How sheer's this thing, they'd want to know, or handle them, testing this one's elasticity, that one's friction. Or inquire after refinements, special merchandise, meticulous as fishermen browsing flies. Let's see. They wanted: French Ticklers, Spanish Daggers, Swedish Surprises, The Chinese Net, The Texas Truss and Gypsy Outrage. They wanted petroleum jellies smooth as syrups.

And I, Pop, all love's avuncular spirit, all smiles, rooting for them, smoothing their way where I could, apparently selfless—they must have thought me some good-sport widower who renewed his memories in their splashy passion—giving the aging Cupid's fond green light. How could they suspect that I learned from them, growing my convictions in their experience? Afterward, casually, I would debrief them. Reviewing the troops: Are Trojans better than Spartans? Cavaliers as good as Commandos? Is your Centurion up to your Cossack? What of the Mercenary? The Guerrilla? How does the Minuteman stand up against the State Trooper? In the end, it was too much for me to have to look on while every male in Hartford above the age of seventeen came in to buy my condoms.

Bea never came back—I had frightened her off

with my wild talk at the bus stop—yet my love was keener than ever. I still kept up my gynecological charts on her, and celebrated twenty-eighth days like sad festivals. I dreamed of her huge vaginal landscape, her loins in terrible cramp. Bernie burns.

I formed a plan. The first step was to get rid of her roommate. I made my first call to Bea that night.

Don't worry. It's not what you think. I didn't disguise my voice or breathe heavily and say nothing, nor any of your dirty-old-man tricks. I'm no phone creep. When Bea answered I told her who it was straight off.

"Miss Dellaspero? Bernie Perk. I don't see you in the drugstore anymore. You took advantage of my bargains but you don't come in."

Embarrassed, she made a few vague excuses which I pretended cleared matters up. "Well that's okay, then," I said. "I just thought you weren't satisfied with the merchandise or something. You can't put a guy in jail for worrying about his business."

In a week I called again. "Bea? Bernie."

This time she was pretty sore. "Listen," she said. "I never heard of a respectable merchant badgering people to trade with him. I was a little flustered when you called last week, but I have the right to trade wherever I want."

"Sure you do, Bea. Forget about that. That was a business call. This is social."

"Social?"

"That's right. I called to ask how you are. After our last conversation I thought I'd be seeing you. Then when you didn't come in I got a little worried. I thought you might be sick or something."

"I'm not sick."

"I'm relieved to hear it. That takes a load off my mind."

"I don't see why my health should be of any concern to you."

"Bea, I'm a *pharmacist*. Is it against the law for

a pharmacist to inquire after the health of one of his customers?"

"Look, I'm not your customer."

"Your privilege, Bea. It's no crime for a man to try to drum up a little trade. Well, as long as you're all right. That's the important thing. If we haven't got our health, what have we got?"

A few days later I called again. "Bernie here. Listen, Bea, I've been thinking. What do you say to dinner tonight? I know a terrific steakhouse in West Hartford. Afterward we could take in a late movie."

"What? Are you crazy?"

"Crazy? I don't get your meaning. Why do you say something like that?"

"Why do I *say* that? Why do you call up all the time?"

"Well, I'm calling to invite you to dinner. Where does it say a man can't invite a young lady to have dinner with him?"

"I don't *know* you."

"Well, *sure* you know me, but even if you didn't, since when is it illegal for a person to try to make another person's acquaintance?"

"Don't call anymore."

"I'm sorry you feel that way, Bea."

"Don't call me Bea."

"That's your name, isn't it? You don't drag a person into court for saying your name. Even your first name."

"I don't know what your trouble is, Mr. Perk—"

"Bernie. Call me Bernie. Bernie's my first name."

*"I don't know what your trouble is, Mr. Perk,* but you're annoying me. You'd better stop calling." She hung up.

I telephoned the next night. "My trouble, Bea, is that I think I'm falling in love with you."

"I don't want to hear this. Please get off the line."

"Bea, dear, you don't lock a fellow up for falling in love."

"You're insane. You must be at least twenty-five years older than I am."

"There *is* a difference in our ages, yes. But they don't arrest people for their birthdays."

She hung up.

My plan was going according to plan. "Bea?"

"I thought I convinced you to stop calling me."

"Bea, don't hang up. Listen, don't hang up. If you hang up I'll just have to call you again. Listen to what I have to say."

"What is it?"

"One of the reasons you're hostile is that you don't know anything about me. That's not my fault, I don't take any responsibility for that. I thought you'd come into the store and gradually we'd learn about each other, but you didn't want it that way. Well, when a person's in love he doesn't stand on ceremonies. I'm going to tell you a few things about myself."

"That can't make any difference."

" 'That can't make any difference.' Listen to her. Of course it can make a difference, Bea. What do you think love between two people is? It's *knowing* a person, understanding him. At least give me a chance to explain a few things. It's not a federal offense for a fellow to try to clear the air. All right?"

"I'll give you a minute."

"Gee, I'd better talk fast."

"You'd better."

"I want to be honest with you. You weren't far off when you said I was twenty-five years older than you are. As a matter of fact, I'm even older than you think. I've got a married son twenty-six years old."

"You're married?"

"Sure I'm married. Since when is it a crime to be married? My wife's name is Barbara. She has the same initial you do. But when I say I'm married I mean that *technically* I'm married. Babs is two years older than I am. A woman ages, Bea darling. All the zip has gone out of her figure. Menopause does that to a girl. I'll tell you the truth: I can't stand to look at her. I used to be so in love that if I saw her on the toilet I'd get excited. I wouldn't even wait for her to wipe herself. Now I see her in her corsets and I wish I were blind. Her hair has turned gray—down *there.* Do you know what that does to a guy?"

"I'm hanging up."

"I'm telling the truth. *Where's it written it's police business when someone tells the truth?*"

I sent over a carton of Kotex and a carton of Tampax, and called her the following week. "Did you get the napkins?"

"I didn't order those. I don't want them."

"Order? Who said anything about order? You can't arrest a man for sending his sweetheart a present. It wouldn't stand up in court."

And the next night.

"It's you, is it? I'm moving," she said. "I'm moving and I'm getting an unlisted number. I hope you're satisfied. I've lost my roommate on account of you. You've made her as nervous as me with these calls. So go ahead and say whatever you want—it's your last chance."

"Come out with me tonight."

"Don't be ridiculous."

"I love you."

"You're insane."

"Listen, go to bed with me. Please. I want to make love to you. Or let me come over and see you naked. I want to know just how big you really are down there."

"You're sick, do you know that? You need help."

"Then help me. Fuck me."

"I actually feel sorry for you. I really do."

*"What are you talking about? I'm not hiding in any bushes. You know who I am. You know all*

*about me. I'm Bernie Perk. My place of business is listed in the Yellow Pages. You could look me up. It isn't a crime to proposition a woman. You can't put a man behind bars for trying."*

"You disgust me."

"Call the police."

"You disgust me."

"Press charges. They'll throw them out."

Her threat about an unlisted number didn't bother me; a simple call to the telephone company the following afternoon straightened *that* out. I gave them my name and told them that Bea had brought in a prescription to be filled. After she'd picked it up I discovered that I had misread it and given her a dangerous overdose. I told them that if I were unable to get in touch with her before she took the first capsule she would die. And they'd better give me her new address as well so that I could get an ambulance to her if she'd already taken the capsule and was unable to answer the phone. Love *always* finds a way!

I gave her time to settle herself in her new apartment and get some of her confidence back. Then, a week later—I couldn't wait longer: it was getting pretty close to her period—I took the package I had prepared and drove to Bea's new address. Her name on the lctter box had been newly stenciled on a shiny black strip of cellulose, the last name only, the little darling—you know how single girls in big cities try to protect themselves by disguising their sex with initials or last names: the poor dears don't realize that it's a dead giveaway—along with her apartment number. I walked up the two flights and knocked on her door.

"Yes?"

"Mr. Giddons from Tiger's." The building was managed by Tiger's Real Estate and there's actually a Mr. Giddons who works there.

"What do you want?"

"We have a report there's some structural damage in 3-E. I want to check the walls in your apartment."

She opened the door, the trusting little cupcake. "It's you."

" 'All's fair in love and war.' "

"What do you want?"

"I'm berserk," I said, "amok with love. If you scream I'll kill you."

I moved into the room and closed the door behind me. What can I say? In the twentieth century there is no disgrace. It happened, so I'll tell you.

I pushed her roughly and turned my back to her while I pulled on the rubber. As I rolled it on I shouted threats to keep her in line. "One false move and I'll kill you. I've got a knife. Don't go for the unlisted phone or I'll slit you from ear to ear. I'll cut your pupick out. Stay away from the window. No tricks. I love you. Bernie burns, the pharmacist on fire. Don't double-cross me. If I miss you with the knife I'll shoot your head with my bullets." At last it was on. Still with my back to her I ordered her to stand still. "Don't make a move. If you make a move I'll strangle you with my bare hands. Don't make a move or you die. I'm wearing a State Trooper. They're the best. I'm smearing K-Y Petroleum Jelly on me. Everything the best, nothing but the best. All right," I said, "almost through. I just have to take this box of Kleenex out of my package and the aerosol douche. I'm unfolding the Venus Folding Feminine Syringe. There: these are for you. *Now.*" I turned to her.

*"My God!"* I said.

She had taken off her dress and brassiere and had pulled down her panties.

"Oh God," I gasped. "It's so *big!*"

"I didn't want you to rip my clothes," she said softly.

"But your legs, your legs are so thin!"

"Pipestems."

"And your poor frail arms."

"Pipecleaners."

"But my God, Bea. Down *there!* Down there you're magnificent!"

I saw the vastnesses, the tropical rain forest that was her pubes, the swollen mons like a freshly made Indian tumulus, labia majora like a great inverted gorge, the lush pudendum.

"Fantastic!"

"I've the vulva of a giantess," she said sadly.

I reached out and hid my hands up to the wrists in her pubic hair. As soon as I touched her I felt myself coming. "Oh, Jesus. Oh, Jesus. I love you—oo—oo—oo!" It was over. The sperm made a warm, independent weight in the bottom of my State Trooper. It swung against me like a third ball. "Oh God," I sighed. "Oh dear. Oh my. Let me just catch my breath. Whew. Holy Cow! Great Scott!

"Okay," I said in a few moments, "now you listen to me. I'm at your mercy. How can you throw a man in the hoosegow when you know as much about him as you do? I didn't jump out at you from an alley or drag you into a car. Look"—I turned my pockets inside out—"I'm not armed. There's no knife. I don't carry a gun. These hands are trained. They fill prescriptions. Do you think they could strangle? Granted I threatened you, but I was afraid you'd scream. Look at it this way. I was protecting *you.* You're just starting out in the neighborhood. It's a first-class building. Would you want a scandal? And didn't I take every precaution? Look at the douche. Everything the best that money can buy. And what did it come to in the end? I never even got close to you. To tell you the truth I thought it might happen just this way. It's not like rape. I love you. How can you ruin a man who loves you? I'm no stranger. You know me. You know my wife's name. I told

you about my son. I'm a grandfather. Take a look
at these pictures of my grandchildren. Did I ever
show you these? This one's Susan. Four years old
and a little imp. Boy, does she keep her parents
hopping! And this is Greg. Greg's the thoughtful
one. He'll be the scholar. Are you going to put a
grandfather in jail? You got me excited. Perk peeks.
The pharmacist in flames. I love you, but I'll never
bother you again. I had to, just this once. Give me
a chance. It would break my wife's heart to find out
about me. Okay, they'd try to hush it up and maybe
the grandkids would never hear about it, but what
about my son? That's another story.

"I'll tell you something else. *You're the last.* A
man's first woman is special, and so's his last. He
never gets over either of them. And how much
time do you think I have left? You saw how I was.
I can't control it. I've had it as a man. I'm through.
Give me a break, Bea. Don't call the police. I love
you. I'm your friend. Though I'll let you in on a
secret. I'd still be your friend in jail. All I really
wanted was to see it. I *still* see it. I'm looking now.
No, I'll be honest: *staring.* I'm staring because I've
never seen anything like it, and I want to remember
it forever. Not that I'll ever forget. I *never* will.
Never."

I was weeping. Bea had started to dress.

"There are jokes," I said when I'd regained control, "about men on motorcycles disappearing inside
women, or getting lost. There's this one about a
rabbi married to a woman who's supposed to be
really fabulous. One day the cleaning lady comes
into the bedroom where the rabbi's wife is taking a
nap. She's lying on the bedspread, all naked except
where she's covered her genitals with the rabbi's
skull cap, and the maid says, 'Oh, my God, I knew
it would happen one day. The rabbi fell in.' I used
to laugh at stories like that, but I never will again.
You're *so* beautiful."

"I didn't scream," she said, "because it was my fate."

"What?"

"People find out about me. In high school, in gym, the girls would see me in the shower, and they'd tell their boyfriends. Then the boys would humiliate me. Worse things were done than what you've done. We had to leave town. In the new high school I got a note from the doctor so that I could be excused from gym, but they still found out. Maybe someone from my old town knew someone in the new town, maybe the doctor himself said something—I don't know. Boys would take me out and . . . want to see. When I graduated I moved away and started all over in a different state. There was a boy . . . I liked him. One day we made love—and *he* told. It was terrible. I can't even wear a bathing suit. You know? Then I came to Hartford. And you found out. I didn't scream because it was my fate. At least you say you love me—"

"Adore you," I said.

She said something I couldn't quite hear.

"What was that?"

"I said it's my burden. Only it carries me. It's as if I were always on horseback," she cried, and rushed toward me and embraced me, and I held her like that for an hour, and when I was ready we made love.

# The  Guest

On Sunday, Bertie walked into an apartment building in St. Louis, a city where, in the past, he had changed trains, waited for buses, or thought about Klaff, and where, more recently, truckers dropped him, or traveling salesmen stopped their Pontiacs downtown just long enough for him to reach into the back seat for his trumpet case and get out. In the hallway he stood before the brass mailboxed wall seeking the name of his friend, his friends' friend really, and his friends' friend's wife. The girl had danced with him at parties in the college town, and one night—he imagined he must have been particularly pathetic, engagingly pathetic—she had kissed him. The man, of course, patronized him, asked him questions that would have been more vicious had they been less naïve. He remembered he rather enjoyed making his long, patient answers. Condescension always brought the truth out of him. It was more appealing than indifference at least, and more necessary to him now. He supposed he didn't

(From *Criers and Kibitzers, Kibitzers and Criers,* 1966.)

care for either of them, but he couldn't go further. He had to rest or he would die.

He found the name on the mailbox—Mr. and Mrs. Richard Preminger—the girl's identity, as he might have guessed, swallowed up in the husband's. It was no way to treat women, he thought gallantly.

He started up the stairs. Turning the corner at the second landing, he saw a man moving cautiously downward, burdened by boxes and suitcases and loose bags. Only as they passed each other did Bertie, through a momentary clearing in the boxes, recognize Richard Preminger.

"Old man, old man," Bertie said.

"Just a minute," Preminger said, forcing a package aside with his chin. Bertie stood, half a staircase above him, leaning against the wall. He grinned in the shadows, conscious of his ridiculous fedora, his eye patch rakishly black against the soft whiteness of his face. Black-suited, tiny, white-fleshed, he posed above Preminger, dapper as a scholarly waiter in a restaurant. He waited until he was recognized.

"Bertie? Bertie? Let me get rid of this stuff. Give me a hand, will you?" Preminger said.

"Sure," Bertie said. "It's on my family crest. One hand washing the other. Here, wait a minute." He passed Preminger on the stairs and held the door for him. He followed him outside.

"Take the key from my pocket, Bertie, and open the trunk. It's the blue convertible."

Bertie put his hand in Preminger's pocket. "You've got nice thighs," he said. To irritate Preminger he pretended to try to force the house key into the trunk lock. Preminger stood impatiently behind him, balancing his heavy burdens. "I've been to Dallas, lived in a palace," Bertie said over his shoulder. "There's this

great Eskimo who blows down there. Would you believe he's cut the best side ever recorded of 'Mood
Indigo'?" Bertie shook the key ring as if it were a
castanet.

Preminger dumped his load on the hood of the car
and took the keys from Bertie. He opened the trunk
and started to throw things into it. "Going somewhere?" Bertie asked.

"Vacation," Preminger said.

"Oh," Bertie said.

Preminger looked toward the apartment house. "I've
got to go up for another suitcase, Bertie."

"Sure," Bertie said.

He went up the stairs behind Preminger. About
halfway up he stopped to catch his breath. Preminger
watched him curiously. He pounded his chest with his
tiny fist and grinned weakly. *"Mea culpa,"* he said.
"Mea booze, Mea sluts. Mea pot. Me-o-mea."

"Come on," Preminger said.

They went inside and Bertie heard a toilet flushing.
Through a hall, through an open door, he saw Norma,
Preminger's wife, staring absently into the bowl. "If
she moves them now you won't have to stop at God
knows what kind of place on the road," Bertie said
brightly.

Norma lifted a big suitcase easily in her big hands
and came into the living room. She stopped when she
saw Bertie. "Bertie! Richard, it's Bertie."

"We bumped into each other in the hall," Preminger
said.

Bertie watched the two of them look at each other.

"You sure picked a time to come visiting, Bertie,"
Preminger said.

"We're leaving on our vacation, Bertie," Norma
said.

"We're going up to New England for a couple of weeks," Preminger told him.

"We can chat for a little with Bertie, can't we, Richard, before we go?"

"Of course," Preminger said. He sat down and pulled the suitcase next to him.

"It's very lovely in New England." Bertie sat down and crossed his legs. "I don't get up there very regularly. Not my territory. I've found that when a man makes it in the Ivy League he tends to forget about old Bertie," he said sadly.

"What are you doing in St. Louis, Bertie?" Preminger's wife asked him.

"It's my Midwestern swing," Bertie said. "I've been down South on the southern sponge. Opened up a whole new territory." He heard himself cackle.

"Who did you see, Bertie?" Norma asked him.

"You wouldn't know her. A cousin of Klaff's."

"Were you living with her?" Preminger asked.

Bertie shook his finger at him. The Premingers stared glumly at each other. Richard rubbed the plastic suitcase handle. In a moment, Bertie thought, he would probably say, "Gosh, Bertie, you should have written. You should have let us know." He should have written! Did the Fuller Brush man write? Who would be home? Who *wouldn't* be on vacation? They were commandos, the Fuller Brush man and he. He was tired, sick. He couldn't move on today. Would they kill him because of their lousy vacation?

Meanwhile the Premingers weren't saying anything. They stared at each other openly, their large eyes in their large heads on their large necks largely. He thought he could wait them out. It was what he *should* do. It should have been the easiest thing in the world to wait out the Premingers, to stare them down. Who was he kidding? It wasn't his forte. He had no forte.

*That* was his forte. He could already hear himself begin to speak.

"Sure," he said. "I almost married that girl. Klaff's lady cousin. The first thing she ever said to me was, 'Bertie, they never build drugstores in the middle of the block. Always on corners.' It was the truth. Well, I thought, this was the woman for me. One time she came out of the ladies' john of a Greyhound bus station and she said, 'Bertie, have you ever noticed how public toilets smell like bubble gum?' That's what it was like all the time. She had these institutional insights. I was sure we could make it together. It didn't work out." He sighed.

Preminger stared at him, but Norma was beginning to soften. He wondered randomly what she would be like in bed. He looked coolly at her long legs, her wide shoulders. Like Klaff's cousin: institutional.

"Bertie, how are your eyes now?" she asked.

"Oh," he said, "still seeing double." He smiled. "Two for one. It's all right when there's something to look at. Other times I use the patch."

Norma seemed sad.

"I have fun with it," he said. "It doesn't make any difference which eye I cover. I'm ambidextrous." He pulled the black elastic band from his forehead. Instantly there were two large Richards, two large Normas. The Four Premingers like a troupe of Jewish acrobats. He felt surrounded. In the two living rooms his four hands fumbled with the two patches. He felt sick to his stomach. He closed one eye and hastily replaced the patch. "I shouldn't try that on an empty stomach," he said.

Preminger watched him narrowly. "Gee, Bertie," he said finally, "maybe we could drop you someplace."

It was out of the question. He couldn't get into a car

again. "Do you go through Minneapolis, Minnesota?"
he asked indifferently.

Preminger looked confused, and Bertie liked him for
a moment. "We were going to catch the Turnpike up
around Chicago, Bertie."

"Oh, Chicago," Bertie said. "I can't go back to
Chicago yet."

Preminger nodded.

"Don't you know anybody else in St. Louis?" Norma asked.

"Klaff used to live across the river, but he's gone,"
Bertie said.

"Look, Bertie . . ." Preminger said.

"I'm fagged," Bertie said helplessly, "locked out."

"Bertie," Preminger said, "do you need any money?
I could let you have twenty dollars."

Bertie put his hand out mechanically.

"This is stupid," Norma said suddenly. "Stay *here*."

"Oh, well—"

"No, I mean it. Stay *here*. We'll be gone for two
weeks. What difference does it make?"

Preminger looked at his wife for a moment and
shrugged. "Sure," he said, "there's no reason you
*couldn't* stay here. As a matter of fact you'd be doing
us a favor. I forgot to cancel the newspaper, the milk.
You'd keep the burglars off. They don't bother a place
if it looks lived in." He put twenty dollars on the coffee
table. "There might be something you need," he explained.

Bertie looked carefully at them both. They seemed
to mean it. Preminger and his wife grinned at him
steadily, relieved at how easily they had come off. He
enjoyed the idea himself. At last he had a real patron,
a real matron. "Okay," he said.

"Then it's settled," Preminger said, rising.

"It's all right?" Bertie said.

"Certainly it's all right," Preminger said. "What harm could you do?"

"I'm harmless," Bertie said.

Preminger picked up the suitcase and led his wife toward the door. "Have a good time," Bertie said, following them. "I'll watch things for you. Rrgghh! Rrrgghhhfff!"

Preminger waved back at him as he went down the stairs. "Hey," Bertie called, leaning over the banister, "did I tell you about that crazy Klaff? You know what nutty Klaff did out at U.C.L.A.? He became a second-story man." They were already outside.

Bertie pressed his back against the door and turned his head slowly across his left shoulder. He imagined himself photographed from underneath. "Odd man in," he said. He bounded into the center of the living room. I'll bet there's a lease, he thought. I'll bet there's a regular lease that goes with this place. He considered this respectfully, a little awed. He couldn't remember ever having been in a place where the tenants actually had to sign a lease. In the dining room he turned on the chandelier lights. "Sure there's a lease," Bertie said. He hugged himself. "How the fallen are mighty," he said.

In the living room he lay down on the couch without taking off his shoes. He sat up and pulled them off, but when he lay down again he was uneasy. He had gotten out of the habit, living the way he did, of sleeping without shoes. In his friends' leaseless basements the nights were cold and he wore them for warmth. He put the shoes on again, but found that he wasn't tired any-more. It was a fact that dependence gave him energy. He was never so alert as when people did him favors. It was having to be on your own that made you tired.

"Certainly," Bertie said to the committee, "it's

scientific. We've suspected it for years, but until our researchers divided up the town of Bloomington, Indiana, we had no proof. What our people found in that community was that the orphans and bastards were sleepy and run-down, while the housewives and people on relief were wide awake, alert, raring to go. We can't positively state the link yet, but we're fairly certain that it's something to do with dependency—in league perhaps with a particularly virulent form of gratitude. Ahem. Ahem."

As he lectured the committee he wandered around the apartment, touring from right to left. He crossed from the living room into the dining room and turned right into the kitchen and then right again into Preminger's small study. "Here's where all the magic happens," Bertie said, glancing at the contour chair near Preminger's desk. He went back into the kitchen. "Here's where all the magic happens," he said, looking at Norma's electric stove. He stepped into the dining room and continued on, passing Norma's paintings of picturesque side streets in Mexico, of picturesque side streets in Italy, of picturesque side streets in Puerto Rico, until he came to a door that led to the back sun parlor. He went through it and found himself in a room with an easel, with paints in sexy little tubes, with brushes, with palettes and turpentine and rags. "Here's where all the magic happens," Bertie said and walked around the room to another door. He opened it and was in the Premingers' master bedroom. He looked at the bed. "Here's where all the magic happens," he said. Through a door at the other end of the room was another small hall. On the right was the toilet. He went in and flushed it. It was one of those toilets with instantly renewable tanks. He flushed it again. And again. "The only kind to have," he said out of the side of his mouth, imagining a rental agent. "I mean, it's like this. Supposing the missus has diarrhea or something. You don't want to have to wait until the tank fills up. Or suppose you're sick. Or suppose you're giving a party and it's mixed company. Well, it's just corny to whistle to cover the noise, know what I mean? 'S jus' corny. On the other hand, you flush it once suppose you're not through, then what happens? There's the damn noise after the water goes down. What have you accomplished? This way"—he reached across and jiggled the little lever and then did it a second time, a third, a fourth—"you never have any embarrassing interim, what we in the trade call 'flush lag.' "

He found the guest bedroom and knew at once that he would never sleep in it, that he would sleep in the Premingers' big bed.

"Nice place you got here," he said when he had finished the tour.

"Dooing de woh eet ees all I tink of, what I fahting foe," the man from the Underground said. "Here ees eet fahrproof, air-condizione and safe from Nazis."

"Stay out of Volkswagens, kid," Bertie said.

He went back into the living room. He wanted music, but it was a cardinal principle with him never to blow alone. He would drink alone, take drugs alone, but somehow for him the depths of depravity were represented by having to play jazz alone. He had a vision of himself in a cheap hotel room sitting on the edge of an iron bedstead. Crumpled packages of cigarettes were scattered throughout the room. Bottles of gin were on top of the Gideon Bible, the Western Union blanks. His trumpet was in his lap. "Perfect," Bertie said. "Norma Preminger could paint it in a picture." He shuddered.

The phonograph was in the hall between the dining room and living room. It was a big thing, with the AM and the FM and the short wave and the place where you plugged in the color television when it was perfected. He found records in Preminger's little room and went through them rapidly. "Ahmad Jamahl, for Christ's sake." Bertie took the record out of its sleeve and broke it across his knee. He stood up slowly and kicked the fragments of the broken recording into a neat pile.

He turned around and scooped up as many of Preminger's recordings as he could carry and brought them to the machine. He piled them on indiscriminately and listened with visible, professional discomfort. He listened to *The New World Symphony,* to Beethoven's *Fifth,* to *My Fair Lady.* The more he listened the more he began to dislike the Premingers. When he could stand it no longer he tore the playing arm viciously away from the record and looked around him. He saw the Premingers' bookcase.

"I'll read," Bertie said.

He took down the Marquis de Sade and Henry Miller and Ronald Firbank and turned the pages desultorily. Nothing happened. He tried reading aloud in front of a mirror. He went back to the bookcase and looked for *The Egg and I* and *Please Don't Eat the Daisies.* The prose of a certain kind of bright housewife always made Bertie erotic. But the Premingers owned neither book. He browsed through Rachel Carson's *Silent Spring* with his fly unzipped, but he felt only a mild lasciviousness.

He went into their bedroom and opened the closet. He found a pair of Norma's shoes and put them on. Although he was no fetishist, he had often promised himself that if he ever had the opportunity he would see what it was like. He got into drag and walked around the apartment in Norma's high heels. All he experienced was a pain in his calves.

In the kitchen he looked into the refrigerator. There were some frozen mixed vegetables in the freezer compartment. "I'll *starve* first," Bertie said.

He found a Billie Holiday record and put it on the phonograph. He hoped that out in Los Angeles, Klaff was being beaten with rubber hoses by the police. He looked up at the kitchen clock. "Nine," he said. "Only seven in L.A. They probably don't start beating them up till later."

"Talk, Klaff," he snarled, "or we'll drag you into the Blood Room."

"Flake off, copper," Klaff said.

"That's enough of that, Klaff. Take that and that and that."

*"Bird lives!"* Bertie screamed suddenly, invoking the dead Charlie Parker. It was his code cry.

"Mama may have," Billie Holiday wailed, "Papa may have, but God bless the child who's got his own, who—oo—zz—"

"Who—oo—zz," Bertie wailed.

"Got his own," Billie said.

"I'll tell him when he comes in, William," Bertie said.

He waited respectfully until Billie was finished and then turned off the music.

He wondered why so many people felt that Norman Mailer was the greatest living American novelist.

He sat down on the Premingers' coffee table and marveled at his being alone in so big and well-furnished an apartment. The Premingers were probably the most substantial people he knew. Though plenty of the others wanted to, Bertie thought bitterly, Preminger was the only one from the old crowd who might make it. Of course he was Jewish, and that helped. Some Jews swung pretty good, but he always suspected that

in the end they would hold out on you. But then who
wouldn't, Bertie wondered. Kamikaze pilots, maybe.
Anyway, this was Bertie's special form of anti-Semi-
tism and he cherished it. Melvin Gimpel, for example,
his old roommate. Every time Melvin tried to kill
himself by sticking his head in the oven he left the
kitchen window open. One time he found Gimpel on
his knees with his head on the oven door, oddly like
the witch in Hansel and Gretel. Bertie closed the window and shook Gimpel awake.

"Mel," he yelled, slapping him. *"Mel."*

"Bertie, go way. Leave me alone, I want to kill
myself."

"Thank God," Bertie said. "Thank God I'm in time.
When I found that window closed I thought it was all
over."

"What, the window was *closed*? My God, was the
*window* closed?"

> "Melvin Gimpel is so simple
> Thinks his nipple is a pimple,"

Bertie recited.

He hugged his knees, and felt again a wave of the
nausea sickness he had experienced that morning. "It's
foreshadowing. One day as I am shoveling my walk I
will collapse and die."

When the nausea left him he thought again about
his situation. He had friends everywhere and made his
way from place to place like an old-time slave on the
Underground Railway. For all the pathos of the figure
he knew he deliberately cut, there were always people
to do him favors, give him money, beer, drugs, to
nurse him back to his normal state of semi-invalidism,
girls to kiss him in the comforting way he liked. This

was probably the first time he had been alone in
months. He felt like a dog whose master has gone
away for the weekend. Just then he heard some people
coming up the stairs and he growled experimentally.
He went down on his hands and knees and scampered
to the door, scratching it with his nails. "Rrrgghhf," he
barked. "Rrgghhfff!" He heard whoever it was fum-
bling to open a door on the floor below him. He
smiled. "Good dog," he said. "Good dog, goodog,
gudug, gudugguduggudug."

He whined. He missed his master. A tear formed in
the corner of his left eye. He crawled to a full-length
mirror in the bathroom. "Ahh," he said. "Ahh." Seeing the patch across his eye, he had an inspiration.
"Here, Patch," he called. "Come on, Patch." He
romped after his own voice.

He moved beside Norma Preminger's easel in the
sun parlor. He lowered his body carefully, pushing
himself slightly backward with his arms. He yawned.
He touched his chest to the wooden floor. He wagged
his tail and then let himself fall heavily on one side. He
pulled his legs up under him and fell asleep.

When Bertie awoke he was hungry. He fingered the
twenty dollars in his pocket that Preminger had given
him. He could order out. The light in the hall where
the phone and phone books were was not good, so he
tore "Restaurants" from the Yellow Pages and brought
the sheets with him into the living room. Only two
places delivered after one A.M. It was already one-
thirty. He dialed the number of a pizza place across
the city.

"Pal, bring over a big one, half shrimp, half mush-
room. And two six-packs." He gave the address. The
man explained that the truck had just gone out and

that he shouldn't expect delivery for at least another hour and a half.

"Put it in a cab," Bertie said. "While Bird lives Bertie spends."

He took out another dozen or so records and piled them on the machine. He sat down on the couch and drummed his trumpet case with his fingers. He opened the case and fit the mouthpiece to the body of the horn. He put the trumpet to his lips and experienced the unpleasant shock of cold metal he always felt. He still thought it strange that men could mouth metal this way, ludicrous that his professional attitude should be a kiss. He blew a few bars in accompaniment to the record and then put the trumpet back in the case. He felt in the side pockets of the trumpet case and took out two pairs of dirty underwear, some handkerchiefs and three pairs of socks. He unrolled one of the pairs of socks and saw with pleasure that the drug was still there. He took out the bottle of carbon tetrachloride. This was what he cleaned his instrument with, and it was what he would use to kill himself when he had finally made the decision.

He held the bottle to the light. "If nothing turns up," he said, "I'll drink this. And to hell with the kitchen window."

The cab driver brought the pizza and Bertie gave him the twenty dollars.

"I can't change that," the driver said.

"Did I ask you to change it?" Bertie said.

"That's twenty bucks there."

"Bird lives. Easy come, easy go go go," Bertie said.

The driver started to thank him.

"Go." He closed the door.

He spread Norma Preminger's largest tablecloth over the dining-room table and then, taking china and

silver from the big breakfront, laid several place settings. He found champagne glasses.

Unwrapping the pizza, he carefully plucked all the
mushrooms from it ("American mushrooms," he said.
"Very square. No visions.") and laid them in a neat
pile on the white linen. ("Many mushloom," he said.
"Mushloom crowd.") He poured some beer into a
champagne glass and rose slowly from his chair.

"Gentlemen," he said, "to the absent Klaff. May the
police in Los Angeles, California, beat his lousy ass
off." He drank off all the beer in one gulp and tossed
the glass behind him over his shoulder. He heard it
shatter and then a soft sizzling sound. Turning around,
he saw that he had hit one of Norma's paintings right
in a picturesque side street. Beer dripped ignobly down
a donkey's leg. "God damn," Bertie said appreciatively,
"*action* painting."

He ate perhaps a quarter of the pizza before rising
from the table, wiping the corner of his lips with a big
linen napkin. "Gentlemen," he said. "I propose that
the ladies retire to the bedroom while we men enjoy
our cigars and port and some good talk."

"*I* propose that we men retire to the bedroom and
enjoy the ladies," he said in Gimpel's voice.

"Here, here," he said in Klaff's voice. "Here, here.
Good talk. Good talk."

"If you will follow me, gentlemen," Bertie said in his
own voice. He began to walk around the apartment. "I
have often been asked the story of my life. These
requests usually follow a personal favor someone has
done me, a supper shared, a bed made available, a ride
in one of the several directions. Indeed, I have become
a sort of troubadour who does not sing so much as
whine for his supper. Most of you—"

"Whine is very good with supper," Gimpel said.

"Gimpel, my dear, why don't you run into the kitchen and play?" Bertie said coolly. "Many of you may know the humble beginnings, the sordid details, the dark Freudian patterns, and those of you who are my friends—"

Klaff belched.

"Those of you who are my *friends,* who do not run off to mix it up with the criminal element in the Far West, have often wondered what will ultimately happen to me, to 'Poor Bertie' as I am known in the trade."

He unbuttoned his shirt and let it fall to the floor. In his undershirt he looked defenseless, his skin pale as something seen in moonlight. "Why, you wonder, doesn't he do something about himself, pull himself up by his bootstraps? Why, for example, doesn't he get his eyes fixed? Well, I've tried."

He kicked off his shoes. "You have all admired my bushy mustache. Do you remember that time two years ago I dropped out of sight for four months? Well, let me tell you what happened that time."

He took off his black pants. "I had been staying with Royal Randle, the distinguished philologist and drunk. You will recall what Royal, Klaff, Myers, Gimpel and myself once were to each other. Regular Whiffenpoofs we were. Damned from here to eternity. Sure, sure." He sighed. "You remember Randle's promises: 'It won't make any difference, Bertie. It won't make any difference, Klaff. It won't make any difference, fellas.' He married the girl in the muu-muu."

He was naked now except for his socks. He shivered once and folded his arms across his chest. "Do you know why the girl in the muu-muu married Randle?" He paused dramatically. *"To get at me, that's why!"* The others she didn't care about. She knew even before I did what they were like. Even what *Klaff* was like. She knew they were corrupt, that they had it in

them to sell me out, to settle down—that all anyone
had to do was wave their deaths in front of them and
they'd come running, that reason and fucking money
and getting it steady would win again. But in me she
recognized the real enemy, the last of the go-to-hell-
god-damn-its. Maybe the first.

"They even took me with them on their honeymoon.
At the time I thought it was a triumph for dependency,
but it was just a trick, that's all. The minute they were
married, this girl in the muu-muu was after Randle to
do something about Bertie. And it wasn't 'Poor' Bertie
this time. It was she who got me the appointment with
the mayor. Do you know what His Honor said to me?
'Shave your mustache and I'll give you a job clerking
in one of my supermarkets.' Christ, friends, do you
know I *did* it? Well, I'm not made of stone. They had
taken me on their honeymoon, for God's sake."

He paused.

*"I worked in that supermarket for three hours.*
Clean-shaved. My mustache sacrificed as an earnest to
the mayor. Well, I'm telling you, you don't know what
square *is* till you've worked in a supermarket for three
hours. They pipe in Mantovani. Mantovani! I cleared
out for four months to raise my mustache again and to
forget. What you see now isn't the original, you understand. It's all second growth, and believe me it's not
the same."

He drew aside the shower curtain and stepped into
the tub. He paused with his hand on the tap. "But I
tell you this, friends. I would rather be a mustached
bum than a clean-shaved clerk. I'll work. Sure I will.
When they pay anarchists! When they subsidize the
hip! When they give grants to throw bombs! When
they shell out for gainsaying!"

Bertie pulled the curtain and turned on the faucet.
The rush of water was like applause.

After his shower Bertie went into the second bedroom and carefully removed the spread from the cot.
Then he punched the pillow and mussed the bed.
"Very clever," he said. "It wouldn't do to let them
think I never slept here." He had once realized with
sudden clarity that he would never, so long as he lived,
make a bed.

Then he went into the other bedroom and ripped the
spread from the big double bed. For some time, in fact
since he had first seen it, Bertie had been thinking
about this bed. It was the biggest bed he would ever
sleep in. He thought invariably in such terms. One
cigarette in a pack would suddenly become distinguished in his mind as the best, or the worst, he would
smoke that day. A homely act, such as tying his
shoelaces, if it had occurred with unusual ease, would
be remembered forever. This lent to his vision an
oblique sadness, conscious as he was that he was
forever encountering experiences which would never
come his way again.

He slipped his naked body between the sheets, but
no sooner had he made himself comfortable than he
became conscious of the phonograph, still playing in
the little hall. He couldn't hear it very well. He thought
about turning up the volume, but he had read somewhere about neighbors. Getting out of bed, he moved
the heavy machine through the living room, pushing it
with difficulty over the seamed, bare wooden floor,
trailing deep scratches. Remember not to walk barefoot there, he thought. At one point one of the legs
caught in a loop of the Premingers' shag rug and Bertie
strained to free it, finally breaking the thick thread and
producing an interesting pucker along one end of the
rug, not unlike the pucker in raised theatrical curtains.
At last he had maneuvered the machine into the hall
just outside the bedroom and plugged it in. He went

back for the Billie Holiday recording he had heard earlier and put it on the phonograph. By fiddling with the machine, he fixed it so that the record would play all night.

Bertie got back into the bed. "Ah," he said, "the *sanctum sanctorum*." He rolled over and over from one side of the bed to the other. He tucked his knees into his chest and went under the covers. "It makes you feel kind of small and insignificant," he said.

"Ladies and gentlemen, this is Graham Macnamee speaking to you from the Cave of the Winds. I have made my way into the heart of this darkness to find my friend, Poor Bertie, who, as you know, entered the bed eight weeks ago. Bertie is with me now, and while there isn't enough light for me to be able to see his condition, his voice may tell us something about his physical state. Bertie, just what *is* the official record?"

"Well, Graham, some couples have been known to stick it out for seventy-five years. Of course, your average is much less than that, but still—"

"Seventy-five years?"

"Seventy-five, yes sir. It's amazing, isn't it, Graham, when you come to think? All that time in one bed."

"It certainly is," Graham Macnamee said. "Do you think you'll be able to go the distance, Bert?"

"Who, me? No, no. A lot of folks have misunderstood my purpose in coming here. I'm rather glad you've given me the opportunity to clear that one up. Actually my work here is scientific. This isn't a stunt or anything like that. I'm here to learn."

"Can you tell us about it, Bert?"

"Graham, it's been a *fascinating* experience, if you know what I mean, but frankly there are many things we still don't understand. *I* don't know why they do it. All that licit love, that regularity. Take the case of Richard and Norma, for example—and incidentally,

you don't want to overlook the significance of that
name 'Norma.' Norma/Normal, you see?"

"Say, I never thought of that."

"Well, I'm trained to think like that, Graham. In my
work you have to."

"Say," Graham Macnamee said.

"Sure. Well, the thing is this, buddy, when I first
came into this bed I felt the aura, know what I mean,
the *power*. I think it's built into the mattress or something."

"Say."

"Shut your face, Graham, and let me speak, will you
please? Well, anyway, you feel surrounded. Respectable. Love is made here, of course, but it's not love as
we know it. There are things that must remain mysteries until we have more facts. I mean, Graham, checks
could be cashed in this bed, for Christ's sake, credit
cards honored. It's ideal for family reunions, high teas.
Graham, it's the kind of place you wouldn't be
ashamed to take your mother."

"Go to sleep, Bert," Graham Macnamee said.

"Say," Bertie said.


Between the third and fourth day of his stay in the
Premingers' apartment Bertie became restless. He had
not been outside the house since the Sunday he arrived, even to bring in the papers Preminger had told
him about. (Indeed, it was by counting the papers that
he knew how long he had been there, though he
couldn't be sure, since he didn't know whether the
Premingers had taken the Sunday paper along with
them.) He could see them on the back porch through
the window of Norma's sun parlor. With the bottles of
milk they made a strange little pile. After all, he was
not a caretaker; he was a guest. Preminger could bring
in his own papers, drink his own damn milk. For the

same reasons he had determined not even to answer the phone when it rang.

One evening he tried to call Klaff at the Los Angeles County Jail, but the desk sergeant wouldn't get him. He wouldn't even take a message.

Although he had not been outside since Sunday, Bertie had only a vague desire to leave the apartment. He weighed this against his real need to rest and his genuine pleasure in being alone in so big a place. Like the man in the joke who does not leave his Miami hotel room because it is costing him so much money, Bertie decided he had better remain inside.

With no money left he was reduced to eating the dry, cold remainder of the pizza, dividing it mathematically into a week's provisions, like someone on a raft. (He actually fancied himself, not on a raft perhaps, but set alone and adrift on, say, the *Queen Mary*.) To supplement the pizza he opened some cans of soup he found in the pantry and drank the contents straight, without heating it or even adding water. Steadily he drank away at the Premingers' modest stock of liquor. The twelve cans of beer had been devoured by the second morning, of course.

After the second full day in the apartment his voices began to desert him. It was only with difficulty that he could manage his imitations, and only for short lengths of time. The glorious discussions that had gone on long into the night were now out of the question. He found he could not do Gimpel's voice anymore, and even Klaff's was increasingly difficult and largely confined to his low, caressing obscenities. Mostly he talked with himself, although it was a real strain to keep up his end of the conversation, and it always made him cry when he said how pathetic he was and asked himself where do you go from here. Oh, to be like Bird, he thought. Not to have to be a bum. To ask, as it were, no quarter.

At various times during the day he would call out "Bird lives" in seeming stunning triumph. But he didn't believe it.

He watched a lot of television. "I'm getting ammunition," he said. "It's scientific."

Twice a day he masturbated in the Premingers' bed.

He settled gradually, then, into restlessness. He knew, of course, that he had it always in his power to bring himself back up to the heights he had known in those wonderful first two days. He was satisfied, however, not to use this power, and thought of himself as a kind of soldier, alone in a foxhole, in enemy territory, at night, at a bad time in the war, with one bullet in his rifle. Oddly, he derived more pride—and comfort, and a queer security—from this single bullet than others might from whole cases of ammunition. It was his *strategic* bullet, the one he would use to get the big one, turn the tide, make the difference. The Premingers would be away two weeks. He would not waste his ammunition. Just as he divided the stale pizza, cherishing each piece as much for the satisfaction he took from possessing it during a time of emergency as for any sustenance it offered, so he enjoyed his knowledge that at any time he could recoup his vanishing spirits. He shared with the squares ("Use their own weapons to beat them, Bertie") a special pride in adversity, in having to do without, in having to expose whatever was left of his character to the narrower straits. It was strange, he thought seriously, it was the paradox of the world and an institutional insight that might have come right out of the mouth of that slut in Dallas, but the most peculiar aspect of the

squares wasn't their lack of imagination or their bland
bad taste, but their ability, like the wildest fanatics,
like the furthest out of the furthest out, to cling to the
illogical, finally untenable notion that they must have
and have in order to live, at the same time that they
realized that it was better not to have. What seemed so
grand to Bertie, who admired all impossible positions,
was that they believed both things with equal intensity,
never suspecting for a moment any inconsistency. And
here was Bertie, Bertie thought, here was Bertie inside
their capitol, on the slopes of their mountains, on their
smooth shores, who believed neither of these proposi-
tions, who believed in not having and in not suffering
too, who yet realized the very same pleasure that they
would in having and not using. It was the strangest
thing that would ever happen to him, he thought.

"Are you listening, Klaff, you second-story fink?"
Bertie yelled. "Do you see how your old pal is developing what is called character?"

And so, master of himself for once, he resolved—
feeling what someone taking a vow feels—not to use
the last of his drugs until the strategic moment of
strategic truth.

That was Wednesday evening. By Thursday morning
he had decided to break his resolution. He had not
yielded to temptation, had not lain fitfully awake
all night—indeed, his resolution had given him the serenity to sleep well—in the sweaty throes of withdrawal. There had been no argument or rationalization, nor
had he decided that he had reached his limit or that
this was the strategic moment he had been waiting for.
He yielded as he always yielded: spontaneously, suddenly, unexpectedly, as the result neither of whim nor
calculation. His important decisions were almost
always reached without his knowledge, and he was
often as surprised as the next one to see what he was

going to do—to see, indeed, that he was already doing it. (Once someone had asked him whether he believed in Free Will, and after considering this for a moment as it applied to himself, Bertie had answered "Free? Hell, it's positively *loose*.")

Having discovered his new intention, he was eager to realize it. As often as he had taken drugs (he never called it anything but drugs, never used the cute or obscene names, never even said "dope"; to him it was always "drugs," medicine for his spirit), they were still a major treat for him. "It's a rich man's game," he had once told Klaff, and then he had leaned back philosophically. "You know, Klaff, it's a good thing I'm poor. When I think of the snobbish ennui of your wealthy junkies, I realize that they don't know how to appreciate their blessings. God keep me humble, Klaff. Abstinence makes the heart grow fonder, a truer word was never spoken."

Nor did a drug ever lose its potency for him. If he graduated from one to another, it was not in order to recover some fading jolt, but to experience a new and different one. He held in contempt all those who professed disenchantment with the drugs they had been raised on, and frequently went back to rediscover the old pleasures of marijuana, as a sentimental father might chew some of his boy's bubble gum. "Loyalty, Gimpel," he exclaimed, "loyalty, do you know what *that* is?"

Bertie would and did try anything, though currently his favorite was mescaline for the visions it induced. Despite what he considered his eclectic tastes in these matters, there were one or two things he would not do, however. He never introduced any drug by hypodermic needle. This he found disgusting and, frankly, painful. He often said he could stand anything but pain and was very proud of his clear, unpunctured skin. "Not a mark on me," he would say, waving his arms like a professional boxer. The other thing he would not do was take his drugs in the presence of other users, for he found the company of addicts offensive. However, he was not above what he called "seductions." A seduction for him was to find some girl and talk her into letting her share his drugs with him. Usually it ended in their lying naked in bed together, both of them serene, absent of all desire and what Bertie called "unclean thoughts."

"You know," he would say to the girl beside him, "I think that if all the world's leaders would take drugs and lie down on the bed naked like this without any unclean thoughts, the cause of world peace would be helped immeasurably. What do you think?"

"I think so too," she would say.

Once he knew he was going to take the drug, Bertie made his preparations. He went first to his trumpet case and took out the last small packet of powder. He opened it carefully, first closing all the windows so that no sudden draft could blow any of it away. This had once happened to a friend of his, and Bertie had never forgotten the warning.

"I am not one on whom a lesson is lost," Bertie said.

"You're okay, Bertie," a Voice said. "Go save France."

He placed the packet on the Premingers' coffee table and carefully spread the paper, exactly like the paper wrapper around a stick of chewing gum, looking almost lustfully at the soft, flat layer of ground white powder. He held out his hand to see how steady it was, and although he was not really shaky he did not trust himself to lift the paper from the table. He brought a water tumbler from the kitchen and gently placed it upside down on top of the powder. He was not yet ready to take it. Bertie was a man who postponed his pleasures as long as he possibly could; he let candy dissolve in his mouth and played with the threads on his tangerine before eating the fruit. It was a weakness in his character perhaps, but he laid it lovingly at the feet of his poverty.

He decided to wait until sundown to take the drug, reasoning that when it wore off, it would be early next morning and he would be ready for bed. Sleep was one of his pleasures too, and he approved of regularity in small things, taking a real pride in being able to keep hours. To pass the time until sundown he looked for something to do. First he found some tools and busied himself by taking Norma's steam iron apart. There was still time left after that, so he took a canvas and painted a picture. Because he did not know how to draw he simply covered the canvas first with one color and then with another, applying layer after layer of the paint thickly. Each block of color he made somewhat smaller than the last, so that the finished painting portrayed successive jagged margins of color. He stepped back and considered his work seriously.

"Well, it has texture, Bertie," Hans Hoffman said.

"Bertie," the Voice said suddenly, "I don't like to interrupt when you're working, but it's sundown."

"So it is," he said, looking up.

He went back into the living room and removed the tumbler. Taking up the paper in his fingers and creasing it as if he were a cowboy rolling a cigarette, Bertie tilted his head far back and inhaled the powder deeply. This part was always uncomfortable for him. "Ooo," he said, "the bubbles." He stuffed the last few grains up his nose with his fingers. "Waste not, want not," he said.

He sat down to wait. After half an hour in which nothing happened, Bertie became uneasy. "It's been cut," he said. "Sure, depend upon friends to do you favors." He was referring to the fact that the mescaline had been a going-away present from friends in Oklahoma City. He decided to give it fifteen more minutes. "Nothing," he said at last, disappointed. "Nothing."

The powder, as it always did, left his throat scratchy, and there was a bitter taste in his mouth. His soft palate prickled. He seized the water tumbler from the coffee table and walked angrily into the kitchen. He ran the cold water, then gargled and spit in the sink. In a few minutes the bitter taste and the prickly sensation subsided and he felt about as he had before he took the drug. He was conscious, however, of a peculiar smell, unpleasant, unfamiliar, nothing like the odor of rotting flowers he associated with the use of drugs. He opened a window and leaned out, breathing the fresh air. But as soon as he came away from the window, the odor was again overpowering. He went to see if he could smell it in the other rooms. When he had made his tour he realized that the stench *must* be coming from the kitchen. Holding his breath, he came back to see if he could locate its source. The kitchen was almost as Norma had left it. He had done no cooking, and although there were some empty soup and beer cans in the sink he knew *they* couldn't be causing the odor. He shrugged. Then he noticed the partially closed door to Preminger's study.

"Of course," Bertie said. "Whatever it is must be in there." He pushed the door open. In the middle of the floor were two blackish mounds that looked like dark sawdust. Bertie stepped back in surprise.

"Camel shit," he said. "My God, how did *that* get in here?" He went closer to investigate. "That's what it is, all right." He had never seen it before but a friend had, and had described it to him. This stuff fitted the description perfectly. He considered what to do.

"I can't leave it there," he said. He found a dustpan and a broom, and propping the pan against the leg of Preminger's chair, began to sweep the stuff up. He was surprised at how remarkably gummy it seemed. When he finished he washed the spot on the floor with a foaming detergent and stepped gingerly to the back door. He lifted the lid of the garbage can and shoved the broom and the contents of the dustpan and the dustpan itself into the can. Then he went to the bathroom and washed his hands.

In the living room he saw the Chinaman. "Jesus," Bertie said breathlessly.

The Chinaman lowered his eyes in a shy, almost demure smile. He said nothing, but motioned Bertie to sit in the chair across from him. Bertie, too frightened to disobey, sat down.

He waited for the Chinaman to tell him what he wanted. After an hour (he heard the chime clock strike nine times and then ten times), when the Chinaman still had not said anything, he began to feel a little calmer. Maybe he was just tired, Bertie thought, and came in to rest. He realized that perhaps he and the Chinaman had more in common than had at first appeared. He looked at the fellow in this new light and saw that he had been foolish to fear him. The Chinaman was small, smaller even than Bertie In fact, he was only two feet tall. Perhaps what made him seem larger was the fact that he was wrapped in wide, voluminous white silk robes. Bertic stared at the robes, fascinated by the delicate filigree trim up and down their length. To see this closer he stood up and walked tentatively toward the Chinaman.

The Chinaman gazed steadily to the front, and Bertie, seeing no threat, continued toward him. He leaned down over the Chinaman, and gently grasping the delicate lacework between his forefinger and his

thumb, drew it toward his eye. "May I?" Bertie asked.
"I know a good deal about this sort of thing."

The Chinaman lowered his eyes.

Bertie examined the weird symbols and designs, and
although he did not understand them, recognized at
once their cabalistic origin.

"Magnificent," Bertie said at last. "My God, the
man hours that must have gone into this. *The sheer
craftsmanship!* That's really a terrific robe you've got
there. Who's your tailor? "

The Chinaman lowered his eyes still further.

Bertie sat down in his chair again. He heard the
clock strike eleven and he smiled at the Chinaman. He
was trying to be sympathetic, patient. He knew the
fellow had his reasons for coming and that in due time
they would be revealed, but he couldn't help being a
little annoyed. First the failure of the drug and then the
camel shit on the floor and now this. However, he
remained very polite.

There was nothing else to do, so he concentrated on
the Chinaman's face.

Then a strange thing happened.

He became aware, as he scrutinized the face, of
some things he hadn't noticed before. First he realized
that it was the oldest face he had ever seen. He knew
that this face was old enough to have looked on Bud-
dha's. It was only *faintly* yellow, really, and he understood with a sweeping insight that originally it must
have been white, as it still largely was, a striking, flat
white, naked as a sheet, bright as teeth, that its yellowness was an intrusion, the intruding yellowness of fantastic age, of pages in ancient books. As soon as he
perceived this he understood the origin and mystery of
the races. All men had at first been white; their different tints were only the shades of their different wis-

doms. Of course, he thought. Of course. It's beautiful. Beautiful!

The second thing Bertie noticed was that the face seemed extraordinarily wise. The longer he stared at it the wiser it seemed. Clearly this was the wisest Chinaman, and thus the wisest man, in the history of the world. Now he was impatient for the Chinaman to speak, to tell him his secrets, but he also understood that so long as he was impatient the Chinaman would *not* speak, that he must become serene, as serene as the Chinaman himself, or else the Chinaman would go away. As this occurred to him the Chinaman smiled and Bertie knew he had been right. He was aware that if he just sat there, deliberately trying to become serene, nothing would happen. He decided that the best way to become serene was to ignore the Chinaman, to go on about his business as if the Chinaman weren't even there.

He stood up. "Am I getting warm?" Bertie asked.

The Chinaman lowered his eyes and smiled.

"Well, then," Bertie said, rubbing his hands, "let's see."

He went into the kitchen to see if there was anything he could do there to make him serene.

He washed out the empty cans of soup.

He strolled into the bedroom and made the bed. This took him an hour. He heard the clock strike twelve and then one.

He took a record off the machine, and starting from the center hole and working to the outer edge, counted all the ridges. This took him fourteen seconds.

He found a suitcase in one of the closets and packed all of Norma's underwear into it.

He got a pail of water and some soap and washed all the walls in the small bedroom.

It was in the dining room, however, that he finally achieved serenity. He studied Norma's pictures of side streets throughout the world and with sudden insight understood what was wrong with them. He took some tubes of white paint and with a brush worked over the figures, painting back into the flesh all their original whiteness. He made the Mexicans white, the Negroes white, feeling as he worked an immense satisfaction, the satisfaction not of the creator, nor even of the reformer, but of the restorer.

Swelling with serenity, Bertie went back into the living room and sat down in his chair. For the first time the Chinaman met his gaze directly, and Bertie realized that something important was going to happen.

Slowly, very slowly, the Chinaman began to open his mouth. Bertie watched the slow parting of the Chinaman's thin lips, the gleaming teeth, white and bright as fence pickets. Gradually the rest of the room darkened and the thinly padded chair on which Bertie sat grew incredibly soft. He knew that they had been transported somehow, that they were now in a sort of theater. The Chinaman was seated on a kind of raised platform. Meanwhile the mouth continued to open, slowly as an ancient drawbridge. Tiny as the Chinaman was, the mouth seemed enormous. Bertie gazed into it, seeing nothing. At last, deep back in the mouth, he saw a brief flashing, as of a small crystal on a dark rock suddenly illuminated by the sun. In a moment he saw it again, brighter now, longer sustained. Soon it was so bright that he had to force himself to look at it. Then the mouth went black. Before he could protest, the brightness was overwhelming again and he saw a cascade of what seemed like diamonds tumble out of the Chinaman's mouth. It was the Chinaman's tongue.

Twisting, turning over and over like magicians' silks

pulled endlessly from a tube, the tongue continued to pour from the Chinaman's mouth. Bertie saw that it had the same whiteness as the rest of his face, and that it was studded with bright, beautiful jewels. On the tongue, long now as an unfurled scroll, were thick black Chinese characters. It was the secret of life, of the world, of the universe. Bertie could barely read for the tears of gratitude in his eyes. Desperately he wiped the tears away with his fists. He looked back at the tongue and stared at the strange words, realizing that he could not read Chinese. He was sobbing helplessly now because he knew there was not much time. The presence of the Chinaman gave him courage and strength and he *forced* himself to read the Chinese. As he concentrated it became easier, the characters some- how re-forming, translating themselves into a sort of decipherable Chinesey script, like the words "Chop Suey" on the neon sign outside a Chinese restaurant. He was breathless from his effort and the stunning glory of what was being revealed to him. Frequently he had to pause, punctuating his experience with queer little squeals. "Oh," he said. "Oh. Oh."

Then it was over.

He was exhausted, but his knowledge glowed in him like fire. "So *that's* it" was all he could say. "So *that's* it. So *that's* it."

Bertie saw that he was no longer in the theater. The Chinaman was gone and Bertie was back in the Prem- ingers' living room. He struggled for control of himself. He knew it was urgent that he tell someone what had happened to him. Desperately he pulled open his trum- pet case. Inside he had pasted sheets with the names, addresses and phone numbers of all his friends.

"Damn Klaff," he said angrily. "Damn Second-Story Klaff in his lousy jail."

He spotted Gimpel's name and the phone number of

his boardinghouse in Cincinnati. Tearing the sheet from where it was pasted inside the lid, he rushed to the phone and placed the call. "Life and death," he screamed at Gimpel's bewildered landlady. "Life and death."

When Gimpel came to the phone Bertie began to tell him, coherently, but with obvious excitement, all that had happened. Gimpel was as excited as himself.

"Then the Chinaman opened his mouth and this tongue with writing on it came out."

"Yeah?" Gimpel said. "Yeah? Yeah?"

"Only it was in Chinese," Bertie shouted.

"Chinese," Gimpel said.

"But I could read it, Gimpel! *I could read it!*"

"I didn't know you could read Chinese," Gimpel said.

"It was the meaning of life."

"Yeah?" Gimpel said. "Yeah? What'd it say? What'd it say?"

"What?" Bertie said.

"What'd it say? What'd the Chink's tongue say was the meaning of life?"

"I forget," Bertie said and hung up.

He slept until two the next afternoon, and when he awoke he felt as if he had been beaten up. His tongue was something that did not quite fit in his mouth, and throughout his body he experienced a looseness of the bones, as though his skeleton were a mobile put together by an amateur. He groaned dispiritedly, his eyes still closed. He knew he had to get up out of the bed and take a shower and shave and dress, that only by making extravagant demands on it would his body give him any service at all. "You *will* make the Death March," he warned it ruthlessly.

He opened his eyes and what he saw disgusted him
and turned his stomach. His eye patch had come off
during the night and now there were two of everything.
He saw one eye patch on one pillow and another eye
patch on another pillow. Hastily he grabbed for it, but
he had chosen the wrong pillow. He reached for the
other eye patch and the other pillow, but somehow he
had put out one of his illusory hands. It did not occur
to him to shut one eye. At last, by covering all visible
space, real or illusory, with all visible fingers, real or
illusory—like one dragging a river—he recovered the
patch and pulled it quickly over one of his heads.

He stood stunned in his hot shower, and then
shaved, cutting his neck badly. He dressed.

"Whan 'e iz through his toilette, *Monsieur* will see
how much better 'e feel," his valet said. He doubted it
and didn't answer.

In the dining room he tried not to look at Norma's
paintings, but could not help noticing that overnight
many of her sunny side streets had become partial
snow scenes. He had done that, he remembered,
though he could not now recall exactly why. It seemed
to have something to do with a great anthropological
the last of the pizza, gagging on it briefly.

Considering the anguish of his body, it suddenly
occurred to him that perhaps he was hooked. Momentarily this appealed to his sense of the dramatic, but
then he realized that it would be a terrible thing to
have happen to him. He could not afford to be hooked,
for he knew with a sense of calm sadness that his
character could no more sustain the responsibility of a
steady drug habit than it could sustain the responsibility of any other kind of pattern.

"Oh, what a miserable bastard I am," Bertie said.

In near-panic he considered leaving the Premingers'

apartment immediately, but he knew that he was in no condition to travel. "You wouldn't make it to the corner," he said.

He felt massively sorry for himself. The more he considered it the more certain it appeared that he was hooked. It was terrible. Where would he get the money to buy the drugs? What would they do to his already depleted physical resources? "Oh, what a miserable bastard I am," he said again.

To steady himself he took a bottle of Scotch from the shelf in the pantry. Bertie did not like hard liquor. Though he drank a lot, it was beer he drank, or, when he could get them, the sweeter cordials. Scotch and bourbon had always seemed vaguely square to him. But he had already finished the few liqueurs that Preminger had, and now nothing was left but Scotch. He poured himself an enormous drink.

Sipping it calmed him—though his body still ached—and he considered what to do. If he *was* hooked, the first thing was to tell his friends. Telling his friends his latest failure was something Bertie regarded as a sort of responsibility. Thus his rare letters to them usually brought Bertie's intimates—he laughed at the word—nothing but bad news. He would write that a mistress had given him up, and, with his talent for mimicry, would set down her last long disappointed speech to him, in which she exposed in angry, honest language the hollowness of his character, his infinite weakness as a man, his vileness. When briefly he had turned to homosexuality to provide himself with funds, the first thing he did was write his friends about it. Or he wrote of being fired from bands when it was discovered how bad a trumpeter he really was. He spared neither himself nor his friends in his passionate self-denunciations.

Almost automatically, then, he went into Preminger's study and began to write all the people he could think of. As he wrote he pulled heavily at the whiskey remaining in the bottle. At first the letters were long, detailed accounts of symptoms and failures and dashed hopes, but as evening came on and he grew inarticulate he realized that it was more important—and, indeed, added to the pathos of his situation—for him just to get the facts to them.

"Dear Klaff," he wrote at last, "I am hooked. I am at the bottom, Klaff. I don't know what to do." Or "Dear Randle, I'm hooked. Tell your wife. I honestly don't know where to turn." And "Dear Myers, how are your wife and kids? Poor Bertie is hooked. He is thinking of suicide."

He had known for a long time that one day he would have to kill himself. It would happen, and even in the way he had imagined. One day he would simply drink the bottle of carbon tetrachloride. But previously he had been in no hurry. Now it seemed like something he might have to do before he had meant to, and what he resented most was the idea of having to change his plans.

He imagined what people would say.

"I let him down, Klaff," Randle said.

"Everybody let him down," Klaff said.

"Everybody let him down," Bertie said. "Everybody let him down."

Weeping, he took a last drink from Preminger's bottle, stumbled into the living room and passed out on the couch.

That night Bertie was awakened by a flashlight shining in his eyes. He threw one arm across his face defensively and struggled to sit up. So clumsy were his efforts that whoever was holding the flashlight started to laugh.

"Stop that," Bertie said indignantly, and thought, I have never been so indignant in the face of danger.

"You said they were out of town," a voice said. The voice did not come from behind the flashlight, and Bertie wondered how many there might be.

"Jesus, I thought so. Nobody's answered the phone for days. I never seen a guy so plastered. He stinks."

"Kill him," the first voice said.

Bertie stopped struggling to get up.

"Kill him," the voice repeated.

"What is this?" Bertie said thickly. "What is this?"

"Come on, he's so drunk he's harmless," the second voice said.

"Kill him," the first voice said again.

"You kill him," the second voice said.

The first voice giggled.

They were playing with him, Bertie knew. Nobody who did not know him could want him dead.

"Turn on the lights," Bertie said.

"Screw that," the second voice said. "You just sit here in the dark, sonny, and you won't get hurt."

"We're wasting time," the first voice said.

A beam from a second flashlight suddenly intersected the beam from the first.

"Say," Bertie said nervously, "it looks like the opening of a supermarket."

Bertie could hear them working in the dark, moving boxes, pulling drawers.

"Are you folks Negroes?" Bertie called. No one answered him. "I mean I dig Negroes, man—*men*. Miles. Jay Jay. Bird lives." He heard a closet door open.

"You *are* robbing the place, right? I mean you're actually *stealing,* aren't you? This isn't just a social call. Maybe you know my friend Klaff."

●

The men came back into the living room. From the sound of his footsteps Bertie knew one of them was carrying something heavy.

"I've got the TV," the first voice said.

"There are some valuable paintings in the dining room," Bertie said.

"Go see," the first voice said.

One of Norma's pictures suddenly popped out of the darkness as the man's light shone on it.

"Crap," the second voice said.

"You cats can't be all bad," Bertie said.

"Any furs?" It was a third voice, and it startled Bertie. Someone flashed a light in Bertie's face. "Hey, you," the voice repeated, "does your wife have any furs?"

"Wait a minute," Bertie said as though it were a fine point they must be made to understand, "you've got it wrong. This isn't *my* place. I'm just taking care of it while my friends are gone." The man laughed.

Now all three flashlights were playing over the apartment. Bertie hoped a beam might illuminate one of the intruders, but this never happened. Then he realized that he didn't want it to happen, that he was safe as long as he didn't recognize any of them. Suddenly a light caught one of the men behind the ear. "Watch that light. Watch that light," Bertie called out involuntarily.

"I found a trumpet," the second voice said.

"Hey, that's mine," Bertie said angrily. Without thinking, he got up and grabbed for the trumpet. In the dark he was able to get his fingers around one of the valves, but the man snatched it away from him easily. Another man pushed him back down on the couch.

"Could you leave the carbon tetrachloride?" Bertie asked miserably.

In another ten minutes they were ready to go. "Shouldn't we do something about the clown?" the third voice said.

"Nah," the second voice said.

They went out the front door.

Bertie sat in the darkness. "I'm drunk," he said after a while. "I'm hooked and drunk. It never happened. It's still the visions. The apartment is a vision. The darkness is. Everything."

In a few minutes he got up and wearily turned on the lights. Magicians, he thought, seeing even in a first glance all that they had taken. Lamps were gone, curtains. He walked through the apartment. The TV was gone. Suits were missing from the closets. Preminger's typewriter was gone, the champagne glasses, the silver. His trumpet was gone.

Bertie wept. He thought of phoning the police, but then wondered what he could tell them. The thieves had been in the apartment for twenty minutes and he hadn't even gotten a look at their faces.

Then he shuddered, realizing the danger he had been in. "Crooks," he said. "Killers." But even as he said it he knew it was an exaggeration. He had never been in any danger. He had the fool's ancient protection, his old immunity against consequence.

He wondered what he could say to the Premingers. They would be furious. Then, as he thought about it, he realized that this too was an exaggeration. They would not be furious. Like the thieves they would make allowances for him, as people always made allowances for him. They would forgive him; possibly they would even try to give him something toward the loss of his trumpet.

Bertie began to grow angry. They had no right to patronize him like that. If he was a clown it was because he had chosen to be. It was a way of life. Why couldn't they respect it? He should have been hit over the head like other men. How dare they forgive him? For a moment it was impossible for him to distinguish between the thieves and the Premingers.

Then he had his idea. As soon as he thought of it he knew it would work. He looked around the apartment to see what he could take. There was some costume jewelry the thieves had thrown on the bed. He scooped it up and stuffed it in his pockets. He looked at the apartment one more time and then got the hell out of there. "Bird lives," he sang to himself as he raced down the stairs. "He lives and lives."

It was wonderful. How they would marvel! He couldn't get away with it. Even the Far West wasn't far enough. How they hounded you if you took something from them! He would be back, no question, and they would send him to jail, but first there would be the confrontation, maybe even in the apartment itself: Bertie in handcuffs, and the Premingers staring at him, not understanding and angry at last, and something in their eyes like fear.

# The  Transient

Everybody dies. Everybody. But no one really believes it. They read the papers. They see the newsreels. They drive past the graveyards on the outskirts of town. Do you think that makes any difference? It does not! No one believes in death. Except me. Boswell. *I* believe in it. Listen, John Burgoyne was born in 1722 and died in 1792. The dates of Louis XVI were 1754 to 1793. (Do you suppose that Louis knew of Burgoyne's death? Do you suppose he said, "Ah, he's gone now, the old campaigner"? Do you suppose he suspected he'd be dead in a year himself?) More. Spenser: 1552(?)–1599. Caesar: 102 (or 100) to 44 B.C. Do you notice how as one goes back the birthdays become less certain while the year of death is always absolute, fixed? Do you think that's an accident? It's because death is realer than life. I saw a sign on U.S. 41 in Kentucky. It said REMEMBER YOU MUST DIE. I remember. But I never needed the sign. I had my own father. My father was a healthy man. Content. Vigor-

(From *Boswell,* 1964.)

166

ous. Powerful. Well. But when he died, he died of everything. The cancer. The blindness. The swollen heart. The failed markets. But even that, the death of one's father in a hospital room, the kiss goodbye inside the oxygen tent, isn't enough for some people. Even if they stretch a point and come to believe in the death of others, they refuse to believe in their own.

I remember reading in the newspaper an interview with the murderer, Braddock, when I was a kid. Braddock, waiting in the death house, told the reporter, "When they pull that switch they'll be pulling it on the whole world. Nobody will outlive me. The warden. The other cons. You. Nobody. Everybody dies when I die." He could believe in a fantastic short circuit that would end the world but not in his own lonely mortality. Do you suppose only a murderer thinks that way? Go on, when they pulled that switch Braddock knew for the first time what it was like to *be* a murderer. He murdered everybody. And don't you think he didn't close his eyes two seconds before he had to, just to make sure? Even my father, my own father, when I kneeled beside his bed in that white, white stinking room, looked at me and there was blood in his eyes. Why he's angry, I thought. He's mad at me.

I'm different. I remember I must die. It explains everything.

Once I wrestled. I was an athlete. (But I am no sportsman. Scores bore me.) To ward off death I built my body. A fortress, I hid in it. I laid low.

The locker room was my hometown, the gymnasium my university. There I moved for years with steamy abandon inside my glazy body, warm under the taped wrist, the hygienically bandaged knee joint, my muscles smoothly piling and meshing like tumblers in a lock. I was interested in a cautious, planned development of the body part, a sort of T.V.A. of the flesh, an aggrandizement of torso and limbs as real and grand as the cultivation of any hothouse bulb. I worked steadily, absently, without either sorrow or joy. Straining at the weights I developed everything, watching with a kind of pride the steady ballooning of my parts, growing taller, wider—expanding, blooming, becoming. For four years I weighed myself each night on the tall, free scale. For four years I sat naked and wet on the low, peeling bench by my locker, making with others the rude, brutal shoptalk of athletes or drying myself with the intense absorption of a soldier cleaning his weapon.

It was death I trained against, I tell you.

I moved out of my room and into the gym. There, lying on the tumblers' mats at night, my covers a half dozen volleyball nets, I wondered what I would do with my life.

What, I asked myself, were the purposes of strength?

Why to pull, to push, to raise, to squeeze, to win— *why to win!*

I answered an ad in a physical-culture magazine. Frank Alconi, the Jersey City manager of wrestlers, needed men. I sent photos, nine-by-eleven glossies of myself under the weights. He sent me fare. I went to Jersey City. I became a wrestler.

Alconi threw me into the ring at once. I was already strong, of course, and Alconi said I was a natural, but for a long time I didn't know what I was doing. I was supposed to lose anyway, so it didn't make much difference to the ring world, but I was traveling up and down the East Coast from Jersey City to Raleigh, North Carolina, in what might be described as a pre-

cariously ambulatory condition. My memories of those
first weeks are chiefly memories of liniment. My body
was like some great northern forest, one part of which
was always on fire. The other wrestlers kept telling me
what a good sport I was and visited me at the rubbing
table afterward. Beating me up made them feel young
again. They liked to feel my muscles. Often, lying on
the rubbing table near unconsciousness and death in
the unheated basement of a civic auditorium, I would
look up into the gap-toothed smile of ancient apes.
They would stand there for a while, lost in wonder,
and then, tracing their prehensile fingers over the
bumps and hollows of my flesh, point with an inverted
pride at their own tough and lumpy bodies, which
looked, from the angle at which I saw them, like great
red hairy mounds of meat. Then these fellows would
shrug, put on their pin-striped businessmen's suits,
snap their *Wall Street Journal*s smartly under their
armpits, and go off with a wave to lose themselves
among the traveling salesmen in the hotel lobby. In
those days druggists went blind mixing special lini-
ments to keep me alive.

When I got back to Jersey City I told Alconi I
would have to have more training.

Alconi grinned. "Tough. I thought you was tough.
Rough, huh? Trip's been rough?"

"A cob, Mr. Alconi."

"Sure. It's the gym does it. All the time developing
yourself against instruments, against metal, when what
you need's contact with human beings. Where's the
fight in a barbell?"

"That must be it," I said.

"Sure," Alconi said. "You need the old smash." He
ground his fist against his palm. "The old kaboom.
The old grrr-rr-agh." He pulled some air down out of

the sky, cradled it in the crook of his right elbow, and strangled it. "The old splat cratch." He kneed an invisible back. "The old fffapp!" He grabbed handfuls of invisible hair and gouged invisible holes in invisible eye sockets.

"With all due respect, Mr. Alconi, that's not what I need. That's what I've got. What I need is to learn to protect myself against that."

"Sure," he said. "I understand, kid. Only I'm not your trainer, you realize. As your manager I get thirty-four percent of your purses. As your trainer I'd be entitled to another"—he considered my bruises—"fifteen percent."

"Sure," I said.

"That would still leave you with fifty-one percent of yourself. You'd be in command."

"Chairman of the Board, as it were," I said.

"Yeah." Alconi laughed. "That's right. Chairman of the Board."

I slept on it. The next day I went up to Alconi again. "Who'd pay expenses?" I asked. I had been paying my own.

Alconi frowned. "What the hell," he said, "we'll take the railroad expenses off the top, the gross. We'll split."

"OK," I said.

We signed a new contract and I went back to my hotel and renewed auld lang syne with a pharmacist I'd been keeping.

In the morning Alconi called me over to his office in the gym. "Boswell," he said, "you lucked out. I got a class of ladies starting Monday and I'm registering you."

"Ladies?"

"*Girls. Fe*male wrestlers."

"You want me to train with girls?"

"Boswell," he said, winking evilly, "it's better than barbells."

"Sure," I said.

"The coming thing," he said. "Lady wrestlers. The wave of the future. I can foresee the time when there'll be girl tag teams, girl midgets, interracial girl wrestling, mixed matches with men."

"Interracial mixed matches with men?"

"Let's go slow," he said.

So I trained with ladies. At first I was shy. After all, it's an odd feeling to see the world strapped across the thick, broad shoulders of some nubile young lady, an extraordinary concept to be struggling for air nuzzled against the breast of some matronly female giant. But I got used to it and even began to enjoy it. Ultimately, for everyone's protection, Alconi's male instructor had to put me on a private crash program. It wasn't the same. I emerged from my training somewhat better prepared for the professional knockabout I had engaged for. I had learned, as Alconi put it, to fall. This is useful knowledge.

I went forth.

I was small-time. I started the evening, or ended it, or filled in on tag teams, but for a year I wrestled everywhere, earning, curiously, different reputations in different parts of the country. In the South, for example, I nearly always won. (Alconi explained why. I was, as Bogolub, the big promoter in Los Angeles, was also to tell me later, clean-cut, a Protestant, Mr. Universe type, Anglo-Saxon all the way up.) But in the coal-mining Middle Atlantic States, and for the same reasons that I was let to win in the South, I always lost. Elsewhere it was the same pattern. Here a winner. There a loser. Only in the democratic racially indifferent West did I win and lose. I was earning a little more money now, though the fact that the instructor had to give me private lessons upped Alconi's take a couple of percent and I was no longer Chairman of the Board.

It went like that, as I say, for about a year. Then, just after Alconi died, I had a row with Bogolub in Los Angeles.

Bogolub insisted his wrestlers have at least three sessions in the gym before they went on. I had complained to him that I thought the act got stale if it was rehearsed too often. "I don't think so," Bogolub said. He's a tiny man, white-faced, like someone with a heart condition. He goes in a limousine which he drives himself to all the gyms in the city to watch his wrestlers. "I don't think so," he said. "I think practice makes perfect."

"I can't agree," I told him. "That's what makes horse racing," he said, pointing vaguely toward the ring. I shrugged and went off with Felix Bush, the Schenectady Stalwart, to work out on the mat. (My kind doesn't even get to use the practice ring.) Bogolub watched me carefully. It was almost half an hour after our talk, but he continued as if there had been no interruption. "In addition," he said, "you are just a tanker. The biggest men, the *biggest,* work out the routine in the gym before a match."

To prove to Bogolub that practice did not make perfect—*to prove nothing of the sort: to reserve to my life a certain limited spontaneity*—I let Felix Bush beat me the next night in a match I was supposed to win.

Bogolub came into the locker room. I was still in the shower.

*"BOSWELL!"*

I pretended not to hear him.

"Boswell, you in there? You hear me? You in there?

Well I hope you're in there because that's where you wash up and that's what you are, you understand? Washed up! No more in L.A. do you wrestle for me in my gardens with the television and the hook-ups to San Francisco and all the way up to Portland in Oregon. That's all finished, tanker. A guy that can't win a fixed fight! Wash up good, you hear me? I'm paying for the soap and I say to you you are welcome because you are washed up in Los Angeles, do you understand me?"

"Yes. Beat it."

"Beat it? Beat it? Do you threaten me, phony? I better not understand you to threaten me because I got guys who sell popcorn for me in this place who can whip you. You're finished."

I came out of the shower and went over to my locker. Bogolub followed and stared at me while I dried myself. It always makes me nervous when people look at me when I'm naked. Even girls. I turned my back.

"Dry up good, do you understand me?" Bogolub said.

"Please, Mr. Bogolub," I said wearily.

"No no, my boy," Bogolub said gently, "you miss my meaning. You shouldn't catch cold. You missed a spot on your back. Where the yellow streak is, *that's still wet!*"

I turned to face him. "Look," I said.

"Show me your behind again. I can't stand to look at your face," Bogolub said.

I shrugged.

"Why did Felix Bush beat you?" Bogolub demanded.

"I was Bushed," I said.

"Pig stink," he said.

"Get out of here, Mr. Bogolub."

"Get out of here, Mr. Bogolub," he mimicked. "Get out of here, Mr. Bogolub." And then, in his own voice, "No tanker tells me to get out of my own place. *You* get out. You get dressed and get out. And that reminds me, I meant to tell you before. Why do you wear those crummy clothes? You look like something in a playground. I pay you. Wrestlers make good money. Ain't you proud of your profession?"

"Wrestling is not my profession."

"That's right. Not no more. Not in Los Angeles it ain't."

"OK."

"OK! You *bet* OK! A tanker who can't win a fight that I go to the trouble to fix it for him. With rehearsals yet. Let me tell you something, Mr. America, let me tell you something about the economics of this profession."

Despite myself I was instantly alert. All shoptalk excites me, everybody's trade secrets are important to me. I can't help it. Men die. Knowledge is power. Power is a sort of health too. It was all I could do to keep from putting my arm around Bogolub, from offering him a swallow of my mineral water.

"You don't know yet the damage you done tonight, do you, tanker? Contracts have been made, do you understand that? How am I going to juggle all those contracts? Bush was supposed to fight Fat Smith here next month. Maybe he won't. Maybe you ruined it for him too. It's something I got to figure it out. How can Smith go against him now? He was on the card last week and lost to the *schvoogie*. Maybe you don't remember the terrific beating you give to the *schvoogie* yourself last time you was here, but the public remembers. So right away it's an overmatch. A winner against a

loser. It's inconsistent. Where's the interest? A guy like
Bush is supposed to lose in Los Angeles. All of a sudden he beats a contender."

"Me?"

"Yes, you. In the long-range geometry. I had plans
for you. Clean-cut. A Mr. Universe type."

"I didn't know about that," I said.

"Big shot. Vigilante. Takes things into his own
hands and doesn't know what he's doing."

"What difference does it make? So Bush wins one
fight. Who's going to think about it that way?"

*"Think* about it? *Think* about it? Who said anything
about anyone thinking about it? It's the *feeling* of the
thing. The *balance*. That's what makes a good card.
You queered that. Now I'll have to readjust outcomes
all the way up the line to get the balance back. And
who pays for all that? You? I pay for it. It means new
routines, new choreography, new identities, new cos-
tumes."

"I'm sorry," I said.

Bogolub wasn't listening. He wasn't even mad anymore. He was just thinking out loud. "Maybe I could
mask somebody. Maybe some old tanker could come
in masked. A new personality. That might fix things."

"I could go against Fat Smith if I wore a mask," I
said. "Bush could fight my man."

Bogolub was silent.

"That would restore the balance," I said.

"Who you supposed to be fighting?" he asked finally. "The Grim Reaper, ain't it?"

"Yes."

"We'll see. I won't make promises."

"I'm really sorry about tonight," I said. "I was
sick."

Look, Alconi had just died. He left no heirs, no

survivors (there *are* no survivors), and my contract
had reverted back to myself. It was like having my
salary suddenly doubled, and with Bogolub sore at me
I stood to lose something for the first time in my life.
*That's* why I apologized.

He looked at me. He didn't believe my excuse, but
he was grateful that I had made one. "You'd have to
change your style," he said.

"Yes," I said. "I'd *have* to change my style."

When I saw him the next day Bogolub explained
that if I assumed a new identity I could no longer
wrestle on the West Coast as myself.

"That's all right," I said.

He looked at me narrowly.

"What's wrong?" I asked.

"Nothing," he said. "Some guys mind."

He wanted me to stay over in Los Angeles a few
days to talk over plans and line up matches (most
of them with men I was already scheduled to meet)
and sign new contracts. I had to cancel contests
in Sacramento and Berkeley, but Bogolub was so excited about launching a new career for someone that
he agreed to split the forfeit fee with me.

I saw him two days later and he asked me if I had
any ideas.

"About what?"

"About *what?* About the costume!"

I tried to seem enthusiastic. I would paint my body
green, I told Bogolub, and wear a monster mask.
There would be fangs, and saliva could drip down from
them like stuff coming off stalactites. I would call
myself The Wolf Man and explain my complexion by
the fact that I was raised in a cave in Belgium until I
was eighteen.

Bogolub listened to me thoughtfully, then frowned. "It's no good," he said. "It's too corny."

"Gee, I liked it," I told him.

"Nah," Bogolub said, "what'd happen when you sweat?"

"When I sweat?"

"Sure," Bogolub said, "the green paint. It's no good."

"How about an executioner's mask? I could wear an executioner's mask down to my shoulders. With big holes for the eyes and the nostrils."

"You ain't got the body for it," he said professionally. "You got a young body. That's what we got to start with."

"Yes," I said. "I suppose that's right."

"Sure," he said. "We got to work on that angle of it. We can't make you into something horrible when you ain't."

"You can't make a sow's ear out of a silk purse," I said.

Bogolub didn't answer. He seemed lost in thought. After a while he smiled and patted his stomach affectionately.

"Have you got an idea?"

"I *think* so, I *think* so. How would this be? We put you in a white silk mask. Like the Lone Ranger's, only white. And you wear white trunks and a beautiful white silk cape. And white shoes. Nothing else. Very simple. You're The Masked Playboy. You wear the mask because you're really a millionaire's kid and you don't want your parents to know that you're wrestling professional—it would break their hearts. THE HIGH-SOCIETY WRESTLER! WHO IS HE? How's that?"

I became The Masked Playboy. This was in the

early days of the baroque wrestler, and Bogolub's
maneuver was very successful. Now it was arranged for
me to win fairly regularly. Bogolub explained the moti-
vation. Why, after all, would a millionaire playboy like
myself continue to wrestle if he got the shit kicked out
of him? He would *have* to be a pretty good wrestler.
Bogolub was pleased with his invention and I began
to have more and more dates on the West Coast. Once
Bogolub told me that my masquerade was actually
helping free enterprise and capitalism. There was far
too much baloney going around about the working
classes, Bogolub said. If Americans were made to see
how tough and clean-cut a rich man's son could be,
they would sit up and take notice and it would be good
for business.

Bogolub was like the rest of us, I thought sadly. It
was like those scenes in Technicolor musicals when
José Iturbi interrupts the classical piece he's playing
and goes into a boogie-woogie riff. It's our instinct to
applaud such acts, to wink at Carmen Miranda with
Esther Williams when the time comes. It's our signal.
The secret handshake of the eye. Classical is only
fancy, but popular is good. Little is big and weak is
strong and poor is rich. What I stood for, what I
demonstrated behind my silk mask, like the Lone
Ranger's, only white, was even better. That rich is
poor, that alive will one day be dead.

I now had four distinct personalities, anyway identities: The Southern Boswell, cheerful, victorious bearer
of the white man's burden—whipper of Wops, Spik
scourger, Hebe hitter, Polack pitcher. The Midatlantic,
Midwest, Midnorthern Tier Boswell, a loser, the Anglo-Saxon toy of first-generation Europeans. Number
three—West Coast. The Masked Playboy. Rich Man's
Son (a kind of Christ, really). The Man in the White

Silk Mask. Who didn't need the money but beat up guys to show he was regular. (Who couldn't use the death, since he was immortal, but who died anyway to show he was regular.) And last, everywhere, myself. The Boswell Boswell. Don't ask. Don't ask.

Without a map it was sometimes difficult to know who I was, good guy or bad. Only the offstage Boswell, the Boswell in the Street, got any peace, and it a fitful one.

For five months I toured, climbing the country in busy, sooty eastern and central tours, a wrestler in industrial towns, comic relief for the day shift. Making the more leisurely long, low southern lope, the white hope of God knows what. Then the western trip. Off with the horn-rims. Into the cape, the mask, the white shoes. The Capitalist's Friend. Free Enterprise's Prize. But still the preliminaries.

Then one evening, six months after putting on the silk mask in Los Angeles, I was having dinner with a promoter in Columbus, Ohio.

"I was out with Barry Bogolub a couple of weeks ago. He came East on a scouting tour. You work for him, don't you?"

"Yes."

"Yeah, he was telling me. Seems you got this gimmick going for you in L.A. Mystery Playboy or something."

"The Masked Playboy."

"Yeah, that's right, he was telling me."

"What about it?"

"It sounds good. Next time you're in Columbus, bring your mask."

So, gradually, slowly, the real Boswell began to fade. Boswell was dead. Long live Boswell. More and more I wrestled as The Masked Playboy. In hick towns

there were write-ups in the paper. I can remember
sitting in more than one lousy hotel room, drinking
expensive Scotch, a silken ascot under my ratty robe,
legs crossed, staring democratically from behind my
mask at the reporter who had come to interview me.

"Yes, thass right. Educated at Cambridge. But I
told Father at the time that I shouldn't be content with
a sedentary rich man's life. He thought it a youth's
threat, of course, and meanwhile I developed my body
to what you see now."

"Were you actually in the Four Hundred?"

"Well, not actually. There was some nasty business
some years ago about an uncle in trade. If I had to
place the family myself, I'd put it somewhere in the
low Five Hundreds."

"I see," the poor fellow would say wearily. "You're
not supporting the family? Of course, it hasn't——"

"Fallen on harder days? I should think not. Otherwise I might be able to take off this damnable mask.
No, no, the Van Bl—, I mean, *the family,* is mon-
eyed."

"They've got a lot of money," he'd say, writing it
down.

"Oh, Lord yes, I should say so. But a fellow likes to
earn a bit of his own, you know."

"Yeah," the man would say.

Yeah. So I died and died and another part of me
was born and born. After a while articles began to
appear about me in the wrestling magazines. The more
sophisticated ones, *The Ring,* for example, treated me
with contempt. My sort of "showmanship" would proliferate, they editorialized, and with the help of un-
scrupulous promoters I would help to discredit even
further a once-noble sport. The other magazines, the
body-building books and that sort, took the story, or

pretended to, at face value, passing it on to their readers—who *were* those people anyway?—so that it actually gained in translation. I wrestled, they said, only in those towns where I had factories or brokerage offices or banks.

I was bigger now, more important than I had ever been as myself, and the lesson was not lost on me. For the first time I began to take the wrestling seriously. As the months went by I gathered more and more of a reputation. There was talk that one day I would be a serious contender for the championship.

Which brings me to my first appearance in a main event.

Bogolub had told me the night he wanted to throw me out of wrestling that I might one day be a contender, that he had had his eye on me. Perhaps it was true. I doubt it, but perhaps it was. Probably he said it to add a fillip to my loss, to start in the young man's mind the old man's myth, "I could have been the champion . . ." We are instinctively ironists, tricky tragedians. But if it was not true when Bogolub said it, a year later it was.

One night I got a call from Bogolub when I was in Fargo, North Dakota.

"Playboy? Barry."

"Yes, Mr. Bogolub?"

"Pete Lancer broke his leg in Philly last night. He was supposed to go against The Grim Reaper in a main event in St. Louis Friday, but there's no question of his making it. I want you to go down and take his place."

"I can't do it," I said. "I'm fighting in Des Moines Friday."

"Called off, kid."

"What about the forfeit fee?"

"Playboy, you're talking regarding peanuts. This is a main event in St. Louis I'm talking about. You're big-time now, Masked. Give me a call when you get to L.A." He started to hang up.

"Mr. Bogolub. Mr. Bogolub?"

"Come on, Boswell, this is long-distance. Fargo ain't Fresno."

"What about the arrangements?"

"Oh, yeah, in my excitement I forgot to tell you. You lose."

"What's that?"

"You lose. Give them a show, you understand, you're an important wrestler, but you lose. I can trust you."

"Mr. Bogolub, the last time I was scheduled to meet him I was supposed to win."

"He's the next champion, Playboy. Be a little patient, please. Give me a ring as soon as you get to L.A."

"Mr. Bogolub, I don't want to fight him. I don't want to fight him Friday." I was talking to myself. Bogolub had hung up.

I went down to the National Guard Armory. I don't even remember who I wrestled. I stumbled through the routine and it was a lousy show, I remember, even though I won. The crowd was booing me. "Hey, masked man, go get Tonto," someone shouted. "Hey, Kemosabe, you stink." "Take off the mask, Prince. The ball is over."

In the locker room afterward, the fellow I beat sat down next to me.

"What's wrong, Boswell?" (The wrestlers, of course, knew who I was. In a way the wrestlers were wonderful. They always played to the other fellow's costume.) "Don't you feel good?"

"Ah, Bogolub called before the match. I fight The Reaper Friday in St. Louis."

"That's terrific," he said. "That's really great. Main eventer?"

"Yes."

"That's marvelous, Boswell. That's really terrific."

"I lose."

"Oh," he said. "Oh, that's different. That's too bad. That's a tough piece of luck."

I didn't understand his reaction, but in the plane that night I suddenly understood. He thought I felt bad because I was supposed to lose. I was a comer, a contender. One day I was supposed to be strictly a main eventer. The Reaper already was. If I was scheduled to lose to him in my first appearance in a main event it probably meant that Bogolub was narrowing the field, was dumping me. I was better off winning the little matches, better off even losing some of them, than losing the big ones. It was too soon for me to go against Reaper and lose. When I realized this, I realized something else. I hadn't been thinking of my career at all. This was personal. I had been thinking of John Sallow.

John Sallow, the Grim Reaper, was the wrestler I had been scheduled to fight in L.A. just before I disappeared out there as Boswell. Sallow had been fighting under one name or another for years. He had been a wrestler before I was even born. He had wrestled when the sport *was* a sport, before it had become an "exhibition." At one time in their careers he had beaten Strangler Lewis, had beaten The Angel, had beaten all the champions. He had fought everywhere— Europe, Asia, Africa, Australia, the Americas, everywhere. It was now impossible to know how many fights he had actually had because many were in days and

towns when and where they didn't keep records, and
because, too, of his many changes of name. He wasn't
very active in the Thirties, though he fought *some*
during the depression, came out of his semi-retirement
during the Second World War when many of the
younger wrestlers were in the service. One day he was
to beat them, too, just as he had defeated the older
champions.

It was phenomenal to see the old man work. The
crowds loved to watch him; they loved to gape, fascinated, at his wily, ancient movements. He was curiously lithe and gave an impression of incredible detachment, suggesting that the body which moved so
gracefully was somehow something he merely inhabit-
ed, oddly like clothes which move always a split second after the agent inside them has already moved. He
seemed to exercise an almost ruthless discipline of his
limbs. His face carried this impression even further. It
was impassive, totally without expression, without the
familiar landmarks of love or hate. Nor did he fit
conveniently into the traditional comic role of hero or
villain in his matches. True, he never employed the
obvious techniques, the blatant eye gougings, hair pull-
ings, finger bendings, choke-holds, which sooner or later
could bring even the most sophisticated crowd to its
feet, to make it scream in manipulated outrage, but there
was latent in his movements, always slow, always oddly prim, a sure viciousness, an indifference to consequence to bone and muscle. If he pulled a punch it
was ultimately strategic, and although he submitted to
the terms of his contracts, winning or losing according
to some higher plan, wrestlers hated to fight him. He
hurt them even when he lost. They could not account
for his steady strength. Some said he was insane, but if
he was, his irrationality never extended to his activities

in the ring. Indeed, he seemed to have a rational body!
His movements were so naturally deft and logical that
it is impossible to imagine his ever stubbing his toe or
ripping his clothes on a nail. Outside the ring, in street
clothes, he was unremarkable, a tall, pale, almost
gaunt man, with black, almost wet-looking hair. He
looked like a farmer, in town to visit by a bedside in a
hospital, perhaps. He did not speak much (indeed, you
could tell that by looking at him) but he must have
had an extraordinary facility with languages. Once,
when I was on a card with him, I heard him explain to
two Japanese Sumo wrestlers who had come over for a
special exhibition what arrangements had been made
for them. The Sumos, delighted that they had found
someone who could speak their language, tried to engage him in further conversation, but Sallow simply
turned away.

It was with relief the year before that I discovered I
would not have to fight him. I could abide the clowns,
good guys and bad guys alike, but to have to struggle
with Sallow's naked dignity, to have to believe that
somehow the match really was of consequence, was
something I could not look forward to. I would have
fought him if I had had to (actually I had been
scheduled to win), but not to have to was much
simpler for me.

In the year I had been making my reputation, Sallow had been remaking his. I heard talk of him wherever I went. Wrestlers spoke in awe of his phenomenal
strength, of his ability simply to rise under the weight
and pressure of any hold. He was now wrestling constantly, wrestling everywhere, winning everywhere. It
was said that suddenly he had simply refused to throw
any more matches. He had never been the champion,
the wrestlers reasoned. Perhaps now, before his career

had ended (surely it was almost over; how old *was* he?
Fifty? Sixty? *More?*), he was eager at last to have the
belt. At any rate, he had been winning steadily.

Knowing Bogolub (who was his manager as well as
my own now), I could not believe that Sallow would
do anything which did not meet with Bogolub's approval, so I doubted the story that he won fights he
had been meant to lose. Still, there was something odd
in the persistence of the rumors, something odder in
his quick, bright fame, the queer fascination of the
crowds that came to watch him. They didn't like him.
They never cheered his victories. I had been in stadi-
ums when he fought and there was no more noise than
there would have been had the crowd never gathered,
had it stayed in its individual homes, watching on
television. They came, one gathered, to watch age beat
youth, not to *see* it, to watch it, to be there when it happened if it had to happen, witnesses at some awful
accident, not personal, not human, a disturbance in
nature itself, some lush imbalance there. Even old people in the crowds watched with distaste his effortless
lifts of men twice his size and half his age. He was not
their hope as in the South I had been. They wanted
nothing to do with his victories. They refused to be
cozened with immortality. Yet—this was the oddest
circumstance—as they never cheered Sallow, neither
did they cheer his opponents. Again, they simply
watched as one watched any inevitable struggle—a fox
against a chicken, say—fascinated and a little frightened.

The papers never let the public forget The Grim
Reaper theme, equating John Sallow with death itself.
"Last night, before a crowd of 7,000 persons in Tulsa's
Civic Auditorium, John Sallow, the Grimmest Reaper,
danced a *danse macabre* with a younger, presumably

stronger man. With slow inevitability the dark visitor"—this was the journalist's imagination; Sallow is pale—"choked all resistance from the helpless body of his opponent." They pretended fear and made John Sallow rich. In February, 1949, however, someone actually died while fighting John Sallow. He was fighting Seldon Faye, the Olympic champion. In the very beginning Sallow lifted Faye off the ground, slammed him down and pinned him. He was declared the winner and he left the ring. Faye did not get up. If Sallow heard the mob he gave no indication, and he went down into his dressing room, showered, dressed and was out of the town before a doctor declared Faye officially dead. It turned out that Faye had a bad heart. He shouldn't have been wrestling at all, but after this The Grim Reaper ceased to be merely a catch phrase and took on the significance of an official title. Some zealous reporter dug up the information that a wrestler named Jack Shallow had killed another wrestler in Johannesburg, South Africa, in 1920. Were Sallow and Shallow the same person? In the myth, of course, they were.

I saw him, I knew, as the crowd saw him, as the papers pretended to see him.

I saw him as the Angel of Death.

Now I had to fight him. Bogolub wanted me to lose but I couldn't. Fixing beyond fixing. It would be the first honest match . . . fight . . . struggle . . . of my career. It was back to the barroom days, one against four, the old odds, the odds that make causes, that make heroes and victims out of winners and losers. That was all right. Come on Sallow, old enemy, Boswell the Big goes against the Angel of Death to save the world. That the public would think me The Masked Playboy was fitting too. Its real heroes are never known to it. Masks beyond masks. No matter. I would save it anyway, anonymously, nom de plumely. In St. Louis I would break old death's old back.

Maybe others think it strange that an overgrown man like myself can believe such things. I say only this in my defense. Why not? Who knows what I believe? If God, why *not* the Angel of Death? Why not ghosts and dragons? Anyway this is the Angel of *Death* I'm talking about. Ah, you don't believe in him? You think you're the one that's going to live forever? Forget it. Forget it! In the meantime don't snicker when somebody fights your battles for you.

I was in St. Louis two days before the match and went to my hotel. *My* hotel. Hah! When I was close enough I read the medallion on the building with approval: HOTEL MISSOURI—TRANSIENTS. You said it, I thought. That's telling them, innkeeper. There should be signs like that all over: on chairs in bank lobbies, on theater seats, on beds in brothels, everywhere. That would change the world. Transients! Put it to them straight. No loitering! Not a command. A warning. Official, brass-plated Dutch-unclery.

I registered. The desk clerk looked familiar to me. (I never forget a face, but it constantly astonishes me when I recognize people in public places—to see the same waiter in a restaurant when I return to a city after five months, the same stewardess on two flights, the same woman who sells tickets in a movie, the same clerk at a desk. That astonishes me. But I know these are the exceptions. The turnover in the world is terrific. Usually the waiter no longer waits for anything. The stewardess is grounded. The woman in the cashier's box files no nails. Neither do they grow. The clerk has checked out.) I took the key from him and went up to my room. By some coincidence my elevator had been inspected by H. R. Fox that very day. That very day. I was safe. H. R. Fox said so. In the elevator. Stay in the elevator. It's been cleared. It wasn't bad advice, but there too I was a transient. H. R. Fox was wrong. Or else I had misunderstood him. Maybe all he meant was that the elevator was safe, not the people in it. H. R. Fox knew his business. He was as sharp as a fox. He gave away nothing. Nothing.

I called room service.

"Yes sir?" a voice answered.

"This is the transient in 814." (Jerk, I thought, it adds up to 13. How come you didn't realize that?) "Send me dinner."

"What's that, sir?"

"Send me dinner."

"What would you like, sir?"

"What difference does it make?"

I hung up.

In a moment the phone rang. It was room service, a different voice than the one I had just spoken to. Already, I thought. The turnover, the turnover. "Is this the gentleman in 814 who just called about his dinner?"

"Yes," I said. "Send it up as soon as it's ready."

"Would the gentleman care for some chateaubriand?"

"Is that expensive?"

"Well . . . ."

"Is it?"

"It is our specialty, sir."

"Fine," I said.

"Very well then, some chateaubriand. And a wine? Should you like to see our wine list?"

"No," I said. "Send up your best wine. Two bottles."

"Certainly, sir. Is the gentleman, is the gentleman—"

"Yes?"

"Is the gentleman entertaining?"

"Only himself, buddy."

"I see, sir. Very good, sir."

"Oh, and buddy?"

"Yes sir?"

"You can't take it with you."

My dinner came and I ate it without enjoyment and drank the two bottles of wine sullenly.

I called the desk.

"Transient in 814. That adds up to 13, did you know that?"

"I beg your pardon, sir?"

"I was in your elevator some while ago," I said, "looking at the control panel."

"Is something wrong, sir?"

"You can drop the 'sir,' buddy. We're all of us transients, you know."

"Sir?"

"Have it your way," I said. "There's no thirteenth floor."

"Sir?"

"There's no thirteenth floor. There's a twelfth floor and a fourteenth floor, but there's no thirteenth floor."

"Sir," the clerk said, humoring the drunken transient from out of town, "that's standard hotel policy. Many of our guests are superstitious and feel—"

"I know all about it," I interrupted him, "but that's the most important floor of all."

The clerk smiled over the telephone.

"Get it back, do you understand?"

"I'll see about it, sir."

"Thank you," I said politely. "I thought you should know." I hung up. I remembered something I had forgotten. I called the desk clerk again.

"Transient in 814," I said.

"Yes sir," the clerk said. He was getting a little tired of me. Fun was fun, he was thinking, but there was a convention in town.

"Has John Sallow checked into this hotel?"

The clerk brightened over the phone.

"Just one moment, sir, I'll check that for you."

The line went dead.

"I'm sorry, sir," the clerk said in a moment, "no such party is registered at the Missouri."

"Standard hotel policy, I suppose, like the foolishness about the thirteenth floor. Superstitious guests, I suppose."

"Shall I check my reservations, sir?" he asked coldly.

"No," I said. "If he shows up, have him get in touch with the transient in 814."

I hung up.

I found a Yellow Pages in the nightstand by the telephone. I opened it to Hotels and called them all alphabetically and asked if John Sallow were there. He was nowhere. Sure, I thought, what do you think, the Angel of Death needs a room? How would he sign the register? How would he have the nerve to walk into one of H. R. Fox's elevators? Besides, he's no transient.

I went to bed.

I was in the gym at eleven o'clock the next morning. I went up to Lee Lee Meadows, the promoter. Lee Lee was wrapped in a big orange camel's-hair coat. He was talking to a reporter. "Lee Lee, is it true you can go fourteen days without water?" the reporter was asking.

"Lee Lee," I said, going up beside him, "I've got to speak to you."

"I'm talking to the press here," Lee Lee said.

The reporter caught the eye of a wrestler and walked over to him. Lee Lee raised his hand to object. The reporter smiled and waved. Lee Lee turned to me. "Yeah, well, what's so important?"

"Is Sallow in town yet? I tried all the hotels."

Lee Lee frowned. "He'll be when he'll be," he said.

"I've got to see him before the match."

Lee Lee looked at me suspiciously. "Hey you," he said, "what's the excitement?"

"I just have to see him," I said.

"Yeah? Bogolub called me about you. He said you ain't too anxious to fight the Reaper. That you don't want to lose."

"No," I said, "I want to fight him."

"Because I got five tankers wild to be whipped by the Reaper."

"No, no, Bogolub misunderstood. I *want* to fight him."

"The Reaper pulls here. You're nothing."

"Of course," I said. "I want to see him because I thought of a new routine."

"He'll be when he'll be."

"He's not in town?"

"How do I know where he is? He could be with a floozy on Market Street. What do I know if he's in town? That old man. That's some old man."

"Lee Lee?"

"What?"

"This business about The Grim Reaper, what do you think about it?"

"A terrific idea. Brilliant."

"Then you don't believe it?"

"Come on," Lee Lee said.

"It's just a stunt," I said, "like The Masked Playboy?"

"Well, that I don't know. I'll say this. I been promoting matches in Louis since 1934. Reaper was one of my first fighters."

"That's only 17 years," I said.

"Kid," he said. "Kid, he was an old man *then!*"

I worked out listlessly with some of the other wrestlers on Friday's card and at two o'clock I went back to my hotel.

I called all the hotels again. It took me an hour and a half. I left messages with all the clerks. Then I slept. I dreamed fitfully of John Sallow and awoke at ten with a headache. I wondered if I had been awakened by the telephone. I had to talk to him. The Masked Playboy unmasked. It was all true about me. As true as it may have been about Sallow. These things were no accidents. Gorgeous George is gorgeous. We were like movie stars playing ourselves. Behind the mask *was* a rich man's son, at least spiritually—a bored darling of no means, of no means at all. I had forgotten about death. Sallow reminded me. My morbidness had led me back to myself. Transients within transients. OK, I thought, here is where I live. Now just let him call.

I didn't leave my room for fear I would miss the Reaper's call. It did not come. I fell asleep fully clothed upon my made bed.

I dreamed bad dreams and finally struggled out of

my sleep like a person trying to move one particular finger on a hand that has gone numb.

In the morning I changed my clothes slowly, ceremoniously, changing from one pair of seven-ninety-five slacks into another pair of seven-ninety-five slacks, like a matador into his suit of lights.

I called the desk.

"Any messages?"

"Who is this, sir?"

"Boswell. 814."

"We would have called you if there were, sir."

"Of course," I said.

I could not eat breakfast. I went to the gymnasium.

"Is Sallow in the city yet?" I asked Lee Lee Meadows.

"As a matter of fact, yeah," he said.

"Did you tell him I wanted to see him?"

"He said he'd see you tonight."

"Where is he staying?"

"Ah, come on, Boswell. I don't know. How should I know where that old man stays?"

"You knew I was looking for him," I said.

"Tonight he'll be in the arena. Conduct your business there."

When I went back to the hotel it had begun to rain. From my room I called the hotels again. He wasn't registered.

"That's impossible," I yelled at the desk clerk when I came to the last hotel on my list.

It was six o'clock and I had not eaten. I had better eat, I told myself. I went downstairs.

I had two steaks for strength. I chewed the meat slowly, the juices and fats filming my lips thickly. I broke the bones and gnawed at the marrow inside. The waiter watched me, his disgust insufficiently masked by a thin indifference.

When I had finished my meat he came to stand beside my plate. "Will there be anything else, sir?" he asked.

"Bring me bread," I told him.

"Bring me red tomatoes," I said when I had chewed and swallowed the bread.

"Bring me ice cream in a soup bowl," I said when I had sucked the tomatoes.

I went upstairs and lay down to wait. At eight o'clock I took my white silk cape, my mask, my tights, my shoes. I wrapped them in newspaper and went downstairs.

The doorman could not get me a cab in the rain. He held an umbrella over me and walked beside me to the corner where I waited for a streetcar.

"I'm going to the arena," I told the conductor.

He saw the silk cape through a rent in the newspaper and nodded indifferently. I sat on the wide, matted straw seat along the side of the car, my shoes damp, their thin soles in shallow, steamy, dirty puddles on the floor. Useless pink streetcar transfers, their cryptic holes curiously clotted with syrupy muck, floated face downward like suicides. Colored round bits from the conductor's punch made a dirty, cheerless confetti on the floor of the car. I read the car ads, depressed by the products of the poor, their salves for pimples, their chewing gum, their sad, lackluster wedding rings. A pale, fleshless nurse, a thick red cross exactly the color of dried blood on her cap, held up a finger in warning. V.D. CAN KILL! spoke the balloon above her. To the side a legend told of cures, of four licensed doctors constantly in attendance, of convenient evening hours that enabled people not to lose their day's pay, of treatments handled in the strictest confidence. There was a phone number and an address, the numerals and letters as thick and black as a scare headline. Above the address, floating on it like a ship tossing on heavy seas, was a drawing of a low gray building which looked like nothing so much as a factory where thin, underpaid girls turned out cheap plastic toys. Across the façade was the name: The St. Louis Institute for the Research and Treatment of Social Diseases and General Skin Disorders. Licensed 1928. The advertisement, though I had never seen it, seemed wearily familiar. Soon it was as if I had never not seen it. It was infinitely boring, depressing. I closed my eyes and saw it on my lids.

Everyone looked shabby, fatigued, their heavy florid faces empty of everything save a kind of dull ache. Those who were not returning from menial jobs were going to them, to wash down office buildings, tend lonely warehouses, stand outside toilet stalls in theaters and nightclubs. Almost everyone carried some worthless thing in some unimportant package—brown paper bags which once contained cheap fruit and now held rolled-up stockings, extra rags, soiled aprons, torn trousers, stale sandwiches and waxy pints of warm milk for two-thirty in the morning.

Only four teen-aged boys standing at the back of the car looked as though they could still be interested in their lives and these looked, despite their youth, disreputable as the others, romanceless in their shiny jackets, their billed motorcycle caps.

Outside, the rain clung listlessly to the barred windows of the streetcar.

The ride was interminable. No one ever seemed to get off. The car would stop and more would climb on, crowding steamily, smelling of wet wool and poverty and dirt, into the overheated, feverish brightness of the car. They swayed dreamily against the poles they held for balance and left greasy smudges on the chipped milkish porcelain.

A colored woman as big as myself sat down heavily next to me with the rough displacement of fatigue. Her knees, spread wide, bounced comfortably against my thighs. Her skirt was so high on her lap that I could see the rolled tops of her stockings, oddly light and obscenely pink against the dark insides of her legs.

I had been glancing repeatedly at the conductor, as much to identify myself as a stranger and thus isolate myself from my fellow passengers as to proclaim my unfamiliarity with the route. He stared back without recognition. "The arena," I mouthed across the colored woman's breasts. He flicked his eyes away impatiently. I closed my eyes and saw again The St. Louis Institute for the Research and Treatment of Social Diseases and General Skin Disorders. In the dark the streetcar slogged forward with a ponderous inevitability.

I thought of the fight. Had I eaten enough? What was the old man's strategy? Did I have any strategy? Was he really the Angel of Death? Would I be able to talk to him beforehand?

An arm shook me.

"You dropped your mask," someone said sullenly.

"What's that?"

"Here's your mask you dropped," the colored woman said. It seemed ridiculously white and silken in her big brown hand, like some intimate undergarment.

"Thank you," I said, embarrassed.

I glanced down at my lap. The clumsy bundle had come loose. One end of the silk cape dragged in a puddle. An old man across the aisle leaned far forward in his seat. I thought he would fall. He retrieved the cape for me. "Thank you," I said and looked nervously toward the conductor.

He held up two fingers to indicate that it would be two more stops. I stood up. "Have a nice party," the old man said huskily. When the car stopped I got off though I knew I had moved prematurely. "Hey," the conductor called as I stepped down. I pretended not to hear him and walked to the arena in the rain.

The trunks were damp when I put them on. Above me I could hear the thin crowd (the rain had held it down) shouting at the referee. It was an unmistakable sound. They thought they saw some infraction he had missed. A strange sound of massed outrage, insular and safe, self-conscious in its anonymity and lack of consequence. If commitment always cost so little, which of us would not be a saint?

I dressed quickly, squeezing uncomfortably and awkwardly into the damp trunks. I laced the high-top silk shoes, fitted the mask securely over my head, and buckled the clasp of the heavy silk cape about my throat. I looked around. Down a row of lockers a couple of college wrestlers who had already fought were rubbing themselves generously with liniment. I went over to them.

"Excuse me, did you see John Sallow?" I asked.

They looked at me and then at each other.

"It's a masked man," one of them said. "Ask him what he wants, Tom."

Tom pretended to hitch up his chaps. "What do you want, masked man?"

"Do you know John Sallow? He's supposed to be on the card tonight. Have you seen him?"

"He went thataway, masked man," the other said.

I walked away from them and went into the toilet.

One of the college boys came in. "Hey, Tom," he called, "there's a masked man in here."

"Knock it off," I said.

"It's all so *corny*," the kid said.

"Knock it off," I said again.

"OK, champ," he said.

"Knock it off."

I left the toilet and went back to my locker. John Sallow was there, one gray leg up on the wooden bench.

"Bogolub tells me you may try to give me some trouble tonight," he said.

"This is my last match," I said. "I'm quitting after tonight." It was true. I hadn't known it was true until I said it. Too often it rained. Too often I had to take the streetcar. Too often I sat too close to the steamy poor. I could still see the nurse. I never forgive a face.

There were excited screams and a prolonged burst of applause above us. Sallow looked up significantly. "Upstairs," he said. "You'll be introduced first. I'm the favorite."

"Look," I said. "I wanted to talk to you."

"Upstairs," he said. "Talk upstairs."

I took my place behind two blue-uniformed ushers at Gate DD. Some boys, just to the right of the entrance, kept turning around to look at me. They laughed and pointed and whispered to each other.

The ring announcer in a tuxedo was climbing through the ropes far in front of me. He walked importantly to the center of the ring, stopping every few steps to turn and pull a microphone wire in snappy, snaking arcs along the surface of the canvas. He tapped the microphone with his fingernail and sent a metal thunk throughout the arena. Then, shooting

his cuffs and clearing this throat, he paused ex-
pectantly. The crowd watched with mild interest.
"First I have some announcements," he said. He told
them of future matches, reading the names of the
wrestlers from a card concealed in his palm. He spoke
each wrestler's name with a calm aplomb and familiar-
ity so that their grotesque titles sounded almost like
real names. He paused. Jerking more microphone cord
into the ring as though he needed all he could get for
what he would say next, he began again. "Ladies and
gentlemen . . . in the main event this evening . . . two
tough . . . wrestlers, both important contenders for the
heavyweight champeenship of the world. The first . . .
that rich man's disguised son . . . who has danced with
debutantes and trains on champagne . . . the muscled
millionaire and eligible bachelor . . . who'd rather
rough and tumble than ride to the hounds . . . from
Nob Hill and Back Bay . . . from Wall Street and the
French Riviera . . . from Newport and the fabled
courts of the eastern potentates . . . weighing 235
pounds without the cape but in the mask . . . the
one . . . the only . . . *Masked Playboy!*"

I pushed the ushers out of the way and bounded
down the long aisle toward the ring. To everyone but
the kids who had spotted me earlier it must have
looked as though I had run up the turnpikes from Wall
Street, over the bridge across the Mississippi and
through the town to the arena. Modest but good-
enough-willed applause paralleled my course down the
aisle as though I were somehow tripping it off automatically as I came abreast of each row. I leaped up
the three steps leading to the ring and hurdled over the
ropes. I unclasped the cape and, arching my shoulders,
let it fall behind me in a heap. Then, swelling my chest

and stretching my long body, I stood on the tips of my high-top silk shoes, seemingly hatched from the cape itself, a crumpled silken eggshell. The crowd cheered. I nodded, lifted the cape with the point of one shoe, slapped it sharply across one arm and tossed it casually to an attendant beneath me. Then I grabbed the thick ropes where they angled at the right post. Without moving my legs I pushed, dead down, against the ropes. Snapping my head up quickly, I pulled against them. I could feel the muscles climbing my back. I looked like a man rowing in place. I let go of the ropes, dropped my weight solidly on my feet and did deep knee bends. Out of the corner of my eye I could see the ring announcer waiting a little impatiently for me to finish while the crowd applauded cheerfully. Suddenly I stood up, made a precise military right face and sprang up onto the ropes, catching the upper rope neatly along my left thigh. I hooked my right foot under the lower rope for balance and folded my arms calmly. I looked like someone on a trapeze. Or, perhaps, like a young, masked sales executive perched casually along the edge of his desk.

Smiling at the ring announcer, I waved my arm grandly, indicating he should go on. He turned away from me. He waited until the crowd was silent. When he began again he sounded oddly sad. "Meeting him in mortal . . . physical . . . one-fall . . . forty-five-minute-time-limit combat tonight . . . is that grim gladiator . . . ancient athlete . . . stalking spectral superman . . . fierce-faced fighter . . . that plague maker . . . that hoary horror . . . that breath-breaking . . . hope-choking . . . death-dealing . . . mortality-making . . . heart-hemorrhaging . . . life-letting—" For the last few seconds the crowd had been applauding in time with the announcer's rhythms. In a way their applause incited him. They incited each other. Now he paused, exhausted. There were a few last false claps and then silence.

"Widow-making," someone yelled from the crowd, applauding four times.

"Coffin-counting," someone else shouted.

"People-pounding," the announcer added weakly.

I slid off the rope. "MUR . . . DER . . . ING," I shouted from the center of the ring. *"All death is murder."*

The ring announcer motioned me angrily to get back. By exercising his authority, the authority of his tuxedo, he seemed to have regained control. "Ladies and gentlemen," he began again more calmly, "in gray trunks, from the Lowlands, John Sallow, The Grim Reaper."

With the rest of the crowd I glanced quickly toward the entrance opposite the one I had used, but from my vantage point I could see that there was no one there. I watched the gate nervously, expecting Sallow to materialize. No one came. Through the entrance gate I could see the long, low concession stand and someone calmly spooning mustard onto a hot dog. Then I heard a gasp from the other end of the arena. Sallow had been spotted. I looked around just in time to see him coming in through the same gate I had used. Of course, I thought. Of course.

He walked slowly. As he came down the aisle toward the ring a few people, more than I would have thought, began to applaud. "He has his fans," I said softly to the referee, who had just come into the ring. Most people, however, particularly those near the aisle, seemed to shrink back as he passed them. Recognizing someone, he suddenly stopped, put his hand on the person's shoulder and leaned down toward him, whispering something into his ear. When Sallow started again, the man he had spoken to stood and left the auditorium.

Sallow came up the three stairs, turned and bowed mockingly to the crowd. They looked at him. He smiled and shrugged and climbed through the ropes. He walked to his corner. I tried to catch his eye but he wouldn't look at me.

"The referee will acquaint the wrestlers with the Missouri rules," the ring announcer said. He stepped back modestly and handed the microphone to the referee. The referee signaled for us to meet at the center of the ring.

"This is a one-fall match, forty-five-minute time limit," he said. "When I signal one of you to break, I want you to break clean and break quickly. Both you men have fought in Missouri before. You're both familiar with the rules in this state. I just want to remind you that if for any reason a man should be out of the ring and not return by the time I count twenty, that man forfeits the fight. Do you understand?"

Sallow nodded placidly. The referee looked at me. I nodded.

"All right. Are there any questions? Reaper? . . . Playboy? OK. Good. Return to your corners. When the bell rings, come out to wrestle."

I had just gotten back to my corner when the bell rang. I whirled around, expecting to find Sallow behind me. He was across the ring. I moved toward him aggressively and locked my arms around his neck. Already my body was wet. Sallow was completely dry.

"Don't you ever sweat?" I whispered.

He twisted out of my neck lock and pushed me away from him.

I went toward him like a sleepwalker, inviting him
to lock fingers in a test of strength. He ignored me and
ducked quickly under my outstretched arms. He
grabbed me around the waist and raised me easily off
the floor. It was humiliating. I felt like some wooden
religious idol carried in a procession. I beat at his neck
and shoulders with the flats of my hands. Sallow in-
creased the pressure of his arms around my body.
Desperately I closed one hand into a fist and chopped
at his ear. He squeezed me tighter. He would crack my
ribs, collapse my lungs. Suddenly he dropped me. I lay
on my side writhing on the canvas. I tried to get to the
ropes, moving across the grainy canvas in a slow side-
stroke like a swimmer lost at sea. The Reaper circled
around toward my head and blocked my progress. I
saw his smooth, marblish shins and tried to hook one
arm around them. It was a trap. He came down quickly on my outstretched arm with all his weight.

"Please," I said. "Please, you'll break my arm."

The Reaper leaned down across my body and
caught me around the hips. He pressed my thighs
together viciously. Raising himself to one knee and
then to the other, he stood up slowly. I hung upside
down. He worked my head between his legs. Then,
without freeing my head, he moved his hands quickly
to my legs and pushed them away from his body,
stretching my neck. I felt my legs go flying backward
and to protect my neck tried to force them again to his
body. I pedaled disgustingly in the air. He grabbed my
legs again.

"Don't," I pleaded.

"If you drop me you'll kill me," I whined.

Again he forced my legs away from his body. Then
suddenly he loosened his terrible grip on my head. I

fell obscenely from between death's legs. Insanely I jerked my head up and broke my fall with my jaw. My body collapsed heavily behind me. It was like one of those clumsy auto wrecks in wet weather when cars pile uselessly up on each other. I had to get outside the ropes. I had a headache. I could not see clearly. I was gasping for air, actually shoveling it with my hands toward my mouth. Blindly I forced my body toward where I thought the ropes must be. Sallow kicked me. I could not get to my knees. My only way of moving was to roll. Helplessly I curled into a ball and rolled back and forth inside the ring. Sallow stood above me like some giant goalie, feinting with his feet and grotesquely seeming to guide my rolling. The crowd laughed. Suddenly I let go of my knees and kicked powerfully toward the ropes. One foot became entangled in them. It was enough to make the referee come between us. He started counting slowly. I moved painfully under the ropes and onto the ring's outer apron. "Seven," the referee intoned. "Eight." Sallow grinned and stepped toward me. He came through the ropes after me. The referee tried to pull him back but he shrugged him off. I had gotten to my feet. "Nine," the referee said. "Ten. One for Reaper. Eleven for Playboy. Two for Reaper. Twelve for Playboy."

The Reaper advanced toward me. I circled along the apron. He pursued me.

"Missouri rules. Missouri rules," I said.

"Natural law. Natural law," he answered.

"Three for Reaper. Thirteen for Playboy."

"Not by default," I shouted. I jumped back inside the ropes.

"Four for Reaper."

"Famine, Flood, War, Pestilence," I hissed.

He came through the ropes. The referee stood between us. When Sallow was standing inside the ring the
referee clapped his hands and stepped back.

I held out my hands again. I was ready to bring
them down powerfully on his neck should he try to go
under them. He hesitated, looking at my long fingers.

"Games?" he said. "With me?"

Slowly he put one hand behind his back. He thrust
the other toward me, the fingers spread wide as a net.
He was challenging me to use both my hands against
his one in a test of strength. The crowd giggled.

"Both," I said, shaking my head.

He slid his arm up higher behind his back. He
looked like a cripple.

I shook my head again. The crowd laughed nervously.

He bent one finger.

"No," I said. "No."

He tucked his thumb into his palm.

I stepped back angrily.

He brought down another finger.

"Use both hands," I yelled. "Beat me, don't humiliate me."

He closed a fourth finger. The crowd was silent. The
finger that remained, the one finger with which he
challenged my ten, was left to point at me. He took a
step backward. He was not pointing. He was beckoning.

"Don't you like the odds?" someone shouted. The
crowd applauded.

"You stink like pus," I yelled at the Reaper.

"Take my hand," he said quietly. "Try to force it
down."

I lost control. I hurled myself toward Sallow's outstretched finger. I would tear it off, I thought. He

stepped back softly, like one pressing himself politely against a wall to allow someone else to pass through a door. The crowd groaned. I looked helplessly at the Reaper. His face was calm, serene, softly satisfied, like one who has spun all the combinations on a lock and can now open it at his leisure. I braced myself too late. My body, remiss, tumbled awkwardly across the ring. The Reaper had brought his fisted hand from behind his back and smashed my unprotected ear. I fell against the rope with my mouth open. My teeth were like so many Chiclets in my mouth. I bled on the golden canvas. The Reaper stalked me. He took my head under his arm almost gently and held my bleeding ear against his chest. "I am old," he whispered, "because I am wily. Because I take nothing for granted. Not the honor of others. Not their determination. Not even their youth and strength."

He would kill me. He had no concern for my life. It was all true—the legends, the myths. Until that moment I hadn't really believed them. He *had* killed the man in South Africa. And how many others? In all those years how many had he maimed and murdered? He wrestled so that he could demonstrate his cruelty, show it in public, with the peculiarly desperate pride of one displaying his cancer in a medical amphitheater. He lived arrogantly, like one who you know will not give way coming toward you down a narrow sidewalk. His strength, his ancient power, was nothing supernatural. It was his indifference. That was what killed us. And it had this advantage—it could not be shorn. He could not be talked out of it. Pain was all our argument. In his arms, my face turning and turning against the bristles in his armpits, I was one with all victims, an everyman through loss and deprivation, knowing the soul's martial law, its sad, harsh curfew. Pain was

all our argument and like all pain, it was wasted. To
live was all his thought, to proliferate his strength in
endless war. The vampire was the truest symbol in the
give and take of the universe.

I called the referee.

"Get him off."

The referee looked down at me helplessly. "It hasn't
lasted long enough," he said. "You've only been at it
ten minutes. You can't quit now."

"Get him off, Goddamn it!"

"These people paid for a main event. Give them a
main event."

*"Get him off!* The main event is my death. He
means to kill me."

"Take it easier with him, Reaper," the referee said.
"Work him toward the ropes. Let him get away a
minute."

"Sure," the Reaper said mildly.

"No," I shouted. "No. I quit."

I tried to turn my neck toward the crowd.

"He means to kill me," I yelled. "They won't let me
quit." They couldn't hear me above their own roar.

The Reaper gathered me toward him. He grabbed
my body—I wasn't even resisting now—and raised me
over his head. He pushed me away as if I were a
medicine ball, and I dropped leadenly at the base of
the ring post.

I knew my man now. To treat flesh as though it
were leather or lead was all his intention. To find the
common denominator in all matter. It was scientific.
He was a kind of alchemist, this fellow. Of course.
Faust and Mephistopheles combined. Fist! I lay still.

"Fight," he demanded.

I didn't answer.

"Fight!" he said savagely.

He could win anytime, but he refused. This was a main event for him too.

"Will you fight?" he asked dangerously.

"Not with you," I said.

The crowd was booing me.

"All right," he said.

He backed away. I watched him. He was bouncing up and down on the balls of his feet in a queer rhythm. His shoulders raised and lowered rapidly, powerfully. His arms seemed actually to lengthen. He came toward me slowly in a leaning stoop, swinging his balled metallic fists inches above the canvas. It was his Reaper movement, the gesture that had given him his name. I had never seen it and I watched fascinated. The crowd had stopped booing now and was screaming for me to get up. The closer he got the more rapidly his fists swept the canvas, but still his pace toward me was slow, deliberate, almost tedious. He loomed above me like some ancient farmer with an invisible scythe. Now the people in the first rows were standing. They rushed toward the ring, pleading with me to get away. At last my resolution broke. I got clumsily to my knees and stumbled away from him. It was too late. His fists were everywhere. They caught me on the legs, the stomach, the neck, the back, the head, the mouth. I felt like some tiny animal—a field mouse—in tall grass trampled by the mower.

I covered my eyes with my hands and dropped to the canvas. I squeezed myself flat against it. I squealed. A fist caught me on one temple, then on the other.

I heard the referee shout, "That's enough."

Then I was unconscious.

In a few seconds I came to, and my head was clear. I could have gotten up. I could have caught one of those fists and pulled him off-balance. I wouldn't. I thought of that phrase they use in the wars—to struggle in vain. They were always praying that battle and injury and death were not in vain. As though anything purchased at some ultimate cost ought to be worth it. It was a well-meant prayer, even a wise one, but not practical. Life was economics. To be alive was to be a consumer. They made a profit on us always. To struggle in vain was stupid, to be on the losing side was stupid. Both were unavoidable. It was all that struggle ever amounted to in a universe like ours, in bodies like our own. I would not get up, I thought. I would not even let them know I was conscious. I lay there, calmer than I had ever been in my life.

"He's dead," someone screamed after a moment. "He's dead," someone else shouted. They took it up, made it a chant. "He's dead. He's dead. He's dead."

The police rushed into the ring. They made a circle around the Reaper and moved off with him through the crowd. They were protecting him, I knew. He was not being arrested. What he did in the ring, that was all right. He was immune to law. Law itself said he was immune. Like someone with diplomatic status. What did that reduce my death to, I wondered. What did that reduce my death to if my murder was not a murder, not some terrible aberration punishable by law? Missouri rules and natural law, they worked hand in hand in the dirty athletics of death.

Lying there on the canvas, in the idiotic nimbus of my blood, no longer sure if I were only feigning unconsciousness, or even whether I still lived, I knew that I could never struggle again, nor plead my pain. I knew, too, that the temptation was always to resist, that there was something glamorous in resistance that led us on, something glamorous in being a man, that to be one was to be a hero, but there was something off-center and sappy and insane in heroes, something clumsy. Fall guys fell. It was the grave gravity of the grave. It was better to take your dive at once, better to conspire, make deals, to keep, however cynically, the trade routes open. It was better, finally, to be a noncombatant, a serene Switzerland of a man, accomplice to one's own death.

The crowd mourned me, crooning grief.

I died.

# Mr. Softee ★★★

From Wolfe's mouth to God's ears.

He'd been driving for hours, on his way from his St. Cloud, Minnesota, Dairy Queen to his Mister Softee in Rapid City, South Dakota—his milk run, as he liked to call it. His right hand had fallen asleep and there was a sharp pain high up in the groin and thigh of his right side.

Mornings he'd been getting up with it. A numbness in his hand and hip, bad circulation, he thought, which left these damned cold zones, warm enough to the touch when he felt them with the freely circulating blood in the fingers of his left hand or lifted his right hand to his face, but, untouched, like icy patches deep in his skin. Perhaps his sleeping habits had changed. Almost unconsciously now he found the right side of the bed. In the night, sleeping alone, even without a twin or triplet beside him, the double bed to himself, some love-altered principle of accommodation or tropism in his body taking him from an absent configuration of flesh to a perimeter of the bed, a yielding without its necessity or reason, a submission and giving

(From *The Franchiser,* 1976.)

212

way to—to what? (And even in his sleep, without naming them, he could tell them apart.) To ride out the night sidesaddle on his own body. (No godfather Julius he, not set in *his* ways, unless this were some new mold into which he was pouring himself.) Pressing his head—heavy as Gertrude's marrowless bones—like a nighttime tourniquet against the flesh of his arm, drawing a knee as high up as a diver's against his belly and chest, to wake in the morning cut off, the lines down and trailing live wires from the heavy storm of his own body. Usually as the day wore on, the sensation wore off, but never completely, some sandy sensitivity laterally vestigial across the tips of his fingers, the sharp pain in the region of his thigh blunted, like a suction cup on the tip of a toy arrow. Bad circulation. Bad.

Unless. Unless— Unless from Wolfe's mouth to God's ears.

He checked into the Hotel Rushmore in Rapid City and asked the clerk for a twin-bedded room. And then, seeing the width of the single bed, requested a rollaway be brought, narrower still. This an experiment. In the narrow bed no place to go, his body occupying both perimeters at once, returned as it had been in the days before he'd shared beds, the pillow beneath his head almost the width of the bed itself, tethered by a perfect displacement, lying, it could be, on his own shadow. But in the morning the sensation still there, if anything worse, not to be shaken off. (Never to be shaken off.)

And a new discovery. At Mister Softee handling the tan cardboard carton of popsicles, as cold to the touch of his right hand as dry ice. He thought his blood had thickened and frozen. Something was wrong.

He got the name of a doctor from his Mister Softee

manager, saw Dr. Gibberd that afternoon, and was oddly moved when the doctor told him that he would like him to go into Rapid City General for observation.

A black woman took him in a wheelchair to his bed.

It was very strange. Having voluntarily admitted himself to the hospital, having driven there under his own steam—his 1971 Caddy was parked in the Visitors' lot—and answered all the questions put to him by the woman at the Admissions Desk, showing them his Blue Cross and Blue Shield cards, his yellow Major Medical, he had become an instant invalid, something seductively agreeable to him as he sat back in the old wheelchair and allowed himself to be shoved up ramps and maneuvered backward—his head and shoulders almost on a level with his knees—across the slight gap between the lobby carpet and the hard floor of an elevator and pushed through what he supposed was the basement, past the kitchens and laundry rooms, past the nurses' cafeteria and the vending machines and the heating plant, lassitude and the valetudinarian on him like climate, though he had almost forgotten his symptoms.

"Where are we going? Is it much farther?"

"No. We almost there." She shoved the brass rod on a set of blue fire doors and they moved across a connector through a second set of fire doors and past a nurses' station, and entered a long, cinder-block, barracks-like ward in which there were perhaps fifteen widely spaced beds down each side of a broad center aisle. Except for what might be behind a folding screen at the far end of the ward, the beds were all empty, the mattresses doubled over on themselves.

"This is the boondocks," Ben said. "Is it a new wing?"

"You got to ask your doctor is it a new wing," she said and left him.

A young nurse came and placed a hospital gown across the back of the wheelchair. She asked Ben if he needed help. He said no but had difficulty with his shirt buttons. Unless he actually saw his fingers on them, he could not be sure he was holding them.

"Here," she said, "let me." She stooped before him and undid the buttons. She unfastened his belt. "Can you get your zipper?"

"Oh sure." But touching the metal was like sticking his hand into an electric socket. The nurse made up the bed. He sat back down in the chair and, watching the fingers on his right hand, carefully attempted to interlace them with the fingers on his left.

"Modest?"

Ben nodded. It was not true. In sickness he understood what he never had in health, that his body, anyone's, everyone's, was something for the public record, something accountable like books for audit, like deeds on file in county courthouses. If he was ashamed it was because he couldn't work his fingers. He stood to take off his pants and shorts. Then he smiled.

"Yes?"

"I was just thinking," he said.

"Yes?"

"I'm Mister Softee." She turned away and completed the last hospital corner. "No," Ben said, "I am. I have the local Mister Softee franchise. It's ice cream." She folded the sheets back. "It's true. Anytime you want a Mister Softee, just go down and ask Zifkovic. Zifkovic's my manager."

"Please put your gown on."

"Tell him Ben Flesh sent you," he said and burst into tears.

"What is it? What's wrong?"

"I don't know," Ben said, "I don't know what's happening to me."

"That's why you're here," she said, "so we can find out." She helped him out of the chair gently, unfolded and held open the gown for him. "Just step into it," she said, "just put your arms through the sleeves." He had to make a fist with his right hand so his fingers wouldn't touch the rough fabric. She came toward him with the gown. His penis moved against her uniform. "Can you turn around?" she said. "I'll tie you up the back."

"I can turn around." He was crying again.

"Please," she said, "please don't do that. You mustn't be afraid. You're going to be fine."

"I can turn around. See?" he sobbed. "Is it smeared? My ass? What there is of it. All belly, no ass. Is it smeared? Is it smeared with shit? Sometimes, I don't know, I try, I try to wipe myself. Sometimes I'm careless."

"You're fine," she said. "You're just fine. Please," she said, "if you shake like that, I won't be able to tie your gown for you."

"No? You won't?" He couldn't stop sobbing. He was grateful they were alone. "So I'd have to be naked. How would that be? This—this body na-naked. Wouldn't that be something—thing? No ass, just two fl-flabby gray pouches and this wi-wide tor-tors-*torso*. They say if you can squeeze a half inch of flab between your forefinger and thumb you're—you're too fat. What's this? Three in-*in*-in*ch*-*ches*? What does that make *me?* I never looked like you're supposed to look on the—on the beach. I've got this terrible body. Well, I'm not the franchise man for nothing. It's—it's like any middle-age man's. I'm so *white*."

"Stop," she demanded. "You just control yourself."

"Yeah? What's that? Shock therapy? Thanks, I needed that? Well, why not? Sure. Thanks, I needed that." He turned to face her. He raised his gown. *"Flesh the flasher!"* He was laughing. "See? I've got this tiny weewee, this undescended cock."

"If you can't control yourself," she said.

"What? You'll call for help? Lady, you just saw for yourself. You don't *need* help. *You* could take me." He sat on the side of the bed, his legs spread wide, his elbows on his thighs, and his head in his palms. But he was calm. "I just never took care of the goddamned thing, my body. I just never took care of it. And the only thing that counts in life is life. You jog?" he asked suddenly.

'What's that?"

"Do you jog?"

"Yes."

"I knew. I knew you did. You smoke?"

"No."

"Right. That's right, Ship-fucking-shape."

"I think one of the interns . . ."

"No," he said calmly, "I'm okay now. No more opera. But you know? I hate joggers. People who breathe properly swimming, who flutter kick. Greedy. Maybe flab is a sign of character and shapelessness is grace. Sure. The good die young, right?"

"Why do you loathe your body so?"

"What'd it ever do for me?"

"Will you be all right now?"

"I told you. Yes. Yeah." He got into bed. When he pulled the covers up his hand tingled. The nurse turned to go. "Listen," he said.

"Yes?"

"Tell Gibberd he can skip the preliminaries, all the observation shit. Tell him to get out his Nation's Leading Crippler of Young Adults kit. The kid's got M.S."

"You don't know what you have."

"Yes. Wolfe the specialist told me. He gave me egg salad and set me straight."

The nurse left him. He tried to feel his pulse with the fingers of his right hand and couldn't. He did five-finger exercises, reaching for the pulse in his throat, his hand doing rescue work, sent down the carefully chiseled tunnels of disaster in a mine shaft, say, to discover signs of life. He brought the fingers away from his neck and waved to the widows. He placed three fingers of his good hand along a finger of his right and, closing his eyes, tried to determine the points where they touched. He couldn't, felt only a suffused, generalized warmth in the deadened finger. He took some change the nurse had put with his watch and wallet in the nightstand by his bed and distributed it on his blanket around his chest and stomach. Still with his eyes closed, he tried to feel for the change and pick it up. He couldn't. He opened his eyes, scooped up a nickel, a dime, and a quarter with his left hand and put them in the palm of his right hand. Closing his eyes again, he very carefully spilled two of the coins onto the blanket—he could determine this by the sound—and made a fist about the coin still in his hand. Concentrating as hard as he had ever concentrated on anything in his life, and trapping the coin under his thumb, he rubbed it up his forefinger, trying to determine the denomination of the remaining coin.

It's the dime, he decided. He was positive. Yes. It's the dime. The inside of his thumb still had some sensitivity. (Though he couldn't be sure, he thought he had felt a trace of pulse under his thumb when he had held the dead necklace of his right hand against his throat.) Definitely the dime. He opened his eyes. His hand was empty. He shoved the change back in the nightstand and closed the drawer.

"I say, are you *really* Mister Softee?" The voice was British and came from behind the screen at the far end of the ward.

"Who's that? Who's there?"

"Are you?"

"Yes."

"Jolly good. They're rather splendid."

"Thanks."

"Mister Softee." The name was drawn out, contemplated, pronounced as if it were being read from a marquee. "Apropos too, yes?"

"Why's that?"

"*Well,* after your performance just now for Sister, I should have thought that would be obvious, wouldn't it?"

"I'm sick."

"Not to worry," the invisible Englishman said cheerfully. "We're all sick here." Ben looked around the empty ward. "Sister was right, you know. You *are* going to be fine. You're in the best tropical medicine ward in either Dakota."

"This is a tropical medicine ward?"

"Oh yes. Indeed. One of the finest in the Dakotas."

"Jesus," Ben said, "a tropical medicine ward."

"Top drawer. Up there with the chief in Rapid City."

"What do you have?" Ben asked.

"One saw you through the crack where the panels of
my screen are joined. One saw everything. One saw
your bum. It *is* smeared, rather. What do *I* have?
Lassa fever, old thing. Came down with a touch of it
last year. Year it was discovered actually. In Nigeria.
Odd that. Well, *I* wasn't in Nigeria. I was in Belize,
Brit Honduras, with RAF. What I meant was, Lassa
*fever* was discovered in Nigeria. Trouble with a clipped
rather precise way of talking, articles left out, refer-
ences left dangling, pronouns understood, is that it's
often imprecise actually, rather."

"What was odd?"

"Beg pardon?"

"You said, 'Odd that.' What was odd?"

"Oh. Sorry. Well. That a disease could be said to be
*discovered*. Of course all that's usually meant is that
they've isolated a particular virus. But I mean, if you
*think* about it the virus must have been there all along,
mustn't it? And I should have thought that people,
well, you know, *natives,* had been coming down with
the bloody thing since *ages*. I mean, when Leif Eric-
son, or whoever, was discovering your States, some
poor devil must have had all the symptoms of Lassa
fever, even dying from it, too, very probably, without
ever knowing that that's what was killing him because
the disease had never been *named,* you see. Now it
has. Officially, I'm only the ninth case—oh yes, I'm in
the literature—but I'll bet populations have died of
it."

"I don't think I understand what—"

"Well, only that I know where I stand, don't I? Just
as you, if you were right about yourself, know where
*you* stand. Is that an ad*van*tage? I wonder. Quite
honestly I don't know. Yes, and that's strange, too,
isn't it, that I know things but don't know what to

make of them? Incubation period one week. Very well.
Weakness? Check. Myositis? Check. And the fever of
course. And ulcerative pharyngitis with oral lesions.
Yellow centers and erythemystositic halos. Rather like
one of your lovely Mister Softee concoctions rather.
Myocarditis, check. Pneumonitis, pleuritis, encephalo-
phitathy, hemorrhagic diathesis? Check. Well, check
some, most. What the hell? Check them *all*. Sooner or
later they'll come. I mean I *expect* they will. Gibberd's
been very straight with me. I think it pleases him how
classic my case has been. Yet one can't tell, can one? I
mean, what about the sleeplessness? *I* sleep like a top.
I was sleeping when you were brought in, wasn't I? It
was only your *rack*et woke me. Well, what *about* the
sleeplessness? Or the slurred speech? One has some
things but not others. There was the headache and leg
rash and even the swollen face, but where was the leg
*pain?* And this is the point, I think: What I have is
incurable and generally fatal. Generally fatal? *Generally? Fatal?* Will this classic condition kill me or not?
Incurable. *Al*ways incurable. But only generally fatal.
Oh, what a hopeful world it is! Even in hospital. So no
more racket, you understand? No more whimpering
and whining. Be *hard,* Mister Softee!"

"All right," Ben said.

"Yes, well," his roommate said. "Are you ambulatory? I couldn't really tell. I saw you stand. But I saw
Sister help. *Are* you? *Amb*ulatory?"

"Yes."

"Oh, good. I wonder if I could trouble you to come
back of the screen. One is rather in need of help."

"You want me to come back there?"

"If you would. If it isn't too much bother. Oh, I see.
The contagion. Well. There's nothing to fear. Lassa
can't be contracted from anyone who's had the disease

for more than thirty-two days. One's had it a year and a half."

One could call the nurse, Ben thought. I have been orphaned and I have been blinded. I am Mister Softee here and Chicken from the Colonel there. Godfathers have called me to their deathbeds to change my life and all this has been grist for my character. I am in one of the go-ahead tropical medicine wards in Rapid City, South Dakota, and a Lassa fever pioneer needs my help. Oh well, he thought, and left his bed and proceeded down the long empty ward toward the screen at its rear. He stood by the screened-in sick man.

"Yes?" Ben said.

"What, here so soon? Well, you *are* ambulatory. Good *show,* Mister Softee! I'm Flight Lieutenant Tanner incidentally. Well then, could you come back of the screen, please just?"

"Come back of it."

"Yes. Would you just?"

Flesh went behind the screen. The Englishman was seated beside his bed in a steel wheelchair. Heavy leather straps circled his weakened chest and wrapped his flaccid legs to hold him upright in it. Flesh looked down meekly at the mandala of spokes, then at the Englishman's bare arms along the chair's wide rests. They were smeared with a perspiration of blood. Tiny droplets of blood freckled the man's forehead, discrete reddish bubbles mitigated by sweat and barely deeper in color than blown bubble gum. A sort of bloodfall trickled like tears from the hollow beneath his left eye and out over the cheekbone and down his face.

"Leukopenia, check," the Englishman said.

"My God, you're bleeding all over."

"No. Not actually *bleeding,* old fellow. It's a sort of

capillary action. It's complicated rather, but the blood
is forced out the pores. It's all explained in the literature. Gibberd told me I might expect it. It was jolly
good luck *your* happening to be by. There's a box of
Kleenex in that nightstand there. Would you mind? If
you'll just tamp at the bloody stuff. Oh, I say, forgive
that last, would you just? I should have thought to
think that would do me rather nicely."

"Maybe I'd better call the nurse."

"She's *rather* busy, I should expect. There are people who really need help, for whom help is of some
help, as it were. As I don't seem to be one of them—
incurable, generally *fatal,* I'm taking the darker view
just now, old boy— I should think you would have
thought we might work this out between ourselves."

"Yeah, between ourselves," Ben said. "Pip." He
took the Kleenex and began to dab at the man's
skin.

"There's a good fellow. That's got the arm, I think,"
the Englishman said.

"This never happened before?"

"No no. Absolutely without precedent. I say, do you
*real*ize?"

"What?"

"That if this disease really *was* discovered in
1970—well, it was, of course, but I mean if it didn't
*exist* before 1970—why, then I'm only the ninth person to have experienced this particular symptom.
We're breaking freshish ground here, you and I."

Ben, working on the bloodfall at its headwaters just
under the Englishman's left eye, started to gag. He
brought the bloodied Kleenex up to his lips.

"Be firm, Mister Softee." Ben swallowed and looked
at him.

"I think that's it, rather," Ben said quietly.

"Yes, well, it would be, wouldn't it, except that the insides of my thighs seem a bit sticky."

"No no. I mean that's *it*. *Generally* fatal. I'm taking the lighter view. I'm calling the nurse."

"Mister Softee."

"What?"

"We've the same doctor."

The same spring that Ben Flesh lay in the tropical medicine ward of Rapid City General—the prime interest rate was 6¾ percent—a record heat wave hit the northern tier of the central plains states. Extraordinary demands on the energy supplies caused breakdowns and brownouts all over. The hospital had its own auxiliary generator, but the power situation was so precarious that the use of electricity, even there, was severely cut back, if not curtailed entirely. There was no electricity to run the patients' television sets, none for air conditioning in any but the most crowded wards, or in those rooms where the heat posed a threat to the lives of the patients. It was forbidden to burn reading lights, or to play radios that did not run on batteries. All available electricity was directed toward keeping the lights and equipment in good order in the operating theaters, maintaining the kitchens with their washers and driers, their toasters and refrigeration units (even at that Flesh suspected that much of what he ate was tainted or turning), to chilling those medications that required it, to operating the laundry services (though the sheets were changed now every third or fourth day instead of daily), and to keeping the power-hungry instruments going that analyzed blood and urine samples and evaluated the more complicated chemistries and tests. The X-ray machines, which required massive doses of electricity, were now used only for emergencies and only the dialysis machine and iron lung, top priorities, were unaffected by the brownout. Even electroshock therapy was suspended for all but the most violent cases, and Flesh was kept awake nights by the shrieks and howls of the nearby mad, people so far gone in their terror and delusion that even powerful tranquilizers like Thorazine were helpless to calm them.

"It isn't the heat," the Englishman said, as they both lay awake one night while the screams of crazed patients in an adjacent ward came through their open windows. (The windows had to be opened, of course, to catch whatever breeze might suddenly stir.) "It's the humidity drives them bonkers."

"They were already bonkers," Flesh said irritably.

"That exacerbated it then," the Englishman said just as irritably.

"Shit."

"You know," the Englishman said, "I don't remember heat like this even in Brit Honduras."

"Brit Honduras, Brit Honduras. Why can't you say British Honduras like everybody else?"

"Everyone in RAF called it Brit Honduras."

"And that's another thing—Raf. Can't you say R.A.F. like any normal human being?"

"I'll say what I bloody well please."

"Then be consistent. Say 'Craf.'" (The Englishman had been on detached duty with the Canadians at their air base in Brandon, Manitoba, when the first symptoms of his Lassa fever had begun to manifest themselves.)

"Why should one say 'Craf' when it's the Royal *Canadian* Air Force? I should have thought you would have heard of the Royal Canadian Air Force *exer*cises. I'd have to say 'RCAF,' wouldn't I? The whole point of an acronym is to save time. One could, I suppose, say '*R*-caf.' That might be all right, I should think. Yes. '*R*-caf.' That's not bad. It has a ring, just. One *could* say that."

"Don't say anything."

"I say. Are you saying, don't say anything?"

"Don't say bloody anything. Shut bloody up. Go to sleep just. Close your eyes and count your symptoms, check."

"Well, we *are* in a temper. You're bloody cheeky, Yank."

" '*Yank.*' Jesus. Where'd you train, on the playing fields of the back lot? Why don't they run my tests? I know what I have anyway. Why don't they read the lumbar puncture thing?"

"Well, they've their priorities, haven't they? The lumbar puncture. *That* was manly. You screaming like a banshee. Louder than our lunatic friends."

"That needle was big as a pencil."

" 'Please stop. *Please!* Oh goddamn it. Oh Jesus. Oh shit. Oh fuck.' Oh me. Oh my. Oh dear. Be adamant, Mister Softee. Be infrangible. Be *stiff*, Mister Softee. Be obdurate, be corn, be kibe!"

Flesh shut his eyes against Tanner's taunts and took the darker view. "I'm taking the darker view," he said quietly. "I'm taking the darker view because I'm going to kill him."

In the morning the nurse came for Ben with a wheelchair. It was more than a hundred degrees in the ward.

"Is it my tests? Are my tests back?"

"You have a phone call. You can take it at the nurses' station."

"A phone call? Gibberd?"

"No."

"I can't think who it could be. No one knows I'm here. Is it a woman?"

"A man."

She wheeled Ben to the phone and put the receiver in his left hand.

"Mr. Flesh?"

"Yes?"

"Zifkovic."

He'd forgotten about his manager. "Yes, Zifkovic, what is it?"

"How you feeling, sir?"

"The same. I'm waiting for my test results. Is anything wrong?"

"The stuff's all turned, sir. It's rancid glop. There must be a ton of it. The Mister Softee's all melted and running. We were working with ice for a time but I can't get no more. It's a high tide of ruined vanilla. The fruit flavors are staining everything in sight. I got the girls working on it with pails and mops but they can't keep up. A truck came down from Fargo with a new shipment today. I told him that with this heat wave we couldn't accept, but he just dumped it anyway. It's outside now. A whole lake of the shit. What should I do, Mr. Flesh? Mr. Flesh?"

"It's a plague," Flesh said. "It's a smoting."

"What? Mr. Flesh? What do you want me to do? You wouldn't believe what this stuff smells like."

"I'd believe it."

"You got any suggestions, Mr. Flesh? I didn't want to trouble you. I know you got your own problems, but I don't know what to do. You got any ideas?"

"Be hard, Mister Softee."

"What? I can hardly hear you."

"Nothing. I have no suggestions." He handed the

phone back to the nurse. "It's the plague," Flesh said. "A fiery lake of Mister Softee, check."

"There you are, Mr. Flesh," another of the nurses said, coming up to him. "Dr. Gibberd has your test results. He's waiting for you."

Flesh nodded, allowed himself to be returned to the ward.

Gibberd, standing at the Englishman's bedside, waved to him. He indicated to the nurse that she set a screen up around Flesh's bed. He was carrying a manila folder with the results of Ben Flesh's tests. They were all positive. It was M.S. all right, Gibberd told him, but of a sensory rather than a motor strain. The chances of its becoming motor were remote. The fact that he'd been in remission all these years was in his favor. He really wasn't in such bad shape. For the time being there would be no treatment. Later, should it shift to a motor M.S., they could give him Ritalin, give him steroids. How would he know? Well, he'd be falling down in the streets, wouldn't he? There'd be speech impairment, wouldn't there? There'd be weakness and he wouldn't be able to tie his shoes, would he? There'd be nystagmus, don't you know? Nystagmus? A sort of rotation of the eyeballs. Anyway, there was no real reason to keep him in the hospital. They needed the beds. Flesh looked around the empty ward.

"As a matter of fact," Gibberd said, "I wish I were going with you. Where you off to now? Someplace cool?"

"I can drive?"

"Of course you can drive. I've told you, there's no strength loss, no motor impairment at all. It's just sensory. A little discomfort in your hand. So what?"

"But it's America's number-one crippler of young adults."

"M.S. is a basket term. You'll be fine. These symptoms should go away in two to three months. Boy, this heat."

"The heat, check."

"Well. Get dressed, why don't you? I'll write up your discharge papers. Be sure to stop by the cashier on the way out. Really. Don't worry about the M.S."

"Sensory discomfort, check."

"I guess you'll be wanting to get back to your Mister Softee stand before you leave. This *heat*. I could use a Mister Softee myself right now."

"The Mister Softees are all melted. The Lord has beaten the Mister Softees back into yogurt cultures."

"What's that?"

"Plague."

"What's all this about plague?"

"The plague is general throughout Dakota. We're being visited and smited."

"Well. Good luck, Mr. Flesh."

"Doctor?"

"Yes?"

"What about him?" Flesh jerked his thumb in the direction of Tanner's screen. The doctor shook his head.

"He'll be shipped off to Guernsey eventually. The R.A.F. maintains a hospital there for incurables."

The doctor extended his hand. A shiver of electric plague ran up Flesh's hand and arm when Gibberd touched him. He felt he could start the hospital's engines just by touching them, that the energy was in his hands now, in the ruined, demyelinating nerves sputtering like live wires in his fingertips.

Gibberd left and Flesh dressed. He was about his business, heading toward the cashier and the Cadillac. (Probably it wouldn't start; the battery dead, check.

Check the oil.) Then suddenly Ben turned back. He stood for a moment in the center aisle, staring in the direction of Tanner's screen. "Tanner," he said, "I don't want you to say a thing. Don't interrupt me. Just listen just.

"Gibberd has given me my walking papers. He has given me my dirty bill of health. It's interesting rather. Here we are, two guys from opposite sides of the world. Yank and Limey. Strangers. Do-be-do-be-doo. Flight Lieutenant Tanner of Eng and Brit Honduras with Nigerian virus in his gut, and me, Ben Flesh, American—don't interrupt, please just—Ben Flesh, American, ranger in Cadillac of Highway this and Interstate that. Yet somehow the both of us ill met in this hotshot trop med ward in Rap Cit S-dak. You know what? Don't, don't answer. You know what? Never mind what, I'll get to what later.

"Well. Strangers. Sickmates on the edge of the Badlands. Both incurable and generally fatal. Oh, I know a lot about *my* disease, too. When Dr. Wolfe first diagnosed my case—you remember, I told you about Dr. Wolfe—I boned up on it in the literature, in *What to Do till the Doctor Comes.* It's progressive, a neurological disorder of the central nervous system, characterized by muscular dysfunction and the formation of sclerotic, or hardening—be hard, Mister Softee—hardening patches in the brain. One's myelin—that's the soft, white fatty substance that encases the axis cylinders of certain nerve fibers: what a piece of work is a man—one's myelin sheath is unraveling like wool. It snags, you see? Like a run in a stocking. I am panty hose, Lieutenant. Vulnerable as.

"Incurable. Generally fatal. Usually slow and often, in its last stages, characterized by an odd euphoria. I was blind once, I tell you that? No family to speak of.

I have heart disease and many businesses. Is this
clear? No, don't answer. The point is, the lines of the
drama of my life are beginning to come together, make
a pattern. I mean, for God's sake, Tanner, just consider what I've been through, I've told you enough about
myself. Look what stands behind me. Theatrical cos-
tumes! Songs! My history given pizzazz and order and
the quality of second- and third-act curtains, coordi-
nated color schemes for the dance numbers, the solos
and show-stoppers, what shows up good in the orches-
tra and the back of the house, and shines like the full
moon in the cheap seats. I got rhythm, dig? Pacing,
timing, and convention have gone into making me. Oh,
Tanner, the prime rate climbs like fever and we ain't
seen nothing yet. Gibberd dooms me. You should have
heard him. He makes it official. He dooms me, but
very soft sell so I can't even be angry with him. It's
getting on, the taxis are gathering, the limos, the cops
are up on their horses in the street, and I don't even
know my lines—though they're coming together—or
begin to understand the character.

"What do you think? Shh, that was rhetorical. What
do you think? You think I should kick my preoccupa-
tions? The stuff about my godfather and my god-
cousins? All the Wandering Jew shit in my late-model
Caddy, going farther than the truckers go, hauling my
ass like cargo? Aach.

"Me and my trademarks. I'm the guy they build the
access roads for, whose signs rise like stiffened pe-
ters—Keep America Beautiful—beyond the hundred-
yard limit of the Interstates. A finger in every logotype.
Ho-Jo's orange roof and the red star of Texaco. D.Q.'s
crimson pout and the Colonel's bucket spinning, spinning. You name it, I'm in it.

"So. Doomed. Why? Shh. Because I am built to

recognize it: a lip reader of big print and the scare
headline. Because I'm one of those birds who ain't
satisfied unless he has a destiny, even though he knows
that destiny sucks. How did I get this way? I used to
be a kid who ate fruit.

"Anyway. As I was saying. You know what? You
know what I think? Shh. Hush. I think you're dead.
Don't bother to correct me if you're not. That's what I
think. I think you're dead there behind your screen,
that you'll never see Guernsey. The dramatic lines
demand it. Theatricality's gravitational pull. Who are
you to go against something like that? You're too
weak. You have to be strapped to your chair, for
God's sake. So. It's nice how you can let your hair
down with strangers. We were strangers, right? Have
we ever met, sir? Do you know me; has there been
communication between us in any way, shape, or form;
have we gotten together before the show; have promises been made to you? *Thank you very much, sir.
Thank you very much, ladies and gentlemen.*

"So it's agreed. We're strangers, locked each into his
own symptoms, you into Lassa fever and me into my
sensory problems. And somehow, as strangers will,
somehow we got to talking, and gradually understood
each other. I wiped your blood up. You saw my
asshole with its spoor of shit. Well, strangers get close
in such situations. Now I have my dirty bill of health
and I'm told to move on and Dr. Gibberd tells me
you're for Guernsey when your orders come through.
And here's where I'm supposed to go behind them
screens and shake hands. Well, I won't! I won't do it.
That ain't going to happen. Because you're dead!
Slumped in that queer way death has of disarraying
things. So that's it. The destiny man thinks you've been

put here on earth to satisfy one more cliché, to be discovered stone cold dead in a Rapid City General wheelchair. For what? So one day I'll be able to say in my impaired speech—'There wash thish time in Shouf Dakota, and I wash on the shame woward wi-with thish young chap from the R.A.F. (He called it "Raf.")— And we got pretty close. The two of us. There was a terrible heat wave and neither of us could sleep. We were kept up half the night by the screams of mental patients who couldn't be quieted because the power was out, and even though the hospital had its own auxiliary generator, there wasn't enough power for electric-shock treatments, so we told each other the story of our life, as fellows will in hospital, and got pretty close to each other, and finally I was discharged and I went over to young Tanner's screen to say goodbye and found him dead.'

"Well, fuck *that,* Lieutenant! I like you too much to use you around fireplaces. We'll just skip it because I ain't going behind no screen to make certain, because if you *are* dead, by Christ, I don't think I could take it. I would grab a scissors and cut the lines of my drama. On the other hand, please don't disabuse me of my sense of the fitness of things. Keep still just. So long, dead guy."

He turned and started to the exit, but just as he got there he heard a loud, ripping, and unruly fart. Well, how do you like that? he thought. What was it, the critique of pure reason? Or only the guy's sphincter relaxing in death? Flesh shoved hard against the handle on the fire doors.

He was like a refugee now. A survivor, the last alive perhaps, the heat a plague and waiting for him in his late-model Cadillac baking in the hospital's open parking lot. He unlocked its doors and opened them wide but did not step in. Whatever was plastic in the car, on the dash, the steering wheel, the push-button knobs on the radio, along the sides of the doors, the wide ledge beneath the rear window, had begun to bubble, boil, the glue melting and the car's great load of padding rising yeast-like, separating, creating seams he'd been unaware of before, like the perforations on Saltines.

What has happened to my car?

It was as if an earthquake had jostled its landscape. Things were not aligned.

He feared for his right, hypersensitive hand, its stripped nerves like peeled electrical wire. If he touched anything metal in the automobile, if he so much as pressed the electric window control, it would ignite. He waited perhaps ten minutes, stuck his head inside to see if the car had cooled off. Imperceptible. Leaving the doors open, he walked back inside the hospital and went up to a fourteen- or fifteen-year-old boy who was sitting in one of the chairs in the waiting room.

"Kid," he said, "I'll give you five dollars if you start my car for me and turn the air conditioning on."

The boy looked at him nervously.

"It's all right. Look. Here." He held the money out to the boy. (It was difficult—his fingers had no discrimination left in them—to separate the bill from the others and remove it from his wallet.) "It's right there on the lot. You can see it from the window. The Cadillac with the doors open. I've just been discharged from the hospital. I'm not supposed to get overheated. Please," he said and started to leave, turning to see if the boy was following. He had not left his chair.

"Well?" Flesh said. "Won't you do it? I'm not supposed to get overheated. Doctor's orders. Look, if you're afraid, I'll stay here. Here, here are my car keys. Go by yourself. Take the money with you."

"I don't drive."

"What? You don't drive? Don't they have driver's training in your high school? That's very important."

"I go to parochial school."

"Oh. Oh, I see. Parochial school. The nuns. If I came with you I could tell you what to do. I could stand outside and tell you just what to do. It's easy. They make it look like a cockpit but it's easy. All I want is for you to start it and turn the air conditioning on High. It's urgent that I get out of the heat. I've been in the hospital and the car has been standing. It's like a blast furnace. If five dollars isn't enough—"

"All right," the boy said uncertainly.

Flesh accompanied him to the car, keeping up a nutty chatter. "Parochial school," he said, "sure. Notre Dame. The Fighting Irish. Tradition. What are you so afraid? Parochial school. Broken-field running. You could be off like a shot if you wanted. What could *I* do? I'm sick. You could dodge. Fake me out. You'd go between the parked cars. What could a sick guy like me do? I couldn't catch you in the Cadillac. Relax please. Who's sick? Maybe I know him?"

"What do you mean?"

"I found you in the waiting room. You're visiting somebody. Who?"

"My dad."

"Oh, your dad. What's his name? We're fellow patients. Maybe I know him."

"Richard Mullen? He had a heart attack."

"Dick Mullen's your pop? *Dick* Mullen?"

"Yes, sir."

"Oh, he'll be fine. I heard the docs talking. He's out of the woods."

"You really heard that?"

"Oh, absolutely. Out of the woods. On the mend. His last two cardiograms have been very exciting. They've definitely stabilized. He mustn't let you see you're worried. I mean, you mustn't let him see you're worried. Who's your patron saint? Pray to your patron saint for a cheerful countenance. Pop's going to be terrific."

The kid began to cry.

"What's this? What's this? What kind of a patron saint are we talking about here? Some deafo?" Flesh looked into the sky. "That's *cheer*ful countenance, not *tear*ful!" He smiled and the boy laughed. They were at the car, Ben standing behind the boy at the driver's side, feeling the terrific heat.

"Get in," he said. The boy hesitated. "What, you think I'm the witch in Hansel and Gretel? You think I could fake *you* out? A broken-field runner from parochial school? Get in, get in." He handed the boy the keys and told him what to do and, once the engine had started, how to work the air conditioning. He had the boy close all the doors. "Let me know when it's cool," he said. "Rap on the window with your knuckles." In a few minutes the boy came out of the car. They changed places. Ben lowered the window and tried to give him the five dollars, but the boy shook his head. "Take it, go on, don't be crazy. Take it, you saved my life."

"Really," the boy said, "it's all right."

"The laborer is worth his hire. Take the money. Buy yourself some Mister Softees."

"No. Please. Really. I don't want the money."

"What, listen, is this a religious thing? Is this something to do with parochial school?"

"What you told me about my father," the boy said. "What you heard from the doctors about his improvement. That's all the payment I, you know, need. Thank you."

Flesh was thinking about his health, the prognosis, the things he'd read since Wolfe had first explained the meaning of his blindness. He was thinking of what one day he could expect to feel in his face, flies walking lightly in place of his cheeks, the heavy sensation of sand between his toes and in his socks even when he was barefoot, of weakness in his limbs, of hunks of deadened flesh along his thighs and torso like queer grafted absences against which the inside of his arms would brush as they might brush against rubber or wood, sensations he could not imagine now, feelings under his thumbnails, the ridges of his cock, things in his pores, stuff in his lip, thinking of the infinite symptoms of the multiple sclerotic.

"Yeah," he said. "I understand. You're a good boy. Tell Mother. She probably needs cheering up, too." And he put the car in gear and drove against the fantastic record heat wave, looking for a hole in it as pioneers traveling west might once have looked for passes through the mountains, as explorers had paddled and portaged to seek a northwest passage. He used side roads and Interstates, paved and unpaved secondary state roads and county, bypasses and alternates, limited-access divided highways and principal thruways, feeling chased by brownouts and power-failed space, civilization's demyelination, slipping safely into temporary zones of remission and waiting in these in motels until the symptoms of the heat wave caught up with him again and the electricity sputtered and was snuffed out like a candle and the air conditioning died.

He gassed up wherever he could. The pumps would not work where the electricity failed, and whenever he came to one of those zones of remission—the heat, constant everywhere, did not in itself insure a brownout; rather the land and towns, invisibly networked with mad zigzag jigsaw power grids, grids like a crossword, secretcoded with electrical messages he couldn't break (in a single block the power might be off in five adjacent buildings but on in the sixth and seventh and off again in an eighth and ninth), had been mysteriously parceled; agreements had been made, contingency plans had gone into effect, Peter robbed here to pay Paul, there permitted to hold his own, a queer but absolute and even visible (the lights, the lights) negotiation and exchange like the complicated maneuvers of foreign currency, the towns seeming to have grown wills, a capacity to conspire, to give and to take; he had an impression of thrown switches, jammed buttons, broken locks—he first sought out service stations, accepting Regular if there was no Premium, refreshing his oil even if it was down by less than a cup, filling exerything: his radiator, his battery, even the container that held the water that sprayed his windshield, to the brim, the brim. Only then did he seek a motel. And, registered, walked to a hardware store, not wanting to use any of his precious gasoline in the wasteful stop-and-start of town driving. In the hardware store he would purchase five-gallon cans and carry them back empty to the gas station closest to his motel to have them filled. These he would store in his trunk, moving his grips and garment bags onto the backseat of his car. (At one time he had as much as sixty gallons in gas cans.) And flashlights, too. And batteries. Bando-

liers of batteries, quivers of them, an ordnance of
Everyready. And in bookstores atlases, guidebooks of
the region to supplement the service-station maps, the
Texaco and Shell and Mobil and Phillips 66 South
Dakotas and Nebraskas and Kansases and Colorados
he already had. Finally to return to the motel, not yet
undressing even, pulling a chair up to the television
and switching from channel to channel—these were
hick towns, the sticks, on cable TV, near the eastern
edges of mountain time, the western edges of central—
to catch the weather reports. (He bought a portable
radio which he took with him into the motels to listen
to the forecasts on the local radio station.) Becoming
in that frantic week and a fraction since he had left
Rapid City behind him, the stench of his spoiled,
dissolved flavors in his nostrils—he'd stopped to see
Zifkovic first, with him investigated the extent of the
damage, the high-water mark of the melted Mister
Softees, the smashed artificial strawberry and broken
chocolate, the ruined crushed banana and pineapple
and decomposed orange, the filmy vanilla and the
serums of lime and lemon, all the scum of melted fruit,
oils now, wet paint—a savant of conditions, an anchor-
man of drought and heat, a seer almost, second-
guessing the brownouts, seeing them coming, a quick
study of the peak hours, and not wanting to be caught
in the motel room when the town stalled, dreading
that, forgetting even his symptoms in his incredible
concentration and prophecy. Hitting at last on tricks,
calling the local power stations and electric companies,
on ruses getting through to the executives themselves,
calling long distance to Omaha even, misrepresenting
himself. (The Mister Softee experience in South Dakota had taught him what to say: "Mr. Rains, Herb
Castiglia here. I'm Innkeeper at the Scotts Bluff Ra-

mada and I've got this problem, sir. I've got an opportunity to buy a ton of ice. Now the son of a bitch who's pushing it wants forty cents a pound for the stuff. That's a cockeyed price and for my dough the guy's no better than a looter. He won't sell less than a ton, and at forty cents a pound that comes to eight hundred bucks. I'm over a barrel, Mr. Rains, but I've got two or three thousand dollars tied up in my meats for my restaurant. What I need to know is if there's going to be a brownout, and, if so, how long you expect it to last. If she blows I'm okay for six to eight hours, but in this heat any longer than that and the stuff will turn into silage. What do I do, Mr. Rains? I got to cover myself. Can you give me a definitive no or a definite yes?") And striking responsive chords in Mr. Rains, in Mr. DeVilbiss, in Mr. Schopf, small businessman to big, getting at last the inside information he could not get on the half dozen or so channels available to him on the cable TV, or the local country-music and farm-report radio stations. And acting on these advices, skipping town, hitting the road. Driving after dark on the hotter days, the hundred-plus scorchers—to cut down on the air conditioning, to keep it on Low instead of High as he'd have to do in the daytime, conserving his gas, four days and he hadn't had to tap the reserves in his trunk—and looking over the broad plains for the lights of a town, any town, a prospector of the electric.

But his body—he'd been sick, he'd been in hospital, M.S. was a stress disease—couldn't adjust to the new hours and he had to return to the old pattern of traveling the highways during the day, thinking to change directions when the radio told him of the brownouts in western Nebraska—he'd been heading for Wyoming, for the high country, mountains, as if electricity followed the laws of gravity, pushing his Cadillac uphill (but that wasted gas, too, didn't it?) toward the headwaters of force—and drop toward Kansas. He couldn't decide. Then, on Interstate 80, he saw detour signs spring up sudden as targets in skeet, the metal diamonds of early warning. He slammed his brakes, slowed to fifty, forty, twenty-five, ten, as the road turned to gravel and dirt at the barricades and the traffic merged two ways. A tall girl in an orange hard hat stood lazily in the road holding up a heavy sign that said SLOW. Her bare arms, more heavily muscled than his own, rubbed death in his face. He yearned for her, her job, her indifference, her strength, her health. He stopped the car and got out. "Tell me," he said, "are you from west of here or east?"

"What? Get back in your car, you're tying up traffic."

"Where do you live? West, east?"

"Get back in that car or I'll drive it off into a field for you."

"Look," he said, "all I want . . ." She raised her arms, lifting her sign high and plunging its metal shaft into the earth, where it quivered for a moment and then stayed, stuck there like an act of state.

"You want to try me?" she threatened.

"I want to know if they've still got power west of here."

"Power's all out west of here. Get back in your car." He lowered his eyes and returned to his car and, going forward slowly and slowly back, made a U-turn in the dirt and gravel narrows.

"Hey," the tall girl shouted. "What the hell—"

On the sixth day, on Interstate 70, between Russell

and Hays—the radio was silent—he looked out the
window and was cheered to see oil rigs—he remembered what they were called: "donkey pumps"—
pumping up oil from the farmers' fields, the ranchers'.
The pumps drove powerful and slow as giant pistons,
turning like the fat metal gear on locomotives just
starting up. Ridiculous things in the open field, spaced
in apparent random, some almost at the very edge of
the highway, that dipped down toward the ground and
up again like novelty birds into glasses of water. Abandoned, churning everywhere unsupervised and unat-
tended for as far as he could see, they gave him an
impression of tremendous reservoirs of power, indifferent opulence, like cars left standing unlocked and keys
in the ignition. There was no brownout here. (Of
course, he thought, *priorities:* oil for the lamps of
Asia, for the tanks and planes of political commitment
and intervention. Flesh was apolitical but nothing so
drove home to him the sense of his nation's real
interests as the sight of these untended donkey pumps
in these obscure Kansas fields. Wichita had been without electricity for two days while the thirsty monsters
of vacant west-central Kansas used up enough to
sustain a city of millions.) He pulled off the Interstate
at Hays and went up the exit ramp, heading for the
Texaco station, the sign for which, high as a three-
story building, he had seen a mile off, a great red star
standing in the daylight.

It wasn't open.

He crossed the road and drove to the entrance of a
Best Western Motel. He went inside. The lobby was
dark. At the desk, the cashier was preparing a guest's
bill by hand. "Is that what you get?" They checked the
addition together.

"I guess," the man said.

"Did you want to register, sir?" the clerk asked Ben.

"What's happening? Why are the lights out? Is your air conditioning working? The TV? What about the restaurant? Will I be able to get a hot meal? Is there iced coffee?"

"There's a power failure," the clerk said. "We can put you up but I'm afraid all the electric is out. You'll have to pay by credit card because we can't get into the register to make change."

"But the pumps," Ben said. "All those pumps are going. I saw them myself. There can't be a brownout. What about those pumps?"

"Those are driven by gasoline engines," the clerk said.

"Oh," Flesh said, "gas. Jesus, that never occurred to me."

"Did you want a room, sir? There's no air conditioning but you can cool off in the pool. Usually there's no swimming after 9 p.m., but because of the power failure we're going to keep it open all night."

"There's no filtration," Flesh said. "It's stagnant water. There's no filtration. It's kids' pee and melted Mister Softees and gallons of sweat."

"It's heavily chlorinated, mister. It's been super-shocked plenty. We're spending a fortune on chlorine and pH minus."

He stayed. He stayed because in an odd way the clerk spoke his language and Flesh had caught hints in the man's speech of his own concerns and obsessions. The motel people had made, he suspected, on their level, the preparations he had made on his. There would *be* a ton of ice to preserve their meats and keep their Cokes cold. There would be flashlights and extra batteries—candles would be too dangerous, Coleman lamps would—on the nightstand and on the sink in the bathroom. He signed the registration card in the gathering dusk.

That was not the first time he was fooled. Two days before he had left Interstate 80 at North Platte, Nebraska, and doubled back east along U.S. 30 to Grand Island. It had already turned dark in Grand Island. The phones were working and he called Nebraska Power and Light. This wasn't a power failure but a localized brownout; he was told that the electricity would be back on by morning. He decided to continue driving. If the brownouts were localized he could probably find a town farther on where there was still juice. He consulted his Shell and Phillips and Mobil maps of Nebraska by the beam of his flashlight. His best bet would be to leave U.S. 30 and get onto 34. That way, heading toward Lincoln, he would hit Aurora and York—York showing in fairly large type on Shell and Mobil—and then Seward, then Lincoln itself. If nothing happened by Seward, State Route 15 looked promising. He could head north to David City and Schuyler or south to the junction with U.S. 6, leave 15, and continue on 6 the three miles to Milford or the twelve to Friend. He would keep his options open. At Schuyler if nothing was happening, he could get back on U.S. 30 and head west again to Columbus, represented on all the maps in type just a little less bold than Grand Island itself.

That's what he did finally. It was very dark now. There was absolutely no moon. It seemed odd to Flesh that after days of such horrendous sunlight there would be no moonlight at all. Did that mean there were clouds? Was the weather about to break? (Yet the air felt no heavier; he could not perceive heat lightning.) He drove with his brights on. State Route 15 was

unimproved road, paved, but gravel kept spitting itself
at the Cadillac, putting great pits in its body and
undercarriage. The gas gauge was dangerously close to
empty, and Flesh pulled off to an improved county
road that he would not have seen at all if he didn't
have his brights on. He stopped the car and went with
his flashlight to the trunk. This was the first time he
had had to use any of the gas from the five-gallon
cans. As he emptied each can he got back into the
driver's seat and read the gas gauge. Five gallons was a
spit in the bucket to the huge Cadillac tank and he
found that he had to empty four cans and part of a
fifth before the gauge read Full. This left him with only
three and a fraction cans in reserve—he had not yet
purchased all twelve five-gallon cans—perhaps seventeen or eighteen gallons at the most.

He closed the lids on the empty cans as tight as he
could—this pained him, aggravating his M.S. as any
contact with metal did—and returned to his car.
Somehow he forgot what he was about and continued
by mistake for perhaps three miles on the dirt road.
The sheer comfort of the ride on the dry, packed
dirt—it was like riding on velvet, the smoothest journey he had ever taken—lulled him, so that finally it
was his comfort itself that warned him of his danger,
that taught him he was lost. Oh, oh, he mourned when
he discovered what had happened. A pretty pass, a
pretty pass when well-being has been so long absent
from me that when I feel it it comes as an alarm, *it* a
symptom. He looked for some place he could turn the
car around and came at last to a turnoff for a farm.
Dogs howled when he pulled into the driveway. He
saw their grim and angry faces in his headlamps and
feared for both them and himself when they disappeared from sight—moving as slowly as I am, they will

be at my tires now—dreading the thump that would
signal he had killed one. But he managed to turn back
up the dirt road he had come down—it no longer
seemed so comfortable a ride—and regained State
Route 15, turning north toward Schuyler.

As he had feared, Schuyler—allowed only the faint-
est print on the map, and not on the Shell map at
all—was nothing but a crossroads, a gas station, a
tavern, a couple of grocery stores, an International
Harvester Agency, and three or four other buildings, a
grange, a picture show, a drugstore, some other things
he could not identify in the dark, homes perhaps, or a
lawyer's or a doctor's office. He stopped the car to
consult his map again.

It would have to be Columbus, eighteen miles west.
The 1970 census put the population at 15,471. A
good-sized town, a small city, in fact. Sure. *Very* respectable. He had high hopes for Columbus and turned
on the radio. He could not pull in Columbus but he
was not discouraged. It was past 2 A.M. after all.
Good-sized town or not, these were solid working
people. They would have no need or use for an all-
night radio station. He started the engine again and
swung left onto U.S. 30. (U.S. 30, yes! A good road, a
respectable road, a first-class road. It went east all the
way to Aurora, Illinois, where it spilled into the Interstates and big-time toll roads that slip into Chicago. It
paralleled Interstate 80 and even merged with it at last
and leaped along with it across 90 percent of Wyoming, touching down at all the big towns, Cheyenne
and Laramie and Rawlins and Rock Springs, before
striking off north on its own toward Boise and Poca-
tello and west to Portland in Oregon. He was satisfied
with U.S. 30. U.S. 30 was just the thing. It would
absolutely lead him out of the wilderness. He was

feeling good.) And when he swung west onto 30 and got a better view of the Schuyler gas station, he saw the pump in the sway of his headlights. *The pump!*

Good God, what a jerk he'd been! Of course. Oh, this night had taught him a lesson all right! That he need never fear the lack of gas again. All he had to do when the gauge got low was to head for the hick towns with their odd old-fashioned gas pumps that didn't give a shit for brownouts or power failures, that worked by—what?—hydraulics, principles of physics that never let you down, capillary action, osmosis, all that sort of thing. He was absolutely cheerful as he tooled along toward Columbus. He was tired and grotty, but he knew that as soon as he hit Columbus things would work themselves out. He would get the best damn motel room in town. If they had a suite—sure, a town like that, better than fifteen thousand, certainly they would have suites—he'd take that. He would sleep, if he wished, with the lights on all night. There was electricity to burn—ha ha—in Columbus. He felt it in his bones.

And sure enough. In fifteen minutes his brights picked up the light-reflecting city-limits sign of Columbus, Nebraska—population 15,471, just like the map said—touched the glass inset sign and seemed to turn it on as you would turn on an electric light. And just past it, somewhere off to his left—and this must still be the *out*skirts—two great shining lights. Probably a party. Two-thirty and probably a party. Oh, what a live-wire town Columbus! He would have to build a franchise here. Tomorrow he'd scout it and decide what kind. Meanwhile, on a whim, tired as he was, he turned left on the street where the two great lights were burning and drove toward them.

He seemed to be driving down an incline in a sort of

park. Probably it wasn't a party as he'd first suspected. Probably it was the Columbus, Nebraska, Tourist Information Center. But open at night? Jesus, what a *town!* What a *live-wire,* go-to-hell-god-damn-it *town!*

Then he was perhaps a hundred or so feet from the lights and in a kind of circular parking lot. He parked and took his flashlight and walked toward the lights.

It was not until he was almost upon them that he saw that they were not electric lights at all, that he saw that they were flickering, that he saw that they were flames, that he saw that they bloomed like two bright flowers from twin pots sunk into the ground, that he saw that they were set beside a brass plaque, that he saw the inscription on the plaque and read that these twin combustions were eternal flames in memory of the dead and missing Columbus Nebraskans of World Wars I and II, Korea, and Vietnam.

"Oh," he groaned aloud, "oh God, oh my God, oh my, my God, oh, oh." And he wept, and his weeping was almost as much for those Columbus Nebraskans as it was for himself. His cheerfulness before, his elevated mood, was it the euphoria? Was it? No, it couldn't have been. It was too soon. Maybe it was only his hope. He hoped it was his hope. Maybe that's all it was and not the euphoria. Feel, feel his tears. He was not euphoric now. His disappointment? No, no, disappointment could not disappoint euphoria. No. He was sad and depressed, so he was still well. Hear him moan, feel his tears, how wet. Taste them, how salty. He remembered, as he was admonished by the inscription on the plaque, the dead soldiers and sailors and marines and coast guardsmen of Columbus who had died in the wars to preserve his freedom. He remembered good old Tanner, dead himself perhaps in Rapid City General, and the father of the kid—though he'd only heard about him—who started his car for him, the man with the heart attack. He prayed that the lie he'd told was true, that the boy's father's cardiograms had stabilized. (He was sorry he'd lied to the boy. See? He was sorry. He felt bad. How's *that* euphoric?) He recalled the boy himself, the broken-field runner.

"Oh, Christ," he said, "I, *I* am the broken-field runner. I, Flesh, am the broken broken-field runner and tomorrow I will look at the map and see where I must go to stop this nonsense and wait out this spell of crazy weather."

Except for the eternal flames, Columbus was black till the sun rose.

So it was not the first time he was fooled. Nor the last.

The last—he stayed on three days in Hays, Kansas, because in the morning the power came back on; he was very tired, exhausted; he needed the rest—was the evening of the day he decided to leave Hays. At five o'clock the power failed again. Rested—he felt he could drive at night once more—he climbed back into the Cadillac and returned to Interstate 70. His gas cans—screw the hick pumps, he'd decided, and had accumulated the twelve cans by then and had had them filled—were in the trunk, his grips and garment bags again on the backseat. He'd eaten at the motel and was ready for the long drive west. (He'd decided to go to Colorado Springs.)

After the layover in Hays it was pleasant to be back on the highway again, pleasant to be driving in the dark, pleasant to be showered, to wear fresh linen, to be insulated from the heat wave in the crisp, sealed environment of the air-conditioned car, to read the soft illuminated figures on the dash, the glowing rounds and ovals like electric fruit.

He leaned forward and turned on the radio, fiddled with the dial that brought up the rear speakers, and blended the sound with those in front. His push buttons, locked in on New York and Chicago stations, yielded nothing but a mellow—he'd adjusted the treble, subordinating it to the bass—static, not finally unpleasant, reassuring him of the distant presence of energies, of storms, far off perhaps but hinting relief. He listened for a while to the sky and then turned the manual dial, surgical—and painful, too; this was his right hand—as a ham, fine tuning, hoping to hone a melody or a human voice from the smear of sound. It was not yet nine o'clock but there was nothing—only more sky.

But of course. I'm on FM, he realized when he had twice swung the dial across its keyboard or wavelength. He switched to AM and moved the dial even more slowly. Suddenly, somewhere in the soprano, a voice broke in commandingly, overriding the static and silence. Flesh turned up the treble. It was a talk show, the signal so firm that Ben assumed—he had left Kansas and crossed the Colorado line—it was Denver.

"The Dick Gibson Show. Go ahead, please, you're on the air."

"Hello?"

"Hello. Go ahead, please."

"Am I on the air? I hear this guy."

"Sir, turn your radio down."

"I can hear this guy talking. Hello? Hello?"

"Turn your radio down or I'll have to go to another caller."

"Hello?"

"We'll go to a commercial."

There was a pause. Then this announcement:

"Tired of your present job? Do you find the routine

boring and unchallenging? Are you underpaid or given
only the most menial tasks? Then a job with the
Monsanto Company may be just what you're looking
for. Monsanto Chemical has exciting openings with
open-ended opportunities for men and women who
have had two years' experience in the field of Sensory
Physiology or at least one year of advanced laboratory
work in research neurophysiology. Preferential treatment will be given to qualified candidates with a back-
ground in ethnobotany and experimental cell biology,
and we are particularly interested in specialists holding
advanced degrees in such areas as the determination of
crystal structures by X-ray analysis, kinetics and mech-
anism, or who have published widely in the fields of
magnetic resonance, molecular orbital theory, quantum
chemistry, and the nuclear synthesis of organic com-
pounds. Applicants will be expected to have a high
degree of competence in structure and spectra and
advanced statistical mechanics. Monsanto is an equal-
opportunity employer."

"The Dick Gibson Show. You're on the air, go
ahead, please."

"Dick?"

"Yes, sir."

"Dick, I've had this fabulous experience and I want
to share it with your audience. I mean it's a believe-it-
or-not situation, a one-in-a-million thing. It's practically a miracle. Can I share this with your audience,
Dick?"

"Sure, go ahead."

"Yes. Thank you. Well, to begin at the beginning,
I'm a brother."

"A brother."

"Yeah. But you see my parents split up when I was
still a little kid and then my mom died and my father

was too sick to take care of us, so my brother and me
were farmed out to different relatives. What I mean is,
I went with my mother's sister, my aunt, but she
couldn't take care of the both of us so my brother went
with an older cousin. I was six and my brother he must
have been around eight at the time. Well, my aunt
married a soldier and they adopted me legally and he
was transferred and we pulled up our roots and we
moved with him, and I was, you know, what do they
call it, an army brat, going from post to post with my
aunt and my new father, the corporal. He was a
thirty-year man and we like traveled all over, pulling
up our roots every three years or so, and when I was
old enough to leave the nest I got a job with this
company, and as time went on I met a girl and we
dated for a while and finally we decided to get married.
Now we have children of our own, a boy seven and a
cute little girl four.

"Well, sir, I'm with the J. C. Penney store, and I
made a good record and Penney's opened up a new
store in the suburbs and about a year ago my department head asked me if I'd consider moving to the new
store with the idea in mind that I could train the new
kitchen-appliance salesmen and be the head of the
department and run my own ship. Well, of course
when an opportunity like that opens up, you jump at
it. Opportunity knocks but once, if you know what I
mean."

"I know what you mean," Dick Gibson said. "What
are you getting at, please?"

"You mean the miracle?"

"Yes, sir."

"That's what I was getting at. Yesterday a guy
comes in for a present for his wife's birthday. He was
thinking in terms of a toaster, but he didn't know

exactly what model he had in mind, so I asked him if he had kids and he said yeah, he had two kids, twin boys, ten years old. 'Well,' I said, 'in that case you probably want the four-slice toaster.' That's our Ezy-Clean pop-up job with an adjustable thermostat control and a crumb tray that opens for easy cleaning in a handsome chrome-plated steel exterior. I have the same toaster in my kitchen."

"Yes?"

"Oh yeah. So he asked to see it and I showed it to him and I told him that he could compare it to any model on the market at the price and it couldn't be beat and that's the truth. Well, to make a long story short, he went for it. I mean, it was just what he had in mind without knowing it and I asked, as I always do, if it would be cash or charge. He said charge. I asked if he wanted to take it with or have it sent. He said take it with. So he gave me his charge plate, and when I went to my machine to write up the sales slip, I couldn't help but notice when I read his charge plate that he was my brother."

"Really?"

"My long-lost brother."

"That *is* a coincidence."

"Wait. When I went back, I was like shaking all over and he noticed it and he asked what was wrong and I said, 'Are *you* Ronald L. Pipe?' And he says, 'Yes. What about it?' And I tell him, I tell him I'm Lou B. Kramer!"

"Oh?"

"Well, I expected him to fall down in a dead faint, but he doesn't bat an eye. Then I realize, I realize Kramer's my *adopted* name, my stepfather's name, the corporal's."

"The thirty-year man's."

"Right. And it's been, what, twenty-eight years since we laid eyes on each other. He's bald, and I'm prematurely gray and I've put on a little weight from all that toast. Of *course* we don't recognize each other. So I tell him his history—our history—that when he was eight years old his folks split up and his mom passed away and he was raised by an older cousin. 'Can this be?' he asked. 'How do you know this?' And I explain everything, who I am and everything, and that if he'd paid cash or if it hadn't been for my habit of reading my customers' names off their Charge-a-Plates we'd never have found each other to this day."

"Well," Dick Gibson said.

"Wait. That's just the beginning of the coincidence. I punched out early and we had a couple of beers together."

"I see."

"We both drink beer!"

"Gee."

"We're both married and have kids!"

"How do you like that?"

"His wife's birthday is the day after tomorrow!"

"Oh?"

"*My* wife was born in the springtime, too!"

"Hmn."

"We both *bowl!*"

"You both do?"

"I average 130, 135."

"And he averages?"

"About 190."

"Do you have anything else in common?"

"We're both Democrats. Neither of us is a millionaire."

"I see. Well, that's really—I'm going to have to take another—"

*"We both watch Monday-night football!"*

"—another . . ."

"When we go out with our wives—when we go out with our wives—"

"Yes?"

*"We both use babysitters!"*

". . . call."

*"Neither of us has been in prison; we both like thick juicy steaks. Dick, Dick, both of us, both of us drive!"*

"Thank you, sir, for sharing your miracle. The Dick Gibson Show. You're on the air, go ahead, please."

Flesh couldn't stop laughing. Things would work out. He left Interstate 70 and turned off onto U.S. 24 to drive the remaining eighty or so miles to Colorado Springs. At Peyton, Colorado, where his headlights ignited a sign that read COLORADO SPRINGS, 24 MILES, the signal was so powerful that he might have been in Chicago listening, say, to the local station of a major network.

When he was almost there, there was a station break. "This is Dick Gibson," Dick Gibson said, "WMIA, Miami Beach."

Then he panicked. It's not, he thought, because it's so close that it's so clear, *it's because all the other stations have failed!* It's because America has everywhere failed, the power broken down!

And that, *that,* was the last time he was fooled.

Yet the lights were on in Colorado Springs.

Colorado Avenue was a garden of neon. The lights of the massage parlors burned like fires. The sequenced circuitry of the drive-ins and motels and theaters and bars was a contagion of light. A giant Big Boy's statue illuminated by spots like a national monument. The golden Shell signs, an old Mobil Pegasus climbing invisible stairs in the sky. The traffic lights, red as bulbs in darkrooms, amber as lawn furniture, green as turf. The city itself, awash in light, suggested boardwalks, carnivals, steel piers, million-dollar miles, and, far off, private homes like upturned dominos or inverted starry nights. Down Cheyenne Mountain and Pikes Peak niagaras of lights were laid out like track. Don't they know? he wondered. Is it Mardi Gras? Don't they know? And he had a sense of connection, the roads that led to Rome, of nexus, the low kindling point of filament, of globe and tubing, as current poured in from every direction, rushing like electric water seeking its own level to ignite every conductor, conflagrating base metals, glass, the white lines down the centers of the avenues bright as tennis shoes, stone itself, the city a kind of full moon into which he'd come at last from behind its hidden darker side. The city like the exposed chassis of an ancient radio, its embered tubes and color-coded wire.

He drove to the Broadmoor Hotel and checked in. Only a suite was available. That was fine, he would take it. How long would he be staying? Open-ended. A bill would be presented every three days. That was acceptable. They did not honor credit cards. No problem. He would pay by check. He could give them two hundred dollars in cash right then if they liked. And was willing to show them his money. That wasn't necessary. All right then. Could he get a bellboy to help with his bags? He was tired. Then he could go to his rooms at once. The boy would take his car keys and bring his bags up when he had parked Mr. Flesh's car for him. Fine. His suite was in the new building. The new building, was that far? Oh no. Not at all. Another boy would show him the way. That was fine. That was just what he wanted.

# The Conventional ★★★
# Wisdom

Ellerbee had been having a bad time of it. He'd had financial reversals. Change would slip out of his pockets and slide down into the crevices of other people's furniture. He dropped deposit bottles and lost money in pay phones and vending machines. He overtipped in dark taxicabs. He had many such financial reversals. He was stuck with Super Bowl tickets when he was suddenly called out of town and with theater and opera tickets when the ice was too slick to move his car out of his driveway. But all this was small potatoes. His portfolio was a disgrace. He had gotten into mutual funds at the wrong time and out at a worse. His house, appraised for tax purposes at many thousands of dollars below its replacement cost, burned down, and recently his once flourishing liquor store, one of the largest in Minneapolis, had drawn the attentions of burly, hopped-up and armed deprivators, ski-masked, head-stockinged. Two of his clerks had been shot, one killed, the other crippled and brain damaged, during

(From *The Living End,* 1979.)

the most recent visitation by these marauders, and
Ellerbee, feeling a sense of responsibility, took it upon
himself to support his clerks' families. His wife re-
proached him for this, which led to bad feeling between them.

"Weren't they insured?"

"I don't know, May. I suppose they had some insurance but how much could it have been? One was just a
kid out of college."

"Whatshisname, the vegetable."

"Harold, May."

"What about whosis? He was no kid out of college."

"George died protecting my store, May."

"Some protection. The black bastards got away with
over fourteen hundred bucks." When the police called
to tell him of the very first robbery, May had asked if
the men had been black. It hurt Ellerbee that this
should have been her first question. "Who's going to
protect you? The insurance companies red-lined that
lousy neighborhood a year ago. We won't get a penny."

"I'm selling the store, May. I can't afford to run it
anymore."

"Selling? Who'd buy it? *Selling!*"

"I'll see what I can get for it," Ellerbee said.

"Social Security pays them benefits," May said,
picking up their quarrel again the next day. "Social
Security pays up to the time the kids are eighteen years
old, and they give to the widow, too. Who do you
think you are, anyway? We lose a house and have to
move into one not half as good because it's all we can
afford, and you want to keep on paying the salaries not
only of two people who no longer work for you, but to

pay them out of a business that you mean to sell! Let
Social Security handle it."

Ellerbee, who had looked into it, answered May.
"Harold started with me this year. Social Security pays
according to what you've put into the system. Dorothy
won't get three hundred a month, May. And George's
girl is twenty. Evelyn won't even get that much."

"Idealist," May said. "Martyr."

"Leave off, will you, May? I'm responsible. I'm
under an obligation."

"Responsible, under an obligation!"

"Indirectly. God damn it, yes. Indirectly. They
worked for me, didn't they? It's a combat zone down
there. I should have had security guards around the
clock."

"Where are you going to get all this money? We've
had financial reverses. You're selling the store. Where's
this money coming from to support three families?"

"We'll get it."

"*We'll* get it? There's no we'll about it, Mister.
*You'll*. The stocks are in joint tenancy. You can't
touch them, and I'm not signing a thing. Not a penny
comes out of my mouth or off my back."

"All right, May," Ellerbee said. "I'll get it."

In fact Ellerbee had a buyer in mind—a syndicate
that specialized in buying up businesses in decaying
neighborhoods—liquor and drugstores, small gro-
ceries—and then put in ex-convicts as personnel,
Green Berets from Vietnam, off-duty policemen, ex-
perts in the martial arts. Once the word was out, no
one ever attempted to rob these places. The syndicate
hiked the price of each item at least 20 percent—and
got it. Ellerbee was fascinated and appalled by their
strong-arm tactics. Indeed, he more than a little sus-

pected that it was the syndicate itself which had been robbing him—all three times his store had been held up he had not been in it—to inspire him to sell, perhaps.

"We read about your trouble in the paper," Mr. Davis, the lawyer for the syndicate, had told him on the occasion of his first robbery. The thieves had gotten away with $300 and there was a four-line notice on the inside pages. "Terrible," he said, "terrible. A fine old neighborhood like this one. And it's the same all over America today. Everywhere it's the same story. Even in Kansas, even in Utah. They shoot you with bullets, they take your property. Terrible. The people I represent have the know-how to run businesses like yours in the spoiled neighborhoods." And then he had been offered a ridiculous price for his store and stock. Of course he turned it down. When he was robbed a second time, the lawyer didn't even bother to come in person. "Terrible. Terrible," he said. "Whoever said lightning doesn't strike twice in the same place was talking through his hat. I'm authorized to offer you ten thousand less than I did the last time." Ellerbee hung up on him.

Now, after his clerks had been shot, it was Ellerbee who called the lawyer. "Awful," the lawyer said. "Outrageous. A merchant shouldn't have to sit still for such things in a democracy."

They gave him even less than the insurance people had given him for his underappraised home. Ellerbee accepted, but decided it was time he at least hint to Davis that he knew what was going on. "I'm selling," he said, "because I don't want anyone else to die."

"Wonderful," Davis said, "wonderful. There should be more Americans like you."

He deposited the money he got from the syndicate in

a separate account so that his wife would have no claims on it and now, while he had no business to go to, he was able to spend more time in the hospital visiting Harold.

"How's Hal today, Mrs. Register?" he asked when he came into the room where the mindless quadraplegic was being cared for. Dorothy Register was a red-haired young woman in her early twenties. Ellerbee felt so terrible about what had happened, so guilty, that he had difficulty talking to her. He knew it would be impossible to visit Harold if he was going to run into his wife when he did so. It was for this reason, too, that he sent the checks rather than drop them off at the apartment, much as he wanted to see Hal's young son, Harold, Jr., in order to reassure the child that there was still a man around to take care of the boy and his young mother.

"Oh, Mr. Ellerbee," the woman wept. Harold seemed to smile at them through his brain damage.

"Please, Mrs. Register," said Ellerbee, "Harold shouldn't see you like this."

"Him? He doesn't understand a thing. You don't understand a thing, do you?" she said, turning on her husband sharply. When she made a move to poke at his eyes with a fork he didn't even blink. "Oh, Mr. Ellerbee," she said, turning away from her husband, "that's not the man I married. It's awful, but I don't feel anything for him. The only reason I come is that the doctors say I cheer him up. Though I can't see how. He smiles that way at his bedpan."

"Please, Mrs. Register," Ellerbee said softly. "You've got to be strong. There's little Hal."

"I know," she moaned, "I know." She wiped the tears from her eyes and sniffed and tossed her hair in a funny little way she had which Ellerbee found appeal-

ing. "I'm sorry," she said. "You've been very kind. I
don't know what I would have done, what *we* would
have done. I can't even thank you," she said helplessly.

"Oh don't think about it, there's no need," Ellerbee
said quickly. "I'm not doing any more for you than I
am for George Lesefario's widow." It was not a boast.
Ellerbee had mentioned the older woman because he
didn't want Mrs. Register to feel compromised. "It's
company policy when these things happen," he said
gruffly.

Dorothy Register nodded. "I heard," she said, "that
you sold your store."

He hastened to reassure her. "Oh now listen," Ellerbee said, "you mustn't give that a thought. The checks
will continue. I'm getting another store. In a very
lovely neighborhood. Near where we used to live before our house burned down."

"Really?"

"Oh yes. I should be hearing about my loan any
time now. I'll probably be in the new place before the
month is out. Well," he said, "speaking of which, I'd
better get going. There are some fixtures I'm supposed
to look at at the Wine and Spirits Mart." He waved to
Harold.

"Mr. Ellerbee?"

"Mrs. Register?"

The tall redhead came close to him and put her
hands on his shoulders. She made that funny little
gesture with her hair again and Ellerbee almost died.
She was about his own height and leaned forward and
kissed him on the mouth. Her fingernails grazed the
back of his neck. Tears came to Ellerbee's eyes and he
turned away from her gently. He hoped she hadn't seen
the small lump in his trousers. He said goodbye with
his back to her.

The loan went through. The new store, as Ellerbee had said, was in one of the finest neighborhoods in the city. In a small shopping mall, it was flanked by a good bookstore and a fine French restaurant. The Ellerbees had often eaten there before their house burned to the ground. There was an art cinema, a florist, and elegant haberdashers and dress shops. The liquor store, called High Spirits, a name Ellerbee decided to keep after he bought the place, stocked, in addition to the usual gins, Scotches, bourbons, vodkas, and blends, some really superior wines, and Ellerbee was forced to become something of an expert in oenology. He listened to his customers—doctors and lawyers, most of them—and in this way was able to pick up a good deal.

The business flourished—doing so well that after only his second month in the new location he no longer felt obliged to stay open on Sundays—though his promise to his clerks' families, which he kept, prevented him from making the inroads into his extravagant debt that he would have liked. Mrs. Register began to come to the store to collect the weekly checks personally. "I thought I'd save you the stamp," she said each time. Though he enjoyed seeing her—she looked rather like one of those splendid wives of the successful doctors who shopped there—he thought he should discourage this. He made it clear to her that he would be sending the checks.

Then she came and said that it was foolish, his continuing to pay her husband's salary, that at least he ought to let her do something to earn it. She saw that the suggestion made him uncomfortable and clarified what she meant.

"Oh no," she said, "all I meant was that you ought to hire me. I was a hostess once. For that matter I could wait on trade."

"Well, I've plenty of help, Mrs. Register. Really. As I may have told you, I've kept on all the people who used to work for Anderson." Anderson was the man from whom he'd bought High Spirits.

"It's not as though you'd be hiring additional help. I'm costing you the money anyway."

It would have been pleasant to have the woman around, but Ellerbee nervously held his ground. "At a time like this," he said, "you ought to be with the boy."

"You're quite a guy," she said. It was the last time they saw each other. A few months later, while he was examining his bank statements, he realized that she had not been cashing his checks. He called her at once.

"I can't," she said. "I'm young. I'm strong." He remembered her fierce embrace in her husband's hospital room. "There's no reason for you to continue to send me those checks. I have a good job now. I can't accept them any longer." It was the last time they spoke.

And then he learned that George's widow was ill. He heard about it indirectly. One of his best customers—a psychiatrist—was beeped on the emergency Medi-Call he carried in his jacket, and asked for change to use Ellerbee's pay phone.

"That's not necessary, Doc," Ellerbee said, "use the phone behind my counter."

"Very kind," the psychiatrist said, and came back of the counter. He dialed his service. "Doctor Potter. What have you got for me, Nancy? What? She did *what?* Just a minute, let me get a pencil.—Bill?" Ellerbee handed him a pencil. "Lesefario, right. I've got that. Give me the surgeon's number. Right. Thanks, Nancy."

"Excuse me, Doctor," Ellerbee said. "I hadn't meant to listen, but Lesefario, that's an unusual name. I know an Evelyn Lesefario."

"That's the one," said the medical man. "Oh," he said, "you're *that* Ellerbee. Well, she's been very depressed. She just tried to kill herself by eating a mile of dental floss."

"I hope she dies," his wife said.

"*May!*" said Ellerbee, shocked.

"It's what she wants, isn't it? I hope she gets what she wants."

"That's harsh, May."

"Yes? Harsh? You see how much good your checks did her? And another thing, how could she afford a high-priced man like Potter on what *you* were paying her?"

He went to visit the woman during her post-operative convalescence, and she introduced him to her sister, her twin she said, though the two women looked nothing alike and the twin seemed to be in her seventies, a good dozen years older than Mrs. Lesefario. "This is Mr. Ellerbee that my husband died protecting his liquor store from the niggers."

"Oh yes?" Mrs. Lesefario's sister said. "Very pleased. I heard so much about you."

"Look what she brought me," Mrs. Lesefario said, pointing to a large brown paper sack.

"Evelyn, don't. You'll strain your stitches. I'll show him." She opened the sack and took out a five-pound bag of sugar.

"Five pounds of sugar," the melancholic woman said.

"You don't come empty-handed to a sick person," her sister said.

"She got it at Kroger's on special. Ninety-nine cents with the coupon," the manic-depressive said gloomily. "She says if I don't like it I can get peach halves."

Ellerbee, who did not want to flaunt his own gift in front of her sister, quietly put the dressing gown, still wrapped, on her tray table. He stayed for another half hour, and rose to go.

"Wait," Mrs. Lesefario said. "Nice try but not so fast."

"I'm sorry?" Ellerbee said.

"The ribbon."

"Ribbon?"

"On the fancy box. The ribbon, the string."

"Oh, your stitches. Sorry. I'll get it."

"I'm a would-be suicide," she said. "I tried it once, I could try it again. You don't bring dangerous ribbon to a desperate, unhappy woman."

In fact Mrs. Lesefario did die. Not of suicide, but of a low-grade infection she had picked up in the hospital and which festered along her stitches, undermining them, burning through them, opening her body like a package.

The Ellerbees were in the clear financially, but his wife's reactions to Ellerbee's efforts to provide for his clerks' families had soured their relationship. She had discovered Ellerbee's private account and accused him of dreadful things. He reminded her that it had been she who had insisted he would have to get the money for the women's support himself—that their joint tenancy was not to be disturbed. She ignored his arguments and accused him further. Ellerbee loved May and did what he could to placate her.

"How about a trip to Phoenix?" he suggested that spring. "The store's doing well and I have complete confidence in Kroll. What about it, May? You like

Phoenix, and we haven't seen the folks in almost a
year."

"Phoenix," she scoffed, "The *folks*. The way you
coddle them. Any other grown man would be
ashamed."

"They raised me, May."

"They raised you. Terrific. They aren't even your
real parents. They only adopted you."

"They're the only parents I ever knew. They took
me out of the Home when I was an infant."

"Look, you want to go to Phoenix, go. Take money
out of your secret accounts and go."

"Please, May. There's no secret account. When Mrs.
Lesefario died I transferred everything back into joint.
Come on, sweetheart, you're awfully goddamn hard on
me."

"Well," she said, drawing the word out. The tone
was one she had used as a bride, and although Ellerbee
had not often heard it since, it melted him. It was her
signal of sudden conciliation, cute surrender, and he
held out his arms and they embraced. They went off to
the bedroom together.

"You know," May said afterwards, "it *would* be
good to run out to Phoenix for a bit. Are you sure the
help can manage?"

"Oh, sure, May, absolutely. They're a first-rate
bunch." He spoke more forcefully than he felt, not
because he lacked confidence in his employees, but
because he was still disturbed by an image he had had
during climax. Momentarily, fleetingly, he had imagined Mrs. Register beneath him.

In the store he was giving last-minute instructions to
Kroll, the man who would be his manager during their
vacation in Phoenix.

"I think the Californias," Ellerbee was saying.

"Some of them beat several of even the more immodest French. Let's do a promotion of a few of the better Californias. What do you think?"

"They're a very competitive group of wines," Kroll said. "I think I'm in basic agreement."

Just then three men walked into the shop.

"Say," one called from the doorway, "you got something like a Closed sign I could hang in the door here?" Ellerbee stared at him. "Well you don't have to look at me as if I was nuts," the man said. "Lots of merchants keep them around. In case they get a sudden toothache or something they can whip out to the dentist. All right, if you ain't you ain't."

"I want," the second man said, coming up to the counter where Ellerbee stood with his manager, "to see your register receipts."

"What is this?" Kroll demanded.

"No, don't," Ellerbee said to Kroll. "Don't resist." He glanced toward the third man to see if he was the one holding the gun, but the man appeared merely to be browsing the bins of Scotch in the back. Evidently he hadn't even heard the first man, and clearly he could not have heard the second. Conceivably he could have been a customer. "Where's your gun?" Ellerbee asked the man at the counter.

"Oh gee," the man said, "I almost forgot. You got so many things to think about during a stickup—the traffic flow, the timing, who stands where—you sometimes forget the basics. Here," he said, "here's my gun, in your kisser," and he took an immense handgun from his pocket and pointed it at Ellerbee's face.

Out of the corner of his eye Ellerbee saw Kroll's hands fly up. It was so blatant a gesture Ellerbee thought his manager might be trying to attract the customer's attention. If that was his idea it had

worked, for the third man had turned away from the
bins and was watching the activity at the counter.
"Look," Ellerbee said, "I don't want anybody hurt."

"What's he say?" said the man at the door who was
also holding a pistol now.

"He don't want nobody hurt," the man at the counter said.

"Sure," said the man at the door, "it's costing him a
fortune paying all them salaries to the widows. He's a
good businessman all right."

"A better one than you," the man at the counter
said to his confederate sharply. "He knows how to
keep his mouth shut."

Why, they're white, Ellerbee thought. They're *white*
men! He felt oddly justified and wished May were
there to see.

"The register receipts," the man at the counter
coaxed. Ellerbee's cash register kept a running total on
what had been taken in. "Just punch Total Tab," the
man instructed Kroll. "Let's see what we got." Kroll
looked at Ellerbee and Ellerbee nodded. The man
reached forward and tore off the tape. He whistled.
"Nice little place you got here," he said.

"What'd we get? What'd we get?" the man at the
door shouted.

Ellerbee cleared his throat. "Do you want to lock
the door?" he asked. "So no one else comes in?" He
glanced toward the third man.

"What, and have you kick the alarm while we're
fucking around trying to figure which key opens the
place?" said the man at the door. "You're cute, you're
a cutie. What'd we get? Let's see." He joined the man
at the counter. "Holy smoke! Jackpot City! We're into
four figures here." In his excitement he did a foolish
thing. He set his revolver down on top of the appetizer

table. It lay on the tins of caviar and smoked oysters, the imported cheeses and roasted peanuts. The third man was no more than four feet from the gun, and though Ellerbee saw that the man had caught the robber's mistake and that by taking one step toward the table he could have picked up the pistol and perhaps foiled the robbery, he made no move. Perhaps he's one of them, Ellerbee thought, or maybe he just doesn't want to get involved. Ellerbee couldn't remember ever having seen him. (By now, of course, he recognized all his repeat customers.) He still didn't know if he were a confederate or just an innocent bystander, but Ellerbee had had enough of violence and hoped that if he *were* a customer he wouldn't try anything dumb. He felt no animus toward the man at all. Kroll's face, however, was all scorn and loathing.

"Let's get to work," the man said who had first read the tape, and then to Kroll and Ellerbee, "Back up there. Go stand by the aperitifs."

The third man fell silently into step beside Ellerbee.

"Listen," Ellerbee explained as gently as he could, "you won't find that much cash in the drawer. A lot of our business is Master Charge. We take personal checks."

"Don't worry," the man said who had set his gun down (and who had taken it up again). "We know about the checks. We got a guy we can sell them to for—what is it, Ron, seventeen cents on the dollar?"

"Fourteen, and why don't you shut your mouth, will you? You want to jeopardize these people? What do you make it?"

Ellerbee went along with his sentiments. He wished the bigmouth would just take the money and not say anything more.

"Oh, jeopardize," the man said. "How jeopardized can you get? These people are way past jeopardized. About six hundred in cash, a fraction in checks. The rest is all credit card paper."

"Take it," Ron said.

"You won't be able to do anything with the charge slips," Kroll said.

"Oh yeah?" Ron's cohort said. "This is modern times, fellow. We got a way we launder Master Charge, BankAmericard, all of it."

Ron shook his head and Ellerbee glanced angrily at his manager.

The whole thing couldn't have taken four minutes. Ron's partner took a fifth of Chivas and a bottle of Lafitte '47. He's a doctor, Ellerbee thought.

"You got a bag?"

"A bag?" Ellerbee said.

"A bag, a paper bag, a doggy bag for the boodle."

"Behind the counter," Ellerbee said hopelessly.

The partner put the cash and the bottle of Chivas into one bag and handed it to Ron, and the wine, checks, and credit charges into a second bag which he held on to himself. They turned to go. They looked exactly like two satisfied customers. They were almost at the door when Ron's partner nudged Ron. "Oh, yeah," Ron said, and turned back to look at them. "My friend, Jay Ladlehaus, is right," he said, "you know too much."

Ellerbee heard two distinct shots before he fell.

When he came to, the third man was bending over him. "You're not hurt," Ellerbee said.

"Me? No."

The pain was terrific, diffuse, but fiercer than anything he had ever felt. He saw himself covered with blood. "Where's Kroll? The other man, my manager?"

"Kroll's all right."

"He is?"

"There, right beside you."

He tried to look. They must have blasted Ellerbee's throat away, half his spinal column. It was impossible for him to move his head. "I can't see him," he moaned.

"Kroll's fine." The man cradled Ellerbee's shoulders and neck and shifted him slightly. "There. See?" Kroll's eyes were shut. Oddly, both were blackened. He had fallen in such a way that he seemed to lie on both his arms, retracted behind him into the small of his back like a yogi. His mouth was open and his tongue floated in blood like meat in soup. A slight man, he seemed strangely bloated, and one shin, exposed to Ellerbee's vision where the trouser leg was hiked up above his sock, was discolored as thundercloud.

The man gently set Ellerbee down again. "Call an ambulance," Ellerbee wheezed through his broken throat.

"No, no. Kroll's fine."

"He's not conscious." It was as if his words were being mashed through the tines of a fork.

"He'll be all right. Kroll's fine."

"Then for *me*. Call one for *me*."

"It's too late for you," the man said.

"For Christ's sake, will you!" Ellerbee gasped. "I can't move. You could have grabbed that hoodlum's gun when he set it down. All right, you were scared, but some of this is your fault. You didn't lift a finger. At least call an ambulance."

"But you're dead," he said gently. "Kroll will recover. You passed away when you said 'move.' "

"Are you crazy? What are you talking about?"

"Do you feel pain?"

"What?"

"Pain. You don't feel any, do you?" Ellerbee stared at him. "Do you?"

He didn't. His pain was gone. "Who are you?" Ellerbee said.

"I'm an angel of death," the angel of death said.

"You're—"

"An angel of death."

Somehow he had left his body. He could see it lying next to Kroll's. "I'm dead? But if I'm dead—you mean there's really an afterlife?"

"Oh boy," the angel of death said.

They went to Heaven.

Ellerbee couldn't have said how they got there or how long it took, though he had the impression that time had passed, and distance. It was rather like a journey in films—a series of quick cuts, of montage. He was probably dreaming, he thought.

"It's what they all think," the angel of death said, "that they're dreaming. But that isn't so."

"I could have dreamed you said that," Ellerbee said, "that you read my mind."

"Yes."

"I could be dreaming all of it, the holdup, everything."

The angel of death looked at him.

"Hobgoblin . . . I could . . ." Ellerbee's voice—if it was a voice—trailed off.

"Look," the angel of death said, "I talk too much. I sound like a cabbie with an out-of-town fare. It's an occupational hazard."

"What?"

"*What?* Pride. The proprietary air. Showing off
death like a booster. Thanatopography. 'If you look to
your left you'll see where . . . Julius Caesar de dum de
dum . . . Shakespeare da da da . . . And dead ahead
our Father Adam heigh ho—' The tall buildings and
the four-star sights. All that Baedeker reality of plaque
place and high history. The Fields of Homer and the
Plains of Myth. Where whosis got locked in a star and
all the Agriculture of the Periodic Table—the South
Forty of the Universe, where Hydrogen first bloomed,
where Lithium, Berylium, Zirconium, Niobium. Where
Lead failed and Argon came a cropper. The furrows of
gold, Bismuth's orchards. . . . Still think you're dreaming?"

"No."

"Why not?"

"The language."

"Just so," the angel of death said. "When you were
alive you had a vocabulary of perhaps seventeen or
eighteen hundred words. Who am I?"

"An eschatological angel," Ellerbee said shyly.

"One hundred percent," the angel of death said.
"Why do we do that?"

"To heighten perception," Ellerbee said, and shuddered.

The angel of death nodded and said nothing more.

When they were close enough to make out the
outlines of Heaven, the angel left him and Ellerbee, not
questioning this, went on alone. From this distance it
looked to Ellerbee rather like a theme park, but what
struck him most forcibly was that it did not seem—for
Heaven—very large.

He traveled as he would on Earth, distance familiar
again, volume, mass, and dimension restored, ordinary.
(*Quotidian,* Ellerbee thought.) Indeed, now that he

was convinced of his death, nothing seemed particularly strange. If anything, it was all a little familiar. He began to miss May. She would have learned of his death by this time. Difficult as the last year had been, they had loved each other. It had been a good marriage. He regretted again that they had been unable to have children. Children—they would be teenagers now—would have been a comfort to his widow. She still had her looks. Perhaps she would remarry. He did not want her to be lonely.

He continued toward Heaven and now, only blocks away, he was able to perceive it in detail. It looked more like a theme park than ever. It was enclosed behind a high milky fence, the uprights smooth and round as the poles in subway trains. Beyond the fence were golden streets, a mixed architecture of minaret-spiked mosques, great cathedrals, the rounded domes of classical synagogues, tall pagodas like holy vertebrae, white frame churches with their beautiful steeples, even what Ellerbee took to be a storefront church. There were many mansions. But where were the people?

Just as he was wondering about this he heard the sound of a gorgeous chorus. It was making a joyful noise. "Oh dem golden slippers," the chorus sang, "Oh dem golden slippers." It's the Heavenly Choir, Ellerbee thought. They've actually got a Heavenly Choir. He went toward the fence and put his hands on the smooth posts and peered through into Heaven. He heard laughter and caught a glimpse of the running heels of children just disappearing around the corner of a golden street. They all wore shoes.

Ellerbee walked along the fence for about a mile and came to gates made out of pearl. The Pearly Gates, he thought. There are actually Pearly Gates. An old man in a long white beard sat behind them, a key attached to a sort of cinch that went about his waist.

"Saint Peter?" Ellerbee ventured. The old man turned his shining countenance upon him. "Saint Peter," Ellerbee said again, "I'm Ellerbee."

"I'm Saint Peter," Saint Peter said.

"Gosh," Ellerbee said, "I can't get over it. It's all true."

"What is?"

"Everything. Heaven. The streets of gold, the Pearly Gates. You. Your key. The Heavenly Choir. The climate."

A soft breeze came up from inside Heaven and Ellerbee sniffed something wonderful in the perfect air. He looked toward the venerable old man.

"Ambrosia," the Saint said.

"There's actually ambrosia," Ellerbee said.

"You know," Saint Peter said, "you never get tired of it, you never even get used to it. He does that to whet our appetite."

"You eat in Heaven?"

"We eat manna."

"There's actually manna," Ellerbee said. An angel floated by on a fleecy cloud playing a harp. Ellerbee shook his head. He had never heard anything so beautiful. "Heaven is everything they say it is," he said.

"It's Paradise," Saint Peter said.

Then Ellerbee saw an affecting sight. Nearby, husbands were reunited with wives, mothers with their small babes, daddies with their sons, brothers with sisters—all the intricate blood loyalties and enlisted loves. He understood all the relationships without being told—his heightened perception. What was most moving, however, were the old people, related or not, some just lifelong friends, people who had lived to-

gether or known one another much the greater part of
their lives and then had lost each other. It was im-
mensely touching to Ellerbee to see them gaze fondly
into one another's eyes and then to watch them reach
out and touch the patient, ancient faces, wrinkled and
even withered but, Ellerbee could tell, unchanged in
the loving eyes of the adoring beholder. If there were
tears they were tears of joy, tears that melded inextri-
cably with tender laughter. There was rejoicing, there
were Hosannas, there was dancing in the golden
streets. "It's wonderful," Ellerbee muttered to himself.
He didn't know where to look first. He would be
staring at the beautiful flowing raiments of the angels—There are actually raiments, he thought, there
are actually angels—so fine, he imagined, to the touch
that just the caress of the cloth must have produced
exquisite sensations not matched by anything in life,
when something else would strike him. The perfectly
proportioned angels' wings like discrete Gothic windows, the beautiful halos—There are actually halos—
like golden quoits, or, in the distance, the lovely green
pastures, delicious as fairway—all the perfectly banked
turns of Heaven's geography. He saw philosophers
deep in conversation. He saw kings and heroes. It was
astonishing to him, like going to an exclusive restaurant one has only read about in columns and spotting,
even at first glance, the celebrities one has read about,
relaxed, passing the time of day, out in the open,
up-front and sharing their high-echelon lives.

"This is for keeps?" he asked Saint Peter. "I mean it
goes on like this?"

"World without end," Saint Peter said.

"Where's . . ."

"That's all right, say His name."

"God?" Ellerbee whispered.

Saint Peter looked around. "I don't see Him
just . . . Oh, wait. *There!*" Ellerbee turned where the
old Saint was pointing. He shaded his eyes. "There's
no need," Saint Peter said.

"But the aura, the light."

"Let it shine."

He took his hand away fearfully and the light spilled
into his eyes like soothing unguents. God was on His
throne in the green pastures, Christ at His right Hand.
To Ellerbee it looked like a picture taken at a summit
conference.

"He's beautiful. I've never . . . It's ecstasy."

"And you're seeing Him from a pretty good distance. You should talk to Him sometime."

"People can talk to Him?"

"Certainly. He loves us."

There were tears in Ellerbee's eyes. He wished May
no harm, but wanted her with him to see it all. "It's
wonderful."

"We like it," Saint Peter said.

"Oh, I do too," Ellerbee said. "I'm going to be very
happy here."

"Go to Hell," Saint Peter said beatifically.

Hell was the ultimate inner city. Its stinking sulfu-
rous streets were unsafe. Everywhere Ellerbee looked
he saw atrocities. Pointless, profitless muggings were
commonplace; joyless rape that punished its victims
and offered no relief to the perpetrator. Everything was
contagious, cancer as common as a cold, plague the
quotidian. There was stomachache, headache, toothache, earache. There was angina and indigestion and
painful third-degree burning itch. Nerves like a hideous
body hair grew long enough to trip over and lay raw

and exposed as live wires or shoelaces that had come undone.

There was no handsomeness, no beauty, no one walked upright, no one had good posture. There was nothing to look at—although it was impossible to shut one's eyes—except the tumbled kaleidoscope variations of warted deformity. This was one reason, Ellerbee supposed, that there was so little conversation in Hell. No one could stand to look at anyone else long enough. Occasionally two or three—lost souls? gargoyles? devils? demons?—of the damned, jumping about in the heat first on one foot then the other, would manage to stand with their backs to each other and perhaps get out a few words—a foul whining. But even this was rare and when it happened that a sufferer had the attention of a fellow sufferer he could howl out only a half-dozen or so words before breaking off in a piercing scream.

Ellerbee, constantly nauseated, eternally in pain, forever befouling himself, longed to find something to do, however tedious or make-work or awful. For a time he made paths through the smoldering cinders, but he had no tools and had to use his bare feet, moving the cinders to one side as a boy shuffles through fallen leaves hunting something lost. It was too painful. Then he thought he would make channels for the vomit and excrement and blood. It was too disgusting. He shouted for others to join him in work details—"Break up the fights, pile up the scabs"—and even ministered to the less aggravated wounds, using his hands to wipe away the gangrenous drool since there was no fabric in Hell, all clothing consumed within minutes of arrival, flesh alone inconsumable, glowing and burning along the bones slow as phosphor. Calling out, suggesting in screams which may have been incoherent, all manner of pointless, arbitrary arrangements—that they organize the damned, that they count them. Demanding that their howls be synchronous.

No one stopped him. No one seemed to be in charge. He saw, that is, no Devil, no Archfiend. There were demons with cloven feet and scaly tails, with horns and pitchforks—They actually have horns, Ellerbee thought, there are actually pitchforks—but these seemed to have no more authority than he had himself, and when they were piqued to wrath by their own torment the jabs they made at the human damned with their sharp arsenal were no more painful—and no less, —than anything else down there.

Then Ellerbee felt he understood something terrible—that the abortive rapes and fights and muggings were simply a refinement of his own attempts to socialize. They did it to make contact, to be friendly.

He was free to wander the vast burning meadows of Hell and to scale its fiery hills—and for many years he did—but it was much the same all over. What he was actually looking for was its Source, Hell's bright engine room, its storm-tossed bridge. It had no engine room, there was no bridge, its energy, all its dreadful combustion coming perhaps from the cumulative, collective agony of the inmates. Nothing could be done.

He was distracted, as he was sure they all were— "Been to Heaven?" he'd managed to gasp to an old man whose back was on fire and the man had nodded—by his memory of Paradise, his long-distance glimpse of God. It was unbearable to think of Heaven in his present condition, his memory of that spectacular place poisoned by the discrepancy between the exaltation of the angels and the plight of the damned. It was the old story of the disappointment of rising expectations. Still, without his bidding, thoughts of Paradise force-fed themselves almost constantly into his skull. They induced sadness, rage.

He remembered the impression he'd had of celebrity when he'd stood looking in at Heaven from beyond the Pearly Gates, and he thought to look out for the historic bad men, the celebrated damned, but either they were kept in a part of Hell he had not yet seen or their sufferings had made them unrecognizable. If there were great men in Hell he did not see them and, curiously, no one ever boasted of his terrible deeds or notoriety. Indeed, except for the outbursts of violence, most of the damned behaved, considering their state, in a respectable fashion, even an exemplary one. Perhaps, Ellerbee thought, it was because they had not yet abandoned hope. (There was actually a sign: "Abandon Hope, All Ye Who Enter Here." Ellerbee had seen it.)

For several years he waited for May, for as long, that is, as he could remember her. Constant pain and perpetual despair chipped away at most of the memories he had of his life. It was possible to recall who and what he had been, but that was as fruitless as any other enterprise in the dark region. Ultimately, like everything else, it worked against him—Hell's fine print. It was best to forget. And that worked against him too.

He took the advice written above Hellgate. He abandoned hope, and with it memory, pity, pride, his projects, the sense he had of injustice—for a little while driving off, along with his sense of identity, even his broken recollection of glory. It was probably what they—whoever they were—wanted. Let them have it. Let them have the straight lines of their trade wind, trade route, through street, thrown stone vengeance.

Let them have everything. Their pastels back and their blues and their greens, the recollection of gratified thirst, and the transient comfort of a sandwich and beer that had hit the spot, all the retrospective of good weather, a good night's sleep, a good joke, a good tune, a good time, the entire mosaic of small satisfactions that made up a life. Let them have his image of his parents and friends, the fading portrait of May he couldn't quite shake, the pleasure he'd had from work, from his body. Let them have all of it, his measly joy, his scrapbook past, his hope, too.

Which left only pure pain, the grand vocabulary they had given him to appreciate it, to discriminate and parse among the exquisite lesions and scored flesh and violated synapses, among the insulted nerves, joints, muscle and tissue, all the boiled kindling points of torment and the body's grief. That was all he was now, staggering Hiroshima'd flesh—a vessel of nausea, a pail of pain.

He continued thus for several years, his amnesia willed—There's Free Will, Ellerbee thought—shuffling Hell in his rote aphasia, his stripped self a sealed environment of indifference. There were years he did not think the name Ellerbee.

And even *that* did not assuage the panic of his burning theater'd, air raid warning'd, red-alert afterlife. (And that was what they wanted, and he knew it, wanting as much as they did for him to persist in his tornado-watch condition, fleeing with others through the crimped, cramped streets of mazy, refugee Hell, dragging his disaster poster avatar like a wounded leg.) He existed like one plugged into superb equipment, interminably terminal—and changed his mind and tried it the other way again, taking back all he had surrendered, Hell's Indian giver, and dredged up from where he had left them the imperfect memories of his former self. (May he saw as she had once been, his breastless, awkward, shapeless childhood sweetheart.) And when that didn't work either—he gave it a few years—he went back to the other way, and then back again, shifting, quickly tiring of each tack as soon as he had taken it, changing fitfully, a man in bed in a hot, airless room rolling position, aggressively altering the surfaces of his pillow. If he hoped—which he came to do whenever he reverted to Ellerbee—it was to go mad, but there was no madness in Hell—the terrific vocabulary of the damned, their poet's knack for rightly naming everything, which was the fail-safe of Reason—and he could find peace nowhere.

He had been there sixty-two years, three generations, older now as a dead man than he had been as a living one. Sixty-two years of nightless days and dayless nights, of aggravated pain and cumulative grief, of escalated desperation, of not getting used to it, to any of it. Sixty-two years Hell's greenhorn, sixty-two years eluding the muggers and evading the rapists, all the joyless joy riders out for a night on his town, steering clear of the wild, stampeding, horizontal avalanche of the damned. And then, spinning out of the path of a charging, burning, screaming inmate, he accidentally backed into the smoldering ruin of a second. Ellerbee leaped away as their bodies touched.

"Ellerbee?"

Who? Ellerbee thought wildly. Who?

"Ellerbee?" the voice repeated.

How? Ellerbee wondered. How can he know me? In this form, how I look . . .

Ellerbee peered closely into the tormented face. It was one of the men who had held him up, not the one who had shot him but his accomplice, his murderer's accomplice. "Ladlehaus?" It was Ellerbee's vocabulary which had recognized him for his face had changed almost completely in the sixty-two years, just as Ellerbee's had, just as it was Ladlehaus's vocabulary which had recognized Ellerbee.

"It is Ellerbee, isn't it?" the man said.

Ellerbee nodded and the man tried to smile, stretching his wounds, the scars which seamed his face, and breaking the knitting flesh, lined, caked as stool, braided as bowel.

"I died," he said, "of natural causes." Ellerbee stared at him. "Of leukemia, stroke, Hodgkin's disease, arteriosclerosis. I was blind the last thirteen years of my life. But I was almost a hundred. I lived to a ripe old age. I was in a Home eighteen years. Still in Minneapolis."

"I suppose," Ellerbee said, "you recall how *I* died."

"I do," Ladlehaus said. "Ron dropped you with one shot. That reminds me," he said. "You had a beautiful wife. May, right? I saw her photograph in the Minneapolis papers after the incident. There was tremendous coverage. There was a TV clip on the Six O'Clock News. They interviewed her. She was—" Ellerbee started to run. "Hey," the accomplice called after him. "Hey, wait."

He ran through the steamy corridors of the Underworld, plunging into Hell's white core, the brightest blazes, Temperature's moving parts. The pain was excruciating, but he knew that it was probably the only way he would shake Ladlehaus so he kept running. And then, exhausted, he came out the other side into an area like shoreline, burning surf. He waded through the flames lapping about his ankles and then, humiliated by fatigue and pain, he did something he had never done before.

He lay down in the fire. He lay down in the slimy excrement and noxious puddles, in the loose evidence of their spilled terror. A few damned souls paused to stare at him, their bad breath dropping over him like an awful steam. Their scabbed faces leaned down toward him, their poisoned blood leaking on him from imperfectly sealed wounds, their baked, hideous visages like blooms in nightmare. It was terrible. He turned over, turned face down in the shallow river of pus and shit. Someone shook him. He didn't move. A man straddled and penetrated him. He didn't move. His attacker groaned. "I can't," he panted, "I can't—I can't see myself in his *blisters*." That's why they do it, Ellerbee thought. The man grunted and dismounted and spat upon him. His fiery spittle burned into an open sore on Ellerbee's neck. He didn't move. "He's dead," the man howled. "I think he's dead. His blisters have gone out!"

He felt a pitchfork rake his back, then turn in the wound it had made as if the demon were trying to pry foreign matter from it.

"Did he die?" Ellerbee heard.

He had Free Will. He wouldn't move.

"Is he dead?"

"How did he do it?"

Hundreds pressed in on him, their collective stench like the swamps of men dead in earthquake, trench warfare—though Ellerbee knew that for all his vocabulary there were no proper analogies in Hell, only the mildest approximations. If he didn't move they would go away. He didn't move.

A pitchfork caught him under the armpit and turned him over.

"He's dead. I think so. I think he's dead."

"No. It can't be."

"I think."

"How? How did he do it?"

"Pull his cock. See."

"No. Make one of the women. If he isn't dead maybe he'll respond."

An ancient harridan stooped down and rubbed him between her palms. It was the first time he had been touched there by a woman in sixty-two years. He had Free Will, he had Free Will. But beneath her hot hands his penis began to smoke.

"Oh God," he screamed. "Leave me alone. Please," he begged. They gazed down at him like teammates over a fallen player.

"Faker," one hissed.

"Shirker," said another scornfully.

"He's not dead," a third cried. "I told you."

"There's no death here."

"World without end," said another.

"Get up," demanded someone else. "Run. Run through Hell. Flee your pain. Keep busy."

They started to lift him. "Let go," Ellerbee shouted. He rolled away from a demon poking at him with a pitchfork. He was on his hands and knees in Hell. Still on all fours he began to push himself up. He was on his knees.

"Looks like he's praying," said the one who had told him to run.

"No."

"Looks like it. I think so."

"How? What for?"

And he started to pray.

"Lord God of Ambush and Unconditional Surrender," he prayed. "Power Play God of Judo Leverage. Grand Guignol, Martial Artist—"

The others shrieked, backed away from him, cordoning Ellerbee off like a disaster area. Ellerbee, caught up, ignoring them, not even hearing them, continued his prayer.

"Browbeater," he prayed, "Bouncer Being, Boss of Bullies—this is Your servant, Ellerbee, sixty-two-year fetus in Eternity, tot, toddler, babe in Hell. Can You hear me? I know You exist because I saw You, avuncular in Your green pastures like an old man on a picnic. The angeled minarets I saw, the gold streets and marble temples and all the flashy summer-palace architecture, all the gorgeous glory locked in Receivership. Your zoned Heaven in Holy Escrow. The miracle props—harps and Saints and popes at tea. All of it—Your manna, Your ambrosia, Your Heavenly Host in their summer whites. So can You *hear* me, pick out my voice from all the others in this din bin? Come on, come on, Old Terrorist, God the Father, God the Godfather! The conventional wisdom is we can talk to You, that You love us, that—"

"I can hear you."

A great awed whine rose from the damned, moans, sharp cries. It was as if Ellerbee alone had not heard. He continued his prayer.

"I hear you," God repeated.

Ellerbee stopped.

God spoke. His voice was pitchless, almost without timbre, almost bland. "What do you want, Ellerbee?"

Confused, Ellerbee forgot the point of his prayer. He looked at the others who were quiet now, perfectly still for once. Only the snap of localized fire could be heard. God was waiting. The damned watched Ellerbee fearfully. Hell burned beneath his knees. "An explanation," Ellerbee said.

"For openers," God roared, "I made the heavens and the earth! Were you there when I laid the foundations of the firmament? When I—"

Splinters of burning bone, incandescent as filament,

glowed in the gouged places along Ellerbee's legs and knees where divots of his flesh had flared and fallen away. "An *explanation*," he cried out, "an *explanation!* None of this what-was-I-doing-when-You-pissed-the-oceans stuff, where I was when You colored the nigger and ignited Hell. I wasn't around when You elected the affinities. I wasn't there when you shaped shit and fashioned cancer. Were *You* there when I loved my neighbor as myself? When I never stole or bore false witness? I don't say when I never killed but when I never even raised a hand or pointed a finger in anger? Where were You when I picked up checks and popped for drinks all round? When I shelled out for charity and voted Yes on the bond issues? So no Job job, no nature in tooth and claw, please. An explanation!"

"You stayed open on the Sabbath!" God thundered.

"I what?"

"You stayed open on the Sabbath. When you were just getting started in your new location."

"You mean because I opened my store on Sundays? That's why?"

"You took My name in vain."

"I took . . ."

"That's right, that's right. You wanted an explanation, I'll give you an explanation. You wanted I/Thou, I'll give you I/Thou. You took It in vain. When your wife was nagging you because you wanted to keep those widows on the payroll. She mocked you when you said you were under an obligation and you said, 'Indirectly. G–d damn it, yes. Indirectly,' 'Come on, sweetheart,' you said, 'you're awfully g–ddamn hard on me.' "

"That's why I'm in Hell? *That's* why?"

"And what about the time you coveted your neighbor's wife? You had a big boner."

"I coveted no one, I was never unfaithful, I practically chased that woman away."

"You didn't honor your father and mother."

Ellerbee was stunned. "I did. I *always* honored my father and mother. I loved them very much. Just before I was killed we were planning a trip to Phoenix to see them."

"Oh, *them*. They only adopted you. I'm talking about your natural parents."

"I was in a Home. I was an *in*fant!"

"Sure, sure," God said.

"And *that's* why? *That's* why?"

"You went dancing. You wore zippers in your pants and drove automobiles. You smoked cigarettes and sold the demon rum."

"These are Your reasons? *This* is Your explanation?"

*"You thought Heaven looked like a theme park!"*

Ellerbee shook his head. Could this be happening? This pettiness signaled across the universe? But anything could happen, everything could, and Ellerbee began again to pray. "Lord," he prayed, "Heavenly Father, Dear God—maybe whatever is is right and maybe whatever is is right isn't, but I've been around now, walking up and down in it, and *every*thing is true. There is nothing that is not true. The philosopher's best idea and the conventional wisdom, too. So I am praying to You now in all humility, asking Your forgiveness and to grant one prayer."

"What is it?" God asked.

Ellerbee heard a strange noise and looked around. The damned, too, were on their knees—all the lost souls, all the gargoyles, all the demons, kneeling in fire, capitulate through Hell like a great ring of the conquered.

"What is it?" He asked.

"To kill us, to end Hell, to close the camp."

"Amen," said Ellerbee and all the damned in a single voice.

"Ha!" God scoffed and lighted up Hell's blazes like the surface of a star. Then God cursed and abused Ellerbee, and Ellerbee wouldn't have had it any other way. *He*'d damned him, no surrogate in Saint's clothing but the real McCoy Son of a Bitch God Whose memory Ellerbee would treasure and eternally repudiate forever, happily ever after, world without end.

But everything was true, even the conventional wisdom, perhaps especially the conventional wisdom—that which had made up Heaven like a shot in the dark and imagined into reality halos and Hell, gargoyles, gates of pearl, and the Pearl of Great Price, that had invented the horns of demons and cleft their feet and conceived angels riding clouds like cowboys on horseback, their harps at their sides like goofy guitars. Everything. Everything was. The self and what you did to protect it, learning the house odds, playing it safe—the honorable percentage baseball of existence.

Forever was a long time. Eternity was. He would seek out Ladlehaus, his murderer's accomplice, let bygones be bygones. They would get close to each other, close as family, closer. There was much to discuss in their fine new vocabularies. They would speak of Minneapolis, swap tales of the Twin Cities. They would talk of Ron, of others in the syndicate. And Ladlehaus had seen May, had caught her in what Ellerbee hoped was her grief on the Six O'Clock News. They would get close. And one day he would look for himself in Ladlehaus's glowing blisters.